CliffsTestPrep®
RICA®

CliffsTestPrep®
RICA®

by

Jerry Bobrow, Ph.D., Beth Andersen, Ph.D.,
Karen Sekeres, M.S., Rhonda Byer, M.A., M.Ed.,
Chris Collins, M.A., M.Ed., Dana Gottlieb, B.A.

Contributing Authors/Consultants

Frieda Bauch, M.A.

Stephen Fisher, M.A.

Terri Battenberg, M.Ed.

WILEY

Wiley Publishing, Inc.

About the Lead Author

Jerry Bobrow, Ph.D., is a national authority in the field of test preparation. As executive director of Bobrow Test Preparation Services, he has been administering test preparation programs at more than 25 California institutions for the past 31 years. Dr. Bobrow has authored more than 40 national best-selling test preparation books, and his books and programs have assisted more than two million test-takers. Dr. Bobrow has assembled an outstanding group of reading and literacy specialists to assist in writing this guide. Each of these specialists has been teaching RICA test preparation programs at universities throughout California.

Author's Acknowledgments

I would like to thank Donna Wright., project editor for Wiley Publishing, Inc., for her careful review of the manuscript. I would also like to thank my wife, Susan; daughter, Jennifer; and sons, Adam and Jonathan; for their moral support and comic relief during the writing process.

Publisher's Acknowledgments

Editorial

Project Editor: Donna Wright

Acquisitions Editor: Greg Tubach

Copy Editor: Kelly D. Henthorne

Production

Proofreader: Vicki Broyles

Wiley Publishing, Inc. Composition Services

CliffsTestPrep® RICA®

Published by:
Wiley Publishing, Inc.
111 River Street
Hoboken, NJ 07030-5774
www.wiley.com

Copyright © 2006 Jerry Bobrow, Ph.D.

Published by Wiley, Hoboken, NJ
Published simultaneously in Canada

CIP data available upon request

ISBN-13 978-0-471-75168-7

ISBN-10 0-471-75168-5

Printed in the United States of America

10 9 8 7 6 5 4 3

1B/RQ/QS/QW/IN

WILEY

Table of Contents

PART III: TWO FULL-LENGTH PRACTICE TESTS

PART IV: FINAL PREPARATION AND SOURCES

This book is dedicated to the memory of two wonderful people, each loving husbands and fathers

Coach
Foster Andersen
March 11, 1940 to April 26, 2004

Architect/Engineer
Jim Collins
November 29, 1943 to October 22, 2005

Their wisdom, caring, insightfulness, and humor
continue to nourish and give strength to those who knew them.

Preface

Be Prepared for the RICA!

The Reading Instruction Competence Assessment (RICA) Written Examination is designed to assess the candidate's knowledge about effective reading instruction in the four RICA domains and the candidate's ability to apply that knowledge. This test includes 70 multiple-choice questions, four regular essays, and one case-study essay.

Because the RICA requires you to use some skills and knowledge that you might not have used in a few years, thorough preparation is the key to doing your best. This fact makes your study time more important than ever; it must be used effectively.

In keeping with the fine tradition of CliffsNotes, this guide was developed by leading experts in the field of test preparation and reading instruction to give you the best preparation possible. The strategies, techniques, and materials presented in this guide have been researched, tested, and evaluated in RICA preparation classes at many leading universities, county offices of education, and school districts. Bobrow Test Preparation Services, a leader in the field of teacher credential exam preparation, is continually offering RICA classes at the request of many California state universities and school districts. This book uses the materials used and developed in these programs.

This guide is divided into an introduction and four parts:

Introduction

A general description of the exam, format, questions commonly asked, and some basic overall strategies

Part I: Analysis of Exam Areas

Focuses on introducing and analyzing each question type with an emphasis on suggested approaches and samples

Part II: Review of Exam Areas

Short intensive reviews including a review of the Content Specifications—the Four Domains, Key Terms and Concepts, and Vocabulary

Part III: Two Full-Length Practice Tests

Two complete full-length practice tests with answers, in-depth explanations, and review charts

Part IV: Final Preparation and Sources

Some final tips and reminders to help you do your best

This guide is not meant to substitute for comprehensive courses in each subject area, but if you follow the Study Guide Checklist on the following page, review subject areas, and study regularly, you will get the best RICA preparation possible.

Good luck!

Study Guide Checklist

❏   1. Read the RICA information materials (registration bulletin) available at the testing office of most undergraduate institutions.

❏   2. Review the information and sample problems available online at www.rica.nesinc.com.

❏   3. Become familiar with the test format, page 1.

❏   4. Read General Description, RICA Scoring, and Questions Commonly Asked about the RICA, starting on pages 1–4.

❏   5. Learn the techniques of A Positive, Systematic Approach to multiple-choice, essay questions, and the case study, starting on pages 5–9.

❏   6. Carefully read Part I: Analysis of Exam Areas, starting on page 13.

❏   7. Read Part II: Review of Exam Areas, starting on page 113.

❏   8. Strictly observing the time allotment, take Practice Test 1, starting on page 159.

❏   9. Check your answers, page 196, and carefully review explanations, starting on page 197.

❏ 10. Read the sample responses, starting on page 203, and use the evaluation sheet s pages 209–213 to evaluate your responses.

❏ 11. Fill out the Analysis/Tally Sheet for Questions Missed, page 208.

❏ 12. Review weak areas as necessary. Remember to review by domain and content areas.

❏ 13. Strictly observing the time allotment, take Practice Test 2 in its entirety, beginning on page 229.

❏ 14. Check your answers, review the explanations, evaluate your essays, and fill in the analysis sheets for Practice Test 2.

❏ 15. Review weak areas as necessary. Now focus your review.

❏ 16. Review Part I: Analysis of Exam Areas, starting on page 13.

❏ 17. Carefully read The Final Touches, page 287.

Introduction

Format

Format of the Examination

Time: 4 Hours for Complete Exam

Multiple-Choice Questions

> **70** questions (only 60 count—10 are experimental)

Focused Educational Problems and Instructional Tasks

> **4** Essays

>> Short essay 1—approximately 50 words (prompt from Domain I)

>> Short essay 2—approximately 50 words (prompt from Domain IV)

>> Longer Essay 1—approximately 150 words (prompt from Domain II)

>> Longer Essay 2—approximately 150 words (prompt from Domain III)

Case Study Based on Student Profile

> **1** Essay—approximately 300 words

Notice that the number of questions and timing could change.

General Description

The Reading Instruction Competence Assessment (RICA) is designed to assess the candidate's knowledge about effective reading instruction in the four RICA domains and the candidate's ability to apply that knowledge. The test is composed of the following:

- **A Multiple-Choice Section** consisting of 70 questions (only 60 questions actually count)
- **A Constructed-Response Section** that requires candidates to write essays
  1. **Focused Educational Problems and Instructional Tasks** (4 essays: 2 short essays of 50 words each and two longer essays of 150 words each—each essay covers one domain)
  2. **Case Study** (1 essay, approximately 300 words in length)

RICA Scoring

Total Possible Multiple-Choice Score: 60 points possible

Total Possible Constructed-Response Scores

Area	Length of Response	Score		Weight		Score Weighted
Domain I	50 word essay	6	×	1	=	6
Domain II	150 word essay	6	×	2	=	12
Domain III	150 word essay	6	×	2	=	12
Domain IV	50 word essay	6	×	1	=	6

(Essays scored 1–3 by 2 scorers giving total possible score of 6)

Case Study	300 word essay	8	×	3	=	<u>24</u>

(Case study scored 1–4 by 2 scorers give total possible score of 8)

Total Points = **60**

Multiple Choice plus Constructed Response equals Total

60 + 60 = 120

Passing Score is 81.

Scoring and passing standards are subject to change.

Note weight score for each essay type.

General Information

- There is no penalty for guessing on multiple-choice or constructed-response questions. Answer all of the questions. Guess if necessary. Always attempt a response.
- Multiple-choice questions have four choices: A, B, C, and D.
- Essays have room for notes at bottom of page.
- The RICA may be taken as often as necessary until a passing score is achieved.
- The information given above is subject to change.

Questions Commonly Asked About the RICA

Q. What is the RICA?

A. The Reading Instruction Competence Assessment (RICA) was adopted by the California Commission on Teacher Credentialing (CCTC) "to measure an individual's knowledge, skill, and ability relative to effective reading instruction." The RICA is composed of two different and separate assessments—the RICA Written Examination and the RICA Video Performance Assessment. **The candidate needs to pass either one of the two assessments to complete the requirement. This book is designed specifically to prepare you for the RICA Written Examination.**

Q. Who administers the RICA?

A. The RICA is administered by National Evaluation Systems (NES®) with guidelines drawn up by the California Commission on Teacher Credentialing.

Q. When and where is the RICA Written Examination given?

A. The RICA Written Examination is administered statewide six times a year. You can get dates and test locations from the RICA Registration Bulletin or from their website at www.rica.nesinc.com. You can also contact the California Commission on Teacher Credentialing to obtain credentialing information at the CCTC website at www.cctc.org.

Q. What materials should I take to the test?

A. Be sure to take your admission ticket, some form of photo and signature identification, several sharpened Number 2 soft lead pencils with good erasers, and a watch to help pace yourself during the exam. No scratch paper, books, or other aids are permitted in the test center.

Q. What is included in the RICA Written Examination?

A. The RICA Written Examination consists of two sections: Section I, 70 multiple-choice questions; and Section II, open-ended questions, which includes essay assignments A, B, C, D, and E. Assignment E is a case study.

Q. How much time do I have to complete the test?

A. You have 4 hours to complete the entire test. You may work on the sections in any order.

Q. What is a passing score?

A. You need 81 points out of the 120 possible points to pass the exam.

Q. When will I get my score report?

A. Your official test score will be mailed to you about 4 to 5 weeks after you take the test. Unofficial scores will be available, for your access only, on the Internet on the score reporting date listed in the bulletin. To get your unofficial score go to www.rica.nesinc.com.

Q. Can I take the RICA Written Examination more than once?

A. Yes. But remember, your plan is to pass on your first try.

Q. Do I need to take both of the sections at one time?

A. Yes.

Q. Should I guess on the test?

A. Yes! Since there is no penalty for guessing, guess if you have to. On the multiple-choice section, first try to eliminate some of the choices to increase your chances of choosing the right answer. But don't leave any of the answer spaces blank. On the open-ended assignment section, be sure to give a response.

Q. May I write on the test?

A. Yes! As scratch paper will not be provided, you must do all of your work in the test booklet. Your answer sheet for the multiple-choice section, however, must have no marks on it other than your personal information (name, registration number, and so on) and your answers.

Q. How should I prepare?

A. Understanding and practicing test-taking strategies will help a great deal. A focused review of the subject matter listed in the Content Specification Domains is invaluable. This guide gives you insights, review, and strategies for the question types. Some universities offer preparation programs to assist you in attaining a passing score. Check with them for further information.

Q. How do I register?

A. The RICA Registration Bulletin is available at most college or university testing offices and teacher preparation programs. The registration bulletin is also available on the website at www.rica.nesinc.com. You can register for the exam by mail by completing the registration form contained in the registration bulletin, electronically on the Internet at www.rica.nesinc.com., or by telephone by calling NES at (916) 928-4004.

Q. How do I get more information about the RICA program?

A. Check the official RICA website. As new information becomes available, it will be posted at www.rica.nesinc.com.

Taking the RICA Written Examination: A Positive Systematic Approach

Strategies for Multiple-Choice Questions

The multiple-choice section appears first, followed by the essays, and finally the case study.

Applying the "Plus-Minus" System

Many who take the RICA don't get their best possible scores because they spend too much time on difficult questions, leaving insufficient time to answer the easy questions. Don't let this happen to you. Since you have about 1 minute per question and each question is worth the same amount, use the following system to avoid getting stuck on any one question.

1. Answer easy questions immediately.
2. When you come to a question that seems impossible to answer, make a large minus sign (–) next to it on your test booklet.
3. Then mark a *guess* answer on your answer sheet and move on to the next question.
4. When you come to a question that seems solvable but appears too time consuming, mark a large plus sign (+) next to that question in your test booklet and register a guess answer on your answer sheet. Then move on to the next question.

Since your time allotment is about 1 minute per question, a time-consuming question is one that you estimate will take you more than 1½ minutes to answer. But don't waste time deciding whether a question is a "+" or a "–". Act quickly, as the intent of the strategy is, in fact, to save you valuable time.

After you work all the easy questions, your test booklet should look something like this:

    1.

+2.

    3.

    4.

–5.

+6.

etc.

5. After answering all the questions you can answer immediately (the easy ones), go back and answer your "+" questions. Change your guess on your answer sheet, if necessary, for those questions you are able to answer. You may instead want to return briefly to the "+" questions in the same subject area before moving on to the next subject area. But do not spend too much time taking a second look at the "+" questions, or you will not complete the section.
6. If you finish the section and have rechecked your "+" questions, then you can either
   - Attempt those "–" questions, the ones that you considered impossible.

   or
   - Don't bother with those impossible questions. Rather, spend your time reviewing your work to be sure that you didn't make any careless mistakes.
7. Allow about 1 minute per question. Never spend more than about 1½ minutes on a question. If it looks like your question is going to take more than 1½ minutes, mark a plus or a minus, take your guess, and move on.

Remember, you do not have to erase the pluses and minuses you make in your test booklet. Be sure to fill in all of your answer spaces—if necessary, with a guess. As there is no penalty for wrong answers, it makes no sense to leave an answer space blank. **Never leave an answer space blank!**

Using the Elimination Strategy

Take advantage of being allowed to mark in your test booklet. As you eliminate an answer choice from consideration, make sure to mark it out in your test booklet as follows:

A̶

?B

C̶

?D

Notice that some choices are marked with question marks, suggesting that they may be possible answers. This technique will help you avoid reconsidering those marked-out choices you have already eliminated and will help you narrow down your possible answers. Remember, you are looking for the best answer of the ones given, which might not be the perfect or ideal answer. This elimination strategy will help you find the best answer. These marks in your test booklet do not need to be erased.

Avoiding the Misread

The most common mistake that test takers make in answering multiple-choice questions is the *misread*. The misread refers to **miss reading** the question, the information given, or the answer choices.

When you misread a question, you are immediately not looking for the answer you should be looking for. When you misread the information given, you are not going where the information and question are leading you. You are not taking advantage of what is given, and, in fact, you could be working from faulty information. Finally, when you misread an answer, you will either not select an answer you should select, or you will select an answer that doesn't mean what you think it means.

A question could ask,

"Which of the following should the teacher consider first, before preparing her lesson?"

or the question may instead have asked,

"Which of the following should the teacher include in her lesson plan?"

Notice that the first question is asking about the FIRST thing that the teacher should consider BEFORE preparing her lesson, whereas the second question simply asks what should be INCLUDED in her lesson plan.

To avoid misreading a question (and, therefore, answering it incorrectly), simply circle or underline what you must answer in the question. In the preceding examples, you would have circled or underlined the questions in your test booklet in this way:

"Which of the following should the teacher <u>consider first</u>, <u>before preparing her lesson</u>?"

or

"Which of the following should the <u>teacher include in her lesson plan</u>?"

You should also circle or underline key words in the information given, and you should focus on key words in the answer choices.

And, once again, these circles or underlines in your test booklet do not have to be erased.

Reviewing the Strategies

When you start reviewing for the multiple-choice section, keep the following items in mind.

1. Remember that the test is composed of 70 multiple-choice questions covering the four domains. The 70 multiple-choice questions appear first. Allow approximately 1 minute per question but never spend more than 1½ minutes on a question. Be sure to pace yourself accordingly.

2. Never leave a question without at least filling in a guess answer. Be careful when skipping questions to make sure that you are marking your answer in the correct space.

3. Try to answer all of the questions but don't deliberate over any one question or group of questions at great length. Remember, each question is of equal value. If you are uncertain, use a process of elimination to choose your response. Since there are only four choices, if you can eliminate one or two, your guessing odds increase tremendously.

4. A common mistake is misreading the question. Be sure to focus on what the question is asking.

5. You are to select the best answer. This means the best of those given, which might not always be an ideal answer.

Strategies for the Regular Essay Questions

There are a total of four regular essay questions on the entire exam and one case-study essay. The two essay questions related to Domains I and IV will require essays of approximately 50 words each. The two essay questions related to Domains II and III will require essays of approximately 150 words each.

Approaching the Questions

First, briefly scan the four essay questions. Do not attempt to answer an individual question at this point. Simply scan for general content to decide which question you will work on first. Select the one with which you feel the most comfortable. If you take the questions out of order, be sure to write your answer on the appropriate essay sheets and be careful not to skip any questions. Some general strategies include:

1. Read and mark the question. That is, circle or underline what the question is asking. For example, does the question ask you to describe what a teacher should do? Does it ask you to explain why a strategy or activity would be effective? Does it ask you for a series of steps or a number of examples?

2. Restate the question to yourself before attempting to answer the item. It is essential that you clearly understand what the question is asking for.

3. Quickly jot down, in the area provided in the test booklet, pertinent facts and information needed to answer the question. You can make a list of individual words or jot down phrases. Do not attempt to make a complete formal outline of your answer. Time constraints limit the effectiveness of detailed formal outlines.

Answering the Question

Follow these guidelines in writing your essay responses.

- Do not restate the question in your introductory sentence. This is considered unnecessary.
- Write in a clear, concise style. Many questions call for an answer to identify a problem or need, recommend a strategy or activity, and explain why this strategy would be effective.
- Answer all parts of an individual question. It's easy to skip part of the question under the time pressure—for example, listing two causes, but forgetting to list the two results.
- Refer back to the question to make sure that your answer is focused. Marking the question will help you maintain focus.
- Essay answers will vary in length from about 50 words (for Domains I and IV) to 150 words (for Domains II and III).
- Specific assessments, activities, materials, and key words (buzzwords) that are used in the field will often help display your knowledge of a subject.

- When you write your essay answer, be very specific answering the question or tasks given. Your answers will be easier to write if you use specific examples. For example, if you are asked to give the benefits of reading a variety of books aloud to a class, it might be much easier to base your answer on a few specific books or types of books, rather than discussing a variety of books in general.

- Do not write more than you need to. That is, keep in mind that two of the essays require 50-word answers and two require 150-word answers. Since the 150-word essays have more value than the 50-word essays, budget your time accordingly. Spend about 15 minutes on each short essay and about 30 minutes on each longer essay. Remember, if you spend too much time on one question, you might not have time to adequately complete your other essays.

- Do not spend an inordinate amount of time on any individual factor in a question that asks for multiple factors. Your overall score will be based on your ability to answer all parts of the question, not simply one part.

- Answer each question. Before skipping a question, read it a few times to see whether you gain insight concerning the question. The questions are generally designed so that you can receive partial credit if you have some knowledge of the subject. Partial answers will get partial credit. Even an answer that receives one point will be added to your total points.

- If you are completely unfamiliar with a question prompt, try a common-sense answer or skip the question. Do not get stuck. Recognize that by skipping a question you know nothing about, you will gain time for other questions, but try to write some sort of answer for each question.

- Unless specifically asked, do not write a conclusion or summary for any question. The question format does not normally require this type of response.

- Remember, these are fairly short essays, not formal three-, four-, or five-paragraph essays. You are trying to show the readers what you know. You may show steps, use bullet points, drawings, and so on.

Checking Your Answer

Keep the following points in mind.

- Keep track of your time. Pace yourself. Make time to briefly scan your responses to make sure that you've answered the question. Look for major errors in focus. Don't be overly concerned with minor spelling or grammar errors.

- Complete each essay in the proper booklet. Then, if time permits, review or reread your responses. You should give a response to each of the four essay questions.

Strategies for the Case Study Essay

The case study essay follows about 7 or 8 pages of information and should be approximately 300 words in length. You should leave about 1 hour to evaluate and write your case study essay.

Approaching the Case Study

When you start reviewing for the case study keep the following items in mind.

1. Read and mark the tasks given. That is, circle or underline what you arc being asked to do. Typically you will be asked to identify strengths and/or weaknesses, describe or recommend a strategy and/or activity, and explain how this strategy/activity will be effective.

2. Quickly jot down, in the area provided in the test booklet, pertinent facts and information needed to answer the question. You can make a list of individual words or jot down phrases. Do not attempt to make a complete formal outline of your answer. Time constraints limit the effectiveness of detailed formal outlines.

Writing the Case Study

Follow these guidelines in writing your case study essay.

- Do not restate the question in your introductory sentence. This is considered unnecessary.

- Write in a clear, concise style.

- Identify the strengths, weaknesses, or needs; recommend a strategy or activity; and explain why this strategy would be effective.

- Answer all of the tasks given. It's easy to skip a part under the time pressure—for example, identifying three weaknesses, describing activities, but forgetting to explain why they will be effective.

- Refer back to the tasks to make sure that your answer is focused. Marking the tasks will help in maintaining focus.

- Specific assessments, activities, materials, and key words (buzzwords) that are used in the field will often help display your knowledge of a subject.

PART I

ANALYSIS OF EXAM AREAS

This section emphasizes **how to approach question types** that you will be seeing on the RICA test. Sample questions are followed by important test-taking strategies and complete explanations.

Read this section carefully. Underline or circle key techniques. Make notes in the margins to help you understand the strategies, suggested approaches, and question types.

Introduction to the Multiple-Choice Questions

The multiple-choice section of the RICA is composed of 70 questions, although only 60 questions actually count toward your score. Ten of the questions are experimental and may be used on future tests. The 70 questions are taken from the four RICA Domains as follows:

Domain I	20% (about 14 questions)
Domain II	30% (about 21 questions)
Domain III	30% (about 21 questions)
Domain IV	20% (about 14 questions)

The 70 multiple-choice questions appear first on the exam. Be sure to allow approximately 1 minute per question, but never spend more than 1½ minutes on a question. Since you are given 4 hours to complete the entire exam, pace yourself accordingly to allow no more than 90 minutes or an hour and a half for the multiple-choice questions.

Some questions will be single questions, but others may be in groups, that is, two or three questions referring to the same information.

Remember to use the strategies mentioned earlier.

Applying the Plus-Minus System

Try to answer all of the questions but don't deliberate over any one question or group of questions at great length. Remember, each question is of equal value. Use the plus-minus system mentioned earlier so you don't get stuck on any one question.

Using the Elimination Strategy

If you are uncertain, use a process of elimination to choose your response. Since there are only four choices, if you can eliminate one or two, your guessing odds increase tremendously. Since there is no penalty for guessing, never leave a question without at least taking a guess.

Avoiding the Misread

Remember to watch out for the common mistake of misreading the question. Be sure to focus on what the question is asking.

Sample RICA Questions and Strategies

The following multiple-choice questions are grouped by domain and identified by content area. Read the sample questions, pay special attention to the strategies given for each question, and then focus carefully on the explanation.

Domain I

Planning and Organizing Reading Instruction Based on Ongoing Assessment

Content Area 1: Conducting Ongoing Assessment of Reading Development

> 1. A first-grade teacher administers running records to assess her students' reading. When listening to one of her students read an unknown text, the teacher notices that the student is able to read most of the words in the text accurately and use appropriate decoding strategies to figure out unknown words. After the student has read the text, the teacher asks him questions about the story. The student is unable to provide any correct answers and responds, "I don't know." What does this information tell the teacher about the student's reading ability and what do the results suggest for the teacher's future reading planning?
>
>   A. This information assists the teacher in selecting books for the student at this reading level and suggests that the classroom needs to provide books for students on many reading levels.
>
>   B. The student is able to comprehend what he has read accurately, and the teacher needs to select more challenging text for the student to read.
>
>   C. The student is able to decode the text but has weak comprehension skills; therefore, the teacher needs to provide direct instruction in comprehension strategies and demonstrate what needs to be understood from the text.
>
>   D. This student is able to decode the text accurately and would benefit from paired reading, flexible guided reading group instruction, and small group instruction on specific phonetic skills.

Strategies to Use

First underline or circle key words. Note that the question includes the grade level of the student—underline "first grade." The question also provides the information that the student can decode accurately but does not comprehend the text adequately—this is necessary information. The question also includes two parts: What does the **information provide** and what are the **next steps for teaching**? Be sure that the answer you choose addresses the two parts asked in the question.

Explanation

The best answer is **C.** The student's comprehension skills are weak if he cannot answer any of the subsequent questions about the story. The teacher will need to address this weakness in planning her future reading lessons. Choice D also correctly surmises that that student can decode accurately but supplies next step strategies that would not wholly address the student's deficits and, therefore, is an incorrect answer. Neither Choice A nor Choice B answers the question correctly. Reading is the active act of combining decoding and comprehension. The goal of all beginning reading programs should be that all students comprehend grade-level material. The teacher should be sure that the student in question is given an opportunity to discuss the meaning of any words or concepts he might not understand, use strategies such as literature circles that promote discussion of text and further facilitate comprehension, support the reader by tapping into any prior knowledge as it relates to the story, discuss the pictures before reading the story, and give clues to the story line beforehand.

Adequate reading comprehension is the ultimate result of effective instruction in reading. If a student is able to decode but not comprehend, then the student is not able to enjoy and understand written language. The knowledge and active application of certain reading strategies are necessary for comprehension.

Additional teaching strategies to develop reading comprehension in all grades, not only first grade, might include the following:

- using open-ended questioning techniques
- using drama activities that are good for supporting literacy development
- guided oral retellings
- question the author
- guided reflection
- small discussion groups
- reciprocal teaching (an approach using multiple strategies to support students in understanding text; students ultimately take on the role of the teacher)
- helping students to make inferences
- think-alouds—teacher modeling the mental processing of print

---

2. At the beginning of the new school term, the school district has provided a fifth-grade teacher with standardized testing results on each of the students enrolled in his class. Each grade level in the school meets to discuss standardized testing results and to utilize them to better know the students' capabilities. What would be the best assessments that the teacher might administer next to provide more information about the students to enable the teacher to better plan reading instruction?

   A. More information is needed on each student in order to plan reading instruction, and the teacher could administer a Phonological Awareness Screening Test, a Phonics Survey, and a reading comprehension assessment to provide him with more data.

   B. The assessments that would provide the most information would be a Spelling Inventory and an Alphabet Recognition Survey.

   C. A Reading Comprehension Test and an Oral Reading Test could be administered next to provide the teacher with diagnostic information that would assist the teacher in planning.

   D. After analyzing each student's performance on standardized tests, a Phonemic Awareness Test and a Phoneme Segmentation Test would help the teacher with planning for classroom instruction in reading.

Strategies to Use

First, circle or underline what you are looking for—in this case, *the best assessment that the teacher might administer next to provide more information*. Notice that this is a fifth-grade classroom. The question is asking about the next steps after analyzing standardized testing data. In general, standardized testing information is not diagnostic and the question asks about how the teacher would obtain more student information for planning instruction.

Explanation

The best answer is **C**. The teacher needs to be competent in selecting appropriate assessments and interpreting their results in order to plan reading instruction. A test that assesses reading comprehension, the ultimate goal of reading, is appropriate for fifth graders. This type of assessment requires that students can accurately decode words; have an understanding of grammar, syntax, and vocabulary; and are able to apply critical reading strategies. This assessment would give the teacher information on which students have reading difficulties and might benefit from additional assessments to help pinpoint their reading difficulties. Additionally, an oral reading test could give an indication of the student's reading fluency and whether the student decodes accurately. Good fluency often impacts a student's comprehension, and a student who reads haltingly with incorrect phasing and intonation will likely have difficulty reading grade level material. In Choice A, a phonological awareness test is mostly appropriate for students in grades K–2, but a phonics survey might be administered to a fifth-grade student who is having difficulty with decoding. In Choice B, a spelling inventory would be an appropriate test for a fifth grader and would give the teacher information on the student's orthographic knowledge, but an alphabet recognition survey would not be an appropriate test for a fifth grader. In Choice D, a phoneme segmentation test would be appropriate for a fifth grader who is significantly behind in reading and would help determine (reveal) where the deficits might be decoding weaknesses, but a phonemic awareness test would not normally be appropriate for this grade level.

Content Area 2: Planning, Organizing, and Managing Reading Instruction

---

3. In a multiple-choice exercise a student who speaks a second language at home is asked to identify the word that matches a picture of a "throne." The choices are:

    a. thrown

    b. throne

    c. throwne

The student chooses answer "a" but doesn't understand why his answer is marked wrong. What could this error suggest to the teacher for further instruction?

    A. This student's difficulty is with correct spelling, and the teacher should recognize that the student would benefit from adding this word to his/her weekly spelling list.

    B. This student is confusing homophones, and the teacher can provide individualized instruction to help the student differentiate between words that sound the same.

    C. The teacher needs to provide an environment that promotes independent reading to help this student with vocabulary.

    D. This student's reading and vocabulary development can be furthered by extra classroom lessons provided by a teacher, aide, or parent volunteer.

Strategies to Use

First, underline or circle key words. Next, focus on the information that is provided with the question. The information states that the student speaks a second language at home and makes an error on a multiple-choice question. Notice the answers that the student has to choose from are homophones. This will help lead you to the best answer to this question. You need to be sure that the answer you choose specifically answers what the question is asking.

Explanation

The best answer is **B.** Confusing "throne" and "thrown" is a very common error for students who might hear another language at home. Additionally, they might be more familiar with the word "thrown" and possibly would have seen it in print before. The teacher should recognize that this student needs some additional individualized instruction to clarify these words. Choice A is incorrect because this student is not experiencing a spelling problem. Although independent reading promotes increased vocabulary, as suggested in Choice C, this is not the best solution to this student's difficulty. Choice D contains correct statements but does not specifically address the question.

Domain II

Developing Phonological and Other Linguistic Processes Related to Reading

Content Area 3: Phonemic Awareness

4. During a phonemic awareness activity, a primary student is unable to blend phonemes said aloud by the teacher. The teacher explains that she will say the sounds in a word very slowly and then the students are to tell her what word she is stretching into sounds. The student listens attentively to the sounds and then orally says an incorrect word, not relying on any of the sounds the teacher has said. For example, after hearing /s/ - /a/ - /t/, the child says, "kitten." What does this information suggest to the teacher?

   A. It would be beneficial to the teacher to include the use of magnetic letters in small group instruction, and the teacher needs to instruct the student in matching sounds to the letters.

   B. The teacher could help this student with blending skills by assigning independent practice with a volunteer or teacher's aide.

   C. The teacher needs to provide this student with explicit instruction in blending and to select appropriate activities and materials to practice sound segmentation and blending.

   D. This student would benefit from additional instruction in phonemic awareness, since phonemic awareness is an essential reading skill and students need to understand how language works in order to be successful readers.

Strategies to Use

First, underline or circle key words in the question. Note that the question provides the exact task and the exact response of the child. Knowing that this is a phonemic awareness task will help you narrow down the choices.

Explanation

The best answer is **C**. Choice A involves matching sounds to letters, not a phonemic awareness task. Choice B would help the student practice the skill with an adult, but this student needs more instruction in the skill before practice can begin. Choice D is true; the student would probably benefit from added instruction in phonemic awareness but is too general an answer and does not specifically address what the question is asking. Choice C specifically addresses this student's weakness. Blending is an important prerequisite to reading, and students need practice and explicit instruction in this skill. In teaching this skill, the teacher needs to select activities and materials that are appropriate for this student's stage of development. Some good activities for this student would be oral games such as play a guessing game by identifying a familiar item in the classroom and say: "What am I thinking of? I'm thinking of something in the room that you can sit at. I'm thinking of a /d/-/e/-/s/-/k/. What am I thinking of?" Or you can use student's names, stretch them into sounds, and ask the students to tell you what name you are saying.

Content Area 4: Concepts About Print

5. After reading a big book to her students who are gathered on the rug at the front of the room, the teacher asks a kindergarten student to find a word on the page of text and to frame that word with her hands. The teacher requests that the student frame any word on the page before her. The student comes to the front of the room where the big book is displayed and uses her hands to frame a whole line of text instead of just one word. After the teacher ascertains that the student has understood the task, what kind of classroom intervention could the teacher plan for this student?

   A. The teacher should engage the student in activities that promote understanding of "word." Some activities that the teacher could use are having the students track print as the teacher reads, counting words, and explaining that there are empty spaces between words.

   B. The ability to frame a word needs to be practiced by this student in order to foster her understanding of phonics. Some activities that could help this student understand the concept of a word are writing in sand, singing songs, cut-and-paste activities, and being read to.

   C. A good intervention for this student is to participate in learning center activities that are carefully planned by the teacher. Some learning centers that would benefit this student are writing centers, listening centers, computer centers, and independent reading.

   D. This student could benefit from additional activities that support these skills. Some suggested intervention activities for this student are letter matching, cut-apart sentences, and oral reading activities.

Strategies to Use

First, underline or circle key words. Next, review the information given carefully. Note that this question describes a classroom scenario in which students are gathered to listen to the teacher read a big book. This is a common activity in early primary classrooms. The task that the teacher is asking the student to perform is described. Additionally, it is noted that the student understands the task.

Explanation

The best answer is **A.** This question deals with Print Concepts. The mastery of Print Concepts is a reliable predictor to reading success.

Some benchmarks in Print Concepts include identifying the front/back of the book, discriminating between a letter and a word, recognizing word and sentence boundaries, knowing where to begin reading on a page, understanding that print goes from top to bottom and left to right. Choice B incorrectly states that framing a word will aid the understanding of phonics. The other activities in the answer are appropriate activities for early primary but would not be appropriate interventions for this student. In Choice C, the learning centers mentioned would not aid this student in mastering Print Concepts. Finally, Choice D suggests intervention activities would not all be appropriate for helping this student in mastering Print Concepts.

Content Area 5: Systemic, Explicit Phonics and Other Word Identification Strategies

6. In small group instruction, the teacher leads her group through the following activities:

First, the teacher segments the following words:

chin	into	/ch/ - /i/ - /n/
reach	into	/r/ - /ea/ - /ch/
cherry	into	/ch/ - /err/ - /y/

Then the students try to guess the word that the teacher is saying.

The teacher then asks what sound was commonly heard in each of the words.

Next, the teacher prints the letters *ch* on the board and shows the students a picture of some cherries. The teacher asks the students to think of some more words that have the /ch/ sound at either the beginning or the end. These words are written on the board and the students practice saying the words.

Finally, the students practice this skill by reading selections on their own in which most of the words are decodable and include *ch* or high frequency words that have already been taught. The teacher carefully monitors each student's reading and makes corrections if necessary.

What are the benefits of using the aforementioned strategies?

A. These strategies reinforce concepts of print and the ability to recognize specific sounds.

B. These strategies will help students recognize this digraph when decoding, spelling, and writing.

C. These strategies will assist students achieve mastery in spelling.

D. Students need to hear the way language sounds and see the print before them for extended periods of time to finally master the skill.

Strategies to Use

First, underline or circle the key words. Note that the question very specifically asks what would be the "benefits" of the lesson. Which response specifically addresses the benefits of the lesson described? There could be other possible benefits to this lesson, but the choices might not provide appropriate answers, so you must eliminate them.

Explanation

The best answer is **B.** This lesson would be a part of systematic, explicit phonics lesson within an organized program. The lesson describes instruction in letter clusters known as digraphs and begins with identifying them in words where they are heard, then seeing how they are written, and finally practicing reading them in connected text. These strategies play a critical role in decoding, reading fluently, and ultimately comprehending text. Therefore, the best answer to this question is B. These strategies do not constitute a phonemics awareness lesson as mentioned in Choice A, nor would it necessarily be a benefit to students to copy the words generated from the board. In Choice C, these strategies certainly would assist students in spelling words that contain the digraph *ch* but would not help students achieve mastery in spelling.

7. In a small group, a first grade nonfluent reader is asked to read the following passage from the first-grade reader.

> Jack and Matt were friends. They had known each other for a very long time. They liked to play together. Sometimes they would play at Jack's house, and sometimes they would play at Matt's house. They were good friends.

The words the student has the most difficulty decoding are "were," "friends," "known," "very," "they," and "would." The student attempts to sound out these words but is not successful and arrives at the completion of the text with limited understanding of what he has just read. What interventions should the teacher plan for this student?

A. If a child reads most words in the text correctly but misses some of the words, the teacher could provide opportunities for this student to practice reading fluently with support. Some activities that could help this student are choral reading, rereading, and listening to stories on tape.

B. If a child misses so many words that comprehension is affected, then the teacher could help this student by activating prior knowledge, encouraging predicting before the text is read, and using graphic organizers.

C. Additional phonics instruction could benefit this student and assist him in improving his decoding. Some activities that would help this student are instruction in word families, playing word games, and doing tongue twisters.

 D. The words that seem to be most difficult for this student are sight words or high frequency words. The teacher should provide some activities that would help this reader such as using word walls, maintaining a personal dictionary, and word study after reading.

Strategies to Use

The key words in this question are "interventions" and "teacher plan." Mark these key words. Note that the question mentions that this is a first-grade classroom and that the student is a nonfluent reader being asked to read a grade-level passage. The primary problem that this student is having is the inability to recognize the high frequency words within the text. Be careful that you are correctly diagnosing what the problem is, in order to arrive at the correct answer.

Explanation

The best answer is **D.** This student apparently is having difficulty in recognizing sight words or high frequency words. These are the errors mentioned in the information given. Readers need to build a repertoire of these words that occur most frequently in text (high frequency words). These are the words that can't be sounded out. It is helpful to try and connect these words to the student's experience to promote long-term memory. It's also beneficial to call students' attention to these words within and out of text. Some activities that help build high frequency word banks are word walls, personal dictionaries, word-study after reading, and student writing. Therefore, the correct choice is D. Choice A doesn't correctly diagnose this student's problem, although the activities mentioned in the answer would promote fluency. Choice B correctly concludes that when a student makes many miscues when reading, comprehension is ultimately affected. This student's understanding of the text must be affected. The strategies mentioned in Choice B would help with comprehension. It's quite likely that if the student could correctly decode the high frequency words, he or she would understand the text, and so difficulty with comprehension would be a secondary problem. Choice C, additional phonics instruction, would not help this student decode the high frequency words that the student is decoding incorrectly and is, therefore, an incorrect answer.

Content Area 6: Spelling Instruction

8. A fourth-grade classroom teacher is asked to submit student writing from her class to be published in a school newspaper. The students in the class are asked to interview a classmate, friend, or relative who immigrated to the United States. The students are to generate a list of questions to ask regarding the person's experience when arriving in a new country. One student submitted the following writing sample:

My Mom

When my mom came, she did not *speek* English because she was born in a *diffirent* country. No one could understand her because of her *axcent*. She was good in *swiming*. I think my mom is *amazzing*.

In analyzing the student's spelling errors, how does the teacher begin to interpret the student's spelling development and how might the teacher plan for further spelling instruction?

A. First of all, the teacher must identify the spelling errors in this student's paper. She can then return the paper to the student for correction. Then, the student can add the misspelled words to the student's weekly spelling list.

B. After identifying the students' spelling errors, the teacher can add these words to her class's weekly spelling list to enable her students to achieve mastery of these words. In future spelling lessons, the teacher can group her students according to the words they are having difficulty spelling and then provide activities to help them with these words.

C. The teacher should identify the misspelled words in this student's writing sample and should add this sample to other samples of this student's work. For further information about this student's spelling development, the teacher should administer a spelling inventory and analyze the results. This would provide her with more information on which to base word study lessons for her class.

D. The teacher notices on this sample that this student has made many errors with words that have doubled consonants, but she needs more information in order to determine this student's spelling development. Future lessons should include activities with the misspelled words of each student.

Strategies to Use

Notice that the question states that this is a fourth-grade class. This student is making appropriate errors for a fourth grader. If the students made errors in other skills that should be mastered by the fourth grade such as beginning/ending consonants or short vowels, further assessments might be necessary. Importantly, the question asks about how the teacher "begins" to interpret her students' spelling development and how the teacher might "plan for further instruction."

Explanation

The best answer is **C.** A good starting point for the instructor is to gain more information about her students' spelling stages by collecting samples of student writing from both formal inventories and from daily writing. Then the teacher can begin to compare the students' spelling abilities. Additionally, administering a spelling inventory to the class will assist the teacher in determining students' spelling stages of development. Although all students will pass through the same stages of development, they pass through at different rates. The inventory can provide the teacher with valuable information about each student's spelling developmental stage and subsequently help her in planning spelling instruction.

Additionally, presenting students with spelling words that are matched to their spelling developmental stage creates lessons in developing concepts rather than memorizing words. That's why Choice A is an incorrect answer. Merely adding the misspelled words to a weekly list will not further this student's spelling development as would doing activities that promote the learning of the skill with which she is having difficulty. Similarly, the first sentence in Choice B is also incorrect although the next sentence suggests appropriate activities to do after spelling assessment to determine the students' developmental spelling levels. In Choice D, the teacher correctly notices the type of errors that the student has made on this particular sample but needs more than this one sample to determine her future spelling instructional plans for this student and the rest of the class.

Domain III

Developing Reading Comprehension and Promoting Independent Reading

Content Area 7: Reading Comprehension

9. A fifth-grade teacher puts the following chart on the board:

Story Title: _____

Setting	
Characters	
Problem	
Solution	

Students receive their own copy of this story map to complete. The students had received instruction and practice with this strategy beforehand when the teacher modeled how to complete the chart while reading a previous story in a whole group setting. The teacher explains that the students are to use the story map to help them identify the key elements in the story they are about to read.

What might be the teacher's purpose for having students complete the story map, and what does this activity demonstrate about her understanding of developing reading comprehension in her students?

A. The teacher is demonstrating her understanding of the reading process by having her students complete this story map. By correctly completing the activity, the students demonstrate their understanding of cause-effect relationships and literal comprehension.

B. This teacher understands that reading comprehension is necessary learning for all students. By having her students complete this story map, she is providing effective instruction in reading comprehension and demonstrating her knowledge of what students need to comprehend the text.

C. The teacher is demonstrating her understanding that a story map assists students in clarifying text. By providing instruction in identifying story elements, this teacher has provided an activity that will help her students identify the important story elements and help her students identify and organize the relationship between them.

D. This teacher is showing how to explicitly demonstrate a comprehension technique. Additionally, she is demonstrating the importance of finding the main idea, something that these students will be able to do after completing this activity.

Strategies to Use

Firstly, review the chart that the question provides. Think about what responses might be appropriate and the purpose for this type of chart. Is it asking for cause-effect relationships? Or is it asking for important story elements? Now focus on key words in the question. Be careful when answering questions that are asking about more than one item—in this case, *the teacher's purpose and what is demonstrated*. Be sure that the answer that you select adequately and specifically answers the complete question. Finally, notice that the question states that this is a fifth-grade classroom. The purposes for this chart might vary with the grade level.

Explanation

The best answer is **C.** This type of activity facilitates student comprehension. Good readers are able to clarify text but need to be taught how to find the most important elements of a story. The teacher needs to create opportunities for students to learn and then independently practice comprehension techniques. Additionally, by having students write, before, during, or after reading, they are deepening their understanding of text. Choice A isn't correct because it makes a very general statement about the teacher demonstrating her understanding of the reading process. This activity does not demonstrate that. Additionally, the purpose of story mapping isn't to teach cause-effect relationships or literal comprehension. Choice B provides correct statements but is not specific. Choice D might also be accurate, but does not address identifying the different story elements, which is a main purpose of this chart.

Content Area 8: Literary Response and Analysis

10. A fourth-grade teacher selects a core literature book for her students to read. After her students have completed reading the book, she asks them to go back through the text and find situations that the main character has experienced that remind the students of something in their own lives. The students are to use a response log to record their ideas. The teacher might choose this strategy as a follow-up to reading the book because:

A. The teacher understands that helping her students connect real-life experiences to those of a character will deepen their understanding of a book, and she can analyze their responses to plan future appropriate instruction.

B. The student responses can be used to evaluate the students' understanding of the text and will provide the teacher with information she can use to plan further assessments and testing.

C. Writing in response logs provides good daily writing practice for students and are an appropriate strategy for fourth graders.

D. Each teacher needs to be familiar with her district's core literature selections in order to provide appropriate material for her students

Strategies to Use

The teacher in the question provides a strategy for her students. You might think of the benefits that this strategy provides for students before reading the choices. Don't let the choices that state correct teaching practices distract you from the correct answer. Remember to find the best answer to the question.

Explanation

The best answer is **A.** Encouraging students to connect text with personal experiences helps students relate what they're reading to their own lives. These types of connections might also be incorporated into students' writing. Besides connecting what they are reading to their experiences, connections can be made between different story versions, books by the same author, and connecting characters to people they know. Choice B is correct in that the teacher can gain information about her students' understanding of the text by reading their responses but is not the *best* answer to this question. Choice C is also correct, but again, is not the *best* answer. Choice D focuses on *the teacher being familiar with the district's core literature selections to provide appropriate material*, which does not answer the question.

Content Area 9: Content-Area Literacy

> **11.** An eighth-grade history teacher is beginning a unit on the history of the Civil Rights Movement in the United States. He begins by systematically collecting documents on the incident that involved a woman being asked to give up her bus seat in the Southern United States in 1955. Besides the school district provided history text, he collects artifacts to be contained within an archive bin that will give the students more information to read about the incident and that are correlated to the text. Some of the documents that the teacher includes regarding the incident are a newspaper article, an interview with the woman, photos, a letter to the woman, and an eyewitness account of the incident written by the woman involved. Next, the teacher involves the students in retrieving information about the incident from the various sources. The students will use the information provided for research, formulating ideas, preparing reports, and taking a test. Some important concepts to be taught about understanding information in this unit are to:
>
> **A.** help students understand the organization of the text, notice the visual clues that will identify the important ideas, and understand the relationship between those ideas.
>
> **B.** help the students understand the features of expository texts by including lessons regarding cause-effect relationships, how to compare/contrast, and how to summarize and identify the main idea.
>
> **C.** have students, with the help of the teacher, complete a K-W-L chart to identify what the students already know about the subject, what they want to learn, and what they have learned when the unit is completed.
>
> **D.** use graphic organizers to provide some important organizational skills for his students to process the information from the various sources.

Strategies to Use

Notice that the question is referring to an eighth-grade history class. All teachers are teachers of reading and need to possess the skills and knowledge to provide access for their students to the content areas. According to the question, all of the information that the students will need to read will be expository text. Also note that the question specifically asks about important concepts to be taught. Eliminate incorrect answers that do not answer the question, even if they are true.

Explanation

The best answer is **A.** The purpose of expository text is to provide facts and information. This type of text can often inform, explain, or persuade. As students progress through the grades, more and more time is devoted to this type of text. Often, this type of text is more difficult for students because it involves more high-level thinking than does narrative text. These are the key concepts that students need to be taught to process this type of text. In addition to the items included in the archive bin mentioned in the question, the Internet could provide students with more information on the topic. According to research, student understanding about the text structure is strongly linked to their comprehension, so any instruction that includes expository text must help students understand how this type of text is organized. Often maps, charts, and diagrams are included in expository text. These items provide visual clues that provide information, and students need to be taught how to use these items to help understand the concepts.

Choice B provides some features that might occur in expository text, but you are not able to infer from the question that these skills need to be taught. Choice C contains an effective strategy for processing expository text, the K-W-L chart (**K**now, **W**ant to know, **L**earned) but again, you cannot infer that the teaching of this strategy will help these students comprehend this specific text. In Choice D, the use of graphic organizers is a good strategy that will help students understand text, but this answer does not provide some key concepts and, therefore, is not as good as Choice A.

Content Area 10: Student Independent Reading

12. What are the best reasons for a teacher to encourage her students to read on their own?

A. Independent reading should be a daily homework assignment, have a reward system for the amount of pages read, and follow teacher read-alouds.

B. Independent reading helps students practice the reading skills they have learned in class, is a good classroom activity for transition periods, provides extra practice for better readers, and can be done after workbook assignments.

C. Independent reading should be conducted outside of school, have a prescribed book list from which students can choose, and can also be done in the school library.

D. Independent reading promotes life-long reading, builds vocabulary, increases reading comprehension, and increases background knowledge.

Strategies to Use

Circle or underline the key words in the question. You are looking for the *best* reasons to encourage students to read independently. Eliminate choices that are not accurate or don't give reasons. Then find the best answer. Remember, sometimes an incorrect answer will be close.

Explanation

The best answer is **D.** All of the items mentioned in this choice—*promotes life-long reading, builds vocabulary, increases reading comprehension,* and *increases background knowledge*—are exactly why students should read on their own. Choice A does not give a reason for a teacher to encourage students. Choice B is a good reason, but not the *best* of the ones given. Choice C is not accurate and does not give a reason for a teacher to encourage students.

13. The best way for a classroom teacher to support student independent reading is by:

A. guiding her students in choosing books at their reading level.

B. making sure that students have a wide variety of choices of books to read within the classroom.

C. providing book bags containing material for the students to read at home with their parents.

D. using a variety of strategies and incentives to motivate her students to read in their spare time and at home.

Strategies to Use

Focus on the key words in the question: best way . . . to support independent reading. Eliminate choices that do not address *student independent reading*.

Explanation

The best answer is **D.** Using motivational strategies and incentives is good way to support independent reading. Choice A is something a teacher should do, but is not specific to supporting independent reading. Choice B refers to books to read within the classroom only, and students need to be encouraged to also read outside of the classroom. Choice C mentions reading at home with their parents. The purpose is to get students to read independently.

Domain IV

Supporting Reading Through Oral and Written Language Development

Content Area 11: Relationships Among Reading, Writing, and Oral Language

---

14. After reading a chapter in their history text, a classroom of eighth graders are asked to form cooperative groups to compare and contrast the systems of transportation of the eighteenth century with those of today. Each group is provided with a chart to complete. The teacher knows that many of her students speak and write other languages at home. How might this strategy support these students' understanding of the text?

A. Since expository text is more difficult for second-language learners to grasp, awareness of language similarities and differences will support student understanding of text varieties.

B. This teacher's support will benefit her students' understanding of the concepts learned in the chapter, and her next step might be to ask each group to prepare a report on their findings.

C. The teacher understands that her students would benefit from using graphic organizers to further student understanding of the ideas in the chapter and help relate them to students' present experiences.

D. The informal language opportunities provided by cooperative group participation will aid student understanding of text.

Strategies to Use

Underline or circle the keys words in the question: strategy support . . . students' understanding. Be aware of the best answer to the question. In some cases, the incorrect choices provide correct information but do not provide the best answer to the question.

Explanation

The best answer is **C.** Choice A provides correct statements but does not address the question. Choices B and D are also correct, but are not the best, most complete or specific answer to the question. Teachers should be aware of the variety of graphic organizers and match the most appropriate one to the text that is being read and to the objective of the lesson. Visual aids help support the learning of the English learner (and of all students). Charts, realia, word organizers, and outlining also support understanding of expository text for all students.

Content Area 12: Vocabulary Development

Use the information below to answer the two questions that follow.

The following diagram is provided for students in a third-grade classroom:

The students are told that one way to understand and remember new words is to think about how they are related. It is explained that one way to do this is to figure out how the word fits in a word hierarchy. This is a diagram in which the words are ranked. The teacher then leads a class discussion about each word, how it relates to the other words, and what the concept is about in each word. She then asks whether the students can add any words to the hierarchy. The students are then divided into small groups and given collections of other words to arrange into hierarchies. Finally, students are given general categories with which to develop word lists to arrange into hierarchies.

---

15. What would be the purpose of using the preceding strategy?

    A. Looking up words in a dictionary and using them in sentences is conducive to effective vocabulary instruction and constitutes purposeful learning at most grade levels.

    B. The purpose of this strategy is to increase students' word knowledge, although the knowledge of words doesn't directly determine how text is understood.

    C. The most important reason for using a similar strategy to teach vocabulary is for comprehending text and aiding students in acquiring new and varied vocabulary.

    D. This strategy will help students understand words with similar meanings and will increase student understanding of how words are related, including differences/similarities between words that have almost the same meaning.

16. The best way for the teacher to determine the words to use in future similar lessons is to use:

    A. recycled words selected from an old lesson including words from past weekly spelling tests.

    B. difficult words that the teacher selects in similar activities from the dictionary.

    C. words that the teacher selects from student writing or story selections read in class.

    D. words that the students select from daily or weekly reading activities.

Strategies to Use

First, underline or circle key words. Next, carefully analyze any chart or diagram included to help you to understand what information is being given. Remember to eliminate answers that are not true or give false information.

Explanation for 15

The best answer is **D.** Students need to have the ability to understand words that are similar in meaning. Oftentimes the inability to understand the shades of meaning of words contributes to poor comprehension of text. Good readers need to know a large number of words that can't only be acquired by wide reading, although encouraging student volume of reading can contribute to an increased vocabulary. This type of lesson can be extended to provide antonyms for the selected words.

Choice A, using the dictionary to look up words, does not contribute to effective vocabulary instruction. Eliminate Choice A. In Choice B, the first part of the statement is correct, but the second part is not true. Knowledge of words does directly determine how text is understood. In Choice C, increasing vocabulary contributes to better comprehension as does an increase in the volume of reading, but instruction in specific words and concepts is needed to produce in-depth vocabulary knowledge. This diagram shows how specific words are related.

Explanation for 16

The best answer is **C.** Although some of the other choices are possible, using words that the students use in writing or speech is probably more meaningful to students. The teacher should select the words to make sure that the students get the most out of the lesson.

Content Area 13: Structure of the English Language

17. What are some effective assessments to use in analyzing student oral and written language in order to determine student understanding and use of effective English structure and conventions?

    A. running records, multiple choice tests, student reports, individual student conferences, and parent conferences

    B. anecdotal records, teacher observation, student conferences, checklists, and collection of writing work samples

    C. mini lessons, cloze procedure tests, oral reading inventories, book lists, retellings, and writing rubrics

    D. analyzing student invented spelling, portfolio assessment, student self-assessment, and student work files

Strategies to Use

Notice that you are looking for effective assessments. You need to be aware of the information that the tests listed provide to the teacher. For example, a running record would help the teacher assess a student's reading level but would not adequately provide information on whether the student is grasping language conventions.

Explanation

The best answer is **B.** Assessing English language structures is an important Structure of the English Language content specification and is an integral part of the teaching process. The teacher frequently observes her students to determine what they already know and what they need to learn. Authentic assessment can provide the teacher with more information about students and the impact of the instructional program in the classroom. Most importantly, authentic assessments inform instruction. Standardized tests will also provide information to the next year's teacher on the students' grasp of the structure of the English Language. The other choices do not adequately address both the oral and written parts of the question.

Introduction to the Essay Questions

The Focused Educational Problems and Instructional Tasks

The essay section is composed of four essay questions as follows:

Question Number	Area Tested	Length	Total Value
Essay 1 (Assignment A)	Domain I	50 words	6 points
Essay 2 (Assignment B)	Domain VI	50 words	6 points
Essay 3 (Assignment C)	Domain II	150 words	12 points
Essay 4 (Assignment D)	Domain III	150 words	12 points

You should plan on spending approximately 15 minutes on each 50-word essay and 25–30 minutes on each 150-word essay. Your total time for the four essays should be about 90 minutes or 1½ hours.

Understanding the Scoring

Let's take a careful look at the scoring system.

Essay Scoring Guide

Score 3

You will receive a score of 3 if the response:

❑ reflects a thorough understanding of the relevant content and academic knowledge from the applicable RICA domain.

❑ fulfills the purpose of the assignment completely.

❑ responds fully to the given task(s).

❑ is very accurate.

❑ demonstrates an effective application of the relevant content and academic knowledge from the applicable RICA domain.

❑ provides strong supporting examples, evidence, and rationale based on the relevant content and academic knowledge from the applicable RICA domain.

Score 2

You will receive a score of 2 if the response:

❑ reflects an adequate understanding of the relevant content and academic knowledge from the applicable RICA domain.

❑ fulfills the purpose of the assignment adequately.

❑ responds adequately to the given task(s).

❑ is generally accurate.

❑ demonstrates a reasonably effective application of the relevant content and academic knowledge from the applicable RICA domain.

❑ provides adequate supporting examples, evidence, and rationale based on the relevant content and academic knowledge from the applicable RICA domain.

Score 1

You will receive a score of 1 if the response:

❑ reflects limited or no understanding of the relevant content and academic knowledge from the applicable RICA domain.

❑ fails to fulfill or partially fulfills the purpose of the assignment.

❑ responds in a limited manner or inadequately to the given task(s).

❑ is inaccurate.

❑ demonstrates an ineffective application of the relevant content and academic knowledge from the applicable RICA domain.

❑ provides limited or no supporting examples, evidence, and rationale based on the relevant content and academic knowledge from the applicable RICA domain.

U

The response will receive a score of U for "unscorable" if it is:

❑ off task.

❑ unrelated to the assigned topic.

❑ illegible.

❑ not of sufficient length to score.

❑ written in a language other than English.

B

The response will receive a score of B if it is blank.

How to Respond to the Essay Questions

Some General Strategies

First, briefly scan the four essay questions. Do not attempt to answer an individual question at this point. Simply scan for general content to decide which question you will work on first. Select the one with which you feel the most comfortable. If you take the questions out of order, **be sure to write your answer on the appropriate essay sheets** and be careful not to skip any questions.

The following steps will help you get started:

1. Read and mark the question. That is, circle or underline what the question is asking. For example, does the question ask you to describe what a teacher should do? Does it ask you to explain why a strategy or activity would be effective? Does it ask you for a series of steps or a number of examples?

2. Restate the question to yourself before attempting to answer the item. It is essential that you clearly understand what the question is asking.

3. Quickly jot down, in the area provided in the test booklet, pertinent facts and information needed to answer the question. You can make a list of individual words or jot down phrases. Do not attempt to make a complete formal outline of your answer. Time constraints limit the effectiveness of detailed formal outlines.

Some General Guidelines for Writing

Follow these guidelines in writing your essay responses.

❑ Write in a clear, concise style.

❑ Many questions call for an answer to identify a problem or need, recommend a strategy or activity, and explain why this strategy would be effective.

❑ Answer all parts of an individual question. It's easy to skip part of the question under the time pressure—for example, listing two causes, but forgetting to list the two results.

❑ Refer back to the question to make sure that your answer is focused. Marking the question will help in maintaining focus.

❑ Essay answers will vary in length from about 50 words (for Domains I and IV) to 150 words (for Domains II and III).

❑ Specific assessments, activities, materials, and key words ("buzzwords") that are used in the field will often help display your knowledge of a subject.

❑ When you write your essay answer, be very specific answering the question or tasks given. Your answers will be easier to write if you use specific examples. For example, if you are asked to give the benefits of reading a variety of books aloud to a class, it might be much easier to base your answer on a few specific books or types of books, rather than discussing a variety of books in general.

❑ Do not write more than you need to write. That is, keep in mind that two of the essays require 50-word answers and two require 150-word answers. Since the 150-word essays have more value than the 50- word essays, budget your time accordingly. Spend about 15 minutes on each short essay and about 30 minutes on each longer essay. Remember, if you spend too much time on one question, you might not have time to adequately complete your other essays.

❑ Do not spend an inordinate amount of time on any individual factor in a question that asks for multiple factors. Your overall score will be based on your ability to answer all parts of the question, not simply one part.

❑ Answer each question. Before skipping a question, read it a few times to see whether you gain insight concerning the question. The questions are generally designed so that you can receive partial credit if you have some knowledge of the subject. Partial answers will get partial credit. Even an answer that receives one point will be added to your total points.

❑ If you are completely unfamiliar with a question prompt, try a common-sense answer or skip the question. Do not get stuck. Recognize that by skipping a question you know nothing about, you will gain time for other questions.

❑ Unless specifically asked, do not write a conclusion or summary for any question. The question format does not normally require this type of response.

❑ Remember, these are fairly short essays, not formal three-, four-, or five-paragraph essays. You are trying to show the readers what you know. You may show steps, use bullet points, drawings, and so on.

Some Points for Checking Your Essay

Keep the following points in mind.

❑ Keep track of your time. Pace yourself. Make time to briefly scan your responses to make sure that you've answered the question. Look for major errors in focus.

❑ Don't be overly concerned with minor spelling or grammar errors.

❑ Complete each essay in the proper booklet. Then, if time permits, review or reread your responses.

❑ Make sure that you write a response to each of the four essay questions.

Now let's take a look at a specific approach with samples from each domain.

The Approach

Understand the situation given.

First, circle or underline the key words in the information.

❑ Note the student's grade.

❑ Also notice the student's history.

❑ Next, focus on the problem or situation.

Carefully read and examine the task.

❑ Underline the key words.

❑ Now focus on the task.

Prewrite—make some notes.

❑ Jot down notes in the area provided.

❑ Keep the notes simple.

Write the essay.

❑ Be clear and concise.

❑ Show what you know.

❑ Give specifics.

❑ Fulfill the task or tasks.

❑ You can use bullet points.

Remember, in many instances you will be asked to:

❑ identify the need.

❑ recommend an instructional strategy/student activity.

❑ explain (when needed).

Watch for these items in analyzing the situation and the task.

Now let's take a closer look at the Educational Problems and Instructional Tasks.

Domain I

Planning and Organizing Reading Instruction Based on Ongoing Assessment

Use the following information to complete the given exercise.

A student enters a first-grade class in November. In reviewing the cumulative folder, the teacher notes that the student attained mastery in phonemic awareness tasks in kindergarten. However, it is noted that he has challenges with sound-symbol relationships.

Examinee Task

Write a response in which you describe what the teacher should do to assist this student in reading.

Your essay should be approximately 50 words in length.

The Approach

Understand the situation given.

- ❑ First, circle or underline the key words in the information.
- ❑ Note the student's grade—*first grade*.
- ❑ Also notice the student's history—*attained mastery in phonemic awareness tasks in kindergarten*.
- ❑ Next, focus on the problem or situation—challenges with sound-symbol relationships.

Carefully read and examine the task.

- ❑ Underline the key words. Your underlining might have looked like this:

  Write a response in which you <u>describe</u> <u>what</u> the <u>teacher should do</u> <u>to assist</u> this student <u>in reading</u>.

- ❑ Now focus on the task of describing what the teacher should do to assist . . . in reading.

Prewrite—make some notes.

Your notes might look like this:

> *Sound-symbol decoding skills*
> *Phonics survey*
> *BPST*
> *Determine skill need*
> *Provide instruction*
> *Provide activities*
> *Reassess*

Write the essay.

Sample Essay

A phonics survey such as the BPST would assist the teacher in identifying gaps or needs in the student's sound-symbol (decoding) skills. Steps the teacher would take include:

- *Administer the phonics survey (BPST).*
- *Analyze and determine phonics skill need.*
- *Provide direct, explicit instruction in the phonics skill.*
- *Provide student activities to practice the identified skill. Practice first in isolation and then in connected text (decodable text).*
- *Reassess with BPST to monitor for skill mastery.*

Evaluating the Essay

The essay fulfills the assignment by identifying the problem—student difficulty in sound-symbol relationships (phonics) and giving the following recommendations. The teacher must assess to find the skill need/gap. She must provide direct instruction and a variety of student activities linked to the skill need. These recommendations are clearly pointed out in a bullet format. The essay could also have mentioned that practice materials in the form of short books or stories that contain words providing children with practice in using specific letter-sound relationships that they are learning would be helpful. Notice that the writer's last bullet deals with reassessing. This shows a clear understanding that it is important to make sure that the problem has been rectified.

Domain II

Developing Phonological and Other Linguistic Processes Related to Reading

> **Use the following information to complete the given exercise.**
>
> The role of phonemic awareness in beginning reading has been well researched. Phonemic awareness is related to reading achievement. Study the following example of a phonemic awareness task.

Sample Phonemic Awareness Task

Students listen to a sequence of separately spoken phonemes. They then combine the phonemes to form a word. They then say the word.

Teacher: What word is /c/ /a/ /t/?

Students: /c/ /a/ /t/ is cat.

Teacher: Good. Now try this word—/s/ /oa/ /p/.

Students: /s/ /oa/ /p/ is soap.

Teacher: Very good. Let's try one more—/f/ /l/ igh//t/.

Students   /f/ /l/ /igh/ /t/ is flight.

Examinee Task

Based on the information given above, write a response in which you:

(1) describe how phonemic awareness is related to beginning reading achievement; (2) identify the phonemic awareness task being taught in the example; and (3) explain why the identified task is essential in developing phonemic awareness.

Your essay should be approximately 150 words in length.

The Approach

Understand the situation given.

- ❏ First, circle or underline the key words in the information.
- ❏ Note the student's *phonemic awareness skill addressed.*
- ❏ Review the example. *What is the teacher asking of the students? What do the students reply?*
- ❏ Focus on the problem or situation.

Carefully read and examine the task.

❑ Underline the key words. Your underlining might have looked like this:

Based on the information given above, write a response in which you:

(1) describe how is phonemic awareness is related to reading achievement;

(2) identify the phonemic awareness task in the example; and

(3) explain why this task is essential in the development of phonemic awareness.

❑ Now focus on the tasks of (1) **describing**; (2) **identifying**; and (3) **explaining**.

Prewrite—make some notes.

Your notes might have looked like this:

> *P.A. strongly related to reading*
> *Stanovich, Adams research*
> *Example—oral blending*
> *Blend individual phonemes spoken word p/i/g*
> *Blend sounds and then identify words*
> *Segment sounds*
> *Fully manipulate sounds*
> *Firm foundation*

Write the essay.

Sample Essay

Phonemic awareness is strongly related to reading achievement. Keith Stanovich's research shows that phonemic awareness is the core causal factor separating normal from disabled readers. Phonemic awareness, as noted in Marilyn Adams' research, is one of the three predictors of success in early reading. Adams notes that if a student does not attain mastery of phonemic awareness, he will probably never be able to read on grade level.

The phonemic awareness task being performed in the example is oral blending. Oral blending is an essential skill in phonemic awareness development. Blending is one of the final areas in phonemic awareness tasks. Students learn to blend individual phonemes into spoken words such as p/i/g. It is essential that students perform this task with mastery. Then they can blend sounds and identify words. When this skill is attained, students then learn to segment the sounds in words rather than blending the sounds. With these skills, putting sounds in words together (blending) and pulling sounds in words apart (segmenting) students are then able to fully manipulate sounds. They have a firm foundation in the auditory skills of phoneme manipulation, and phonemic awareness, an essential element in reading achievement, is mastered.

<u>**Evaluating the Essay**</u>

The essay clearly informs the reader that phonemic awareness is directly related to reading achievement. The author then notes two researchers who support this statement. Next, the author fulfills the second part of the task with the answer that oral blending is the phonemic awareness task used in the example.

The third part of the examinee tasks asks for a rationale. Why is the identified task essential? The essay clearly explains that oral blending is essential in hearing and identifying sounds put together to form words. Putting sounds together, blending, and identifying words forms the necessary foundation in the alphabetic code for putting sounds and symbols together to identify words and, thus, begin reading.

Domain III

Developing Reading Comprehension and Promoting Independent Reading

Use the following information to complete the given exercise.

Understanding what we read or reading comprehension is the reason for reading. It is not enough to first read the words; we must understand the meaning. Therefore, capable seventh-grade readers, as they read, are both purposeful and active readers. They are purposeful for a number of reasons, depending on the content of the text. Good readers are engaged in actively thinking about what they read. They use their prior knowledge and reading comprehension strategies to make sense of text.

<u>**Comprehension Strategy Examples**</u>

1. The reader thinks to herself:

   "I don't understand that paragraph."

   "I don't get what the author means."

   "Oh, yes, the author means that . . ."

   "The author talked about the characters in the previous chapter. I think I will reread that chapter to understand the character better."

2. The reader is reading a chapter comparing mammals and reptiles. To help himself to understand the likeness and differences he might create a visual such as this:

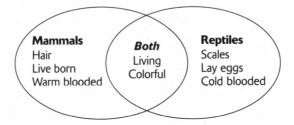

Mammals
Hair
Live born
Warm blooded

Both
Living
Colorful

Reptiles
Scales
Lay eggs
Cold blooded

<u>**Examinee Task**</u>

Based on the information given and using your knowledge of reading comprehension, write a response in which you (1) identify each comprehension strategy in the example; (2) describe the strategy; and (3) clearly state how the strategy helps the reader in comprehension or understanding.

The Approach

Understand the situation given.

- ❏ First, circle or underline the key words in the information.
- ❏ Note the grade level—*seventh grade.*
- ❏ Note each *comprehension strategy in the example.*
- ❏ Also, identify *each comprehension strategy.*
- ❏ Next, focus on the problem: *Explain how each strategy helps the reader to comprehend.*

Carefully read and examine the task.

- ❏ Underline the key words. Your underlining might have looked like this:

   Based on the information given and using your knowledge of reading comprehension, write a response in which you (1) <u>identify</u> <u>each comprehension strategy</u> in the example; (2) <u>describe</u> the <u>strategy</u>; and (3) clearly <u>explain</u> <u>how the strategy helps</u> the reader in <u>comprehension</u> or understanding.

- ❏ Now focus on the tasks of (1) **identifying;** (2) **describing;** and (3) **explaining.**

Prewrite—make some notes.

Your notes might have looked like this:

> *#1 comprehension monitoring*
> *aware of understanding*
> *use fix-up strategies*
> *reader questions, adjusts*
> *problem solves*
>
> *strategy helps understanding*
> *aware of what they understand*
> *identify what they don't get*
>
> *#2 graphic organizer*
> *visuals, illustrate concepts and relationships*
> *list types of organizers*
> *help students see how ideas are related*
> *help students remember and focus*
> *tools for understanding text, summarizing*

Write the essay.

Sample Essay

The first example is comprehension monitoring. It involves the reader being aware of her understanding of the text and using specific fix-up strategies when needed. Comprehension monitoring is a form of thinking about one's thinking or metacognition. The reader questions, adjusts, modifies, clarifies as she is reading to "get" (comprehend) the meaning in the text.

This strategy helps readers in understanding or comprehension because they are consistently aware of what they do understand. In addition, they can identify what they do not get or understand and they are able to use fix-up strategies to solve problems in understanding. Fix-up strategies appropriate for the example are identifying that there is a difficulty, identifying what the difficulty is, restating what the author means and re-reading for meaning.

The second example is using a graphic organizer. Graphic organizers are visuals that illustrate concepts and relationships among concepts in a text. There are many types of graphic organizers such as: semantic maps, webs, charts, graphs, and the type used in the example; Venn diagrams. Graphic organizers help students to organize ideas and concepts and to see how ideas are interrelated. They also help the reader to remember the information. Graphic organizers provide visual tools for students to use in understanding and representing text. In addition, they help students in "putting it all together," understanding, and summarizing text.

Evaluating the Essay

The essay fulfills the task by addressing each comprehension strategy in the example separately. First, the comprehension strategy is identified or named. Next, the author tells what it is or describes the strategy. The descriptions are very clear—almost definitions. The explanations with the descriptions tell the reader that the author understands the strategy in depth. After the description, the author explains how this strategy helps the reader to understand or gain meaning from the text. It is key to let the reader know that the author knows how each strategy assists students in understanding. They are tools. How does each help? In comprehension monitoring, the key ideas of "I get it, don't get it, or I know how to solve the problem" are addressed. The author carefully discusses how graphic organizers assist the reader in seeing relationships and summarizing.

Domain IV

Supporting Reading Through Oral and Written Language Development

> **Use the following information below to complete the given exercise.**
>
> In a third-grade class, many of the students are English language learners. The teacher is planning study skills and/or learning strategies that will assist students in understanding written materials and retaining information.
>
> ### Examinee Task
>
> Describe two strategies the teacher might use to enhance the students' ability to understand written material and to retain information.

The Approach

Understand the situation given.

- ❏ First, circle or underline the key words in the information.
- ❏ Note the students' grade—*third grade.*
- ❏ Also, note the students' history—*many English language learners*
- ❏ Next, focus on the problem—understanding written materials and retaining information.

Carefully read and examine the task.

- ❏ Underline the key words. Your underlining might have looked like this:

  Describe two strategies the teacher might use to enhance the students' ability to understand written materials and to retain information.

- ❏ Now focus on the task of: describing the two strategies.

Prewrite—make some notes.

Your notes might have looked something like this:

> *Variety of strategies*
> *Strategy 1*
> *Word organizers*
> *Brainstorming, mapping, clustering*
> *Strategy 2*
> *Visual aids*
> *Real objects, pictures, DVDs, charts*

Write the essay.

Sample Essay

The third-grade teacher could use a variety of strategies to aid students in understanding concepts and vocabulary in written language. Word organizers and realia are tools that assist students' understanding of vocabulary and concepts. Word organizers such as brainstorming, mapping, and clustering are strategies that help students in linking prior knowledge and in developing necessary vocabulary. A second strategy is using visual aides such as real objects, pictures, DVDs, and charts to make concepts more comprehensible.

Evaluating the Essay

The essay addresses the task of describing at least two strategies to help students to understand written material and retain information. Research has shown that graphic organizers are some of the best tools to increase comprehension/ understanding and to assist students in retaining information. The essay names several graphic word organizers to enhance the description.

The second strategy of using visuals is a classic, very well-accepted strategy. Using real items (**realia**) helps to provide a bridge (**scaffold**) from the student's prior knowledge to the concept addressed in the lesson, thus, making concepts more comprehensible to second language learners. Both graphic organizers and visuals aid in understanding by providing a linkage between students' prior knowledge and the new knowledge to be learned.

39

Extra Practice

Domain I

Practice Essay Topic 1

Use the following information to complete the given exercise.

A kindergarten student writes, "I love my kitty" underneath his drawing of child and a pet.

Examinee Task

Write a response in which you explain what this tells the teacher about his understanding of print and his readiness to read. Explain how the teacher should follow up.

Your essay should be approximately 50 words in length.

You may use the space below to make notes. The notes will not be scored.

Practice Essay for Topic 1

RICA Practice Essay Evaluation Form

Use this checklist to evaluate your essay:

1. To what extent does this response reflect an **understanding of the relevant content** and academic knowledge from the applicable RICA domain?

thorough	**adequate**	**limited or no**
understanding	understanding	understanding

2. To what extent does this response fulfill the purpose of the **assignment?**

completely	**adequately**	**partially**
fulfills	fulfills	fulfills or fails to

3. To what extent does this essay **respond to the given task(s)?**

fully	**adequately**	**limited or inadequately**
responds	responds	responds

4. How **accurate** is the response?

very	**generally**	**inaccurate**
accurate	accurate	

5. Does the response **demonstrate an effective application** of the relevant content and academic knowledge from the applicable RICA domain?

yes	**reasonably**	**no**
effective	effective	ineffective and inaccuracies

6. To what extent does the response **provide supporting examples, evidence, and rationale** based on the relevant content and academic knowledge from the applicable RICA domain?

strong	**adequate**	**limited or no**
support	support	support

Important Points

Some of the points your essay could have covered for Practice Topic 1 were as follows:

- ❑ The student is connecting print to meaning and is progressing through the stages of writing development.
- ❑ Writing and reading are closely connected, and the student's ability to connect his print to his picture most likely predicts his readiness for reading. It is important that the teacher asks him to read his story to her and that she praises him.
- ❑ Often this situation presents a teachable moment for writing and spelling instruction.
- ❑ Teacher needs to give numerous opportunities for meaningful writing experiences for her students (that is, writing on self-selected topics, practicing invented/temporary spelling, and reading story aloud to audience).

Domain II

Practice Essay Topic 2

Use the following information to complete the given exercise.

A fifth-grade teacher uses an essay assignment to survey student writing ability. In reading the essays he can see that more than half of his class seems to be having difficulty with spelling.

Examinee Task

Write a response that describes some steps the teacher should take to assist his students in the area of spelling.

Your essay should be approximately 150 words in length.

You may use the space below to make notes. The notes will not be scored.

Practice Essay for Topic 2

RICA Practice Essay Evaluation Form

Use this checklist to evaluate your essay:

1. To what extent does this response reflect an **understanding of the relevant content** and academic knowledge from the applicable RICA domain?

thorough	**adequate**	**limited or no**
understanding	understanding	understanding

2. To what extent does this response fulfill the purpose of the assignment?

completely	**adequately**	**partially**
fulfills	fulfills	fulfills or fails to

3. To what extent does this essay **respond to the given task(s)?**

fully	**adequately**	**limited or inadequately**
responds	responds	responds

4. How **accurate** is the response?

very	**generally**	**inaccurate**
accurate	accurate	

5. Does the response **demonstrate an effective application** of the relevant content and academic knowledge from the applicable RICA domain?

yes	**reasonably**	**no**
effective	effective	ineffective and inaccuracies

6. To what extent does the response **provide supporting examples, evidence, and rationale** based on the relevant content and academic knowledge from the applicable RICA domain?

strong	**adequate**	**limited or no**
support	support	support

Important Points

Some of the steps your essay could have described for Practice Topic 2 were as follows:

1. Use a developmental model to assess students' spelling level. *The Synchrony of Reading, Writing, and Spelling Development* by Bear is an excellent tool to pinpoint spelling levels as linked with reading and writing levels.

2. Use informal, diagnostic teaching tools such as Bear's *Qualitative Spelling Checklist*, collect spelling samples, and analyze for the stages of spelling development. Hendersen (1974) noted the following stages of spelling development.

   - Pre-Literate
   - Early Letter Name
   - Middle and Late Letter Name
   - Within Word Pattern
   - Syllable Juncture
   - Derivational Constancy

3. Plan instruction and monitor growth. Questions to ask in monitoring include what does the student know? Use but confuse? What developmental stage? Where in the stage (beginning/middle/end)?

Domain II

Practice Essay Topic 3

Use the following information to complete the given exercise.

An eighth-grade English teacher is concerned that the students entering her class do not possess strong enough spelling/reading skills, so she gives her students the "Upper Level Qualitative Spelling Inventory" at the beginning of each school year.

Examinee Task

Using your knowledge of reading, write a response in which you explain why this is a good practice.

Your essay should be approximately 150 words in length.

You may use the space below to make notes. The notes will not be scored.

Practice Essay for Topic 3

RICA Practice Essay Evaluation Form

Use this checklist to evaluate your essay:

1. To what extent does this response reflect an **understanding of the relevant content** and academic knowledge from the applicable RICA domain?

thorough	**adequate**	**limited or no**
understanding	understanding	understanding

2. To what extent does this response fulfill the purpose of the assignment?

completely	**adequately**	**partially**
fulfills	fulfills	fulfills or fails to

3. To what extent does this essay **respond to the given task(s)?**

fully	**adequately**	**limited or inadequately**
Responds	responds	responds

4. How **accurate** is the response?

very	**generally**	**inaccurate**
accurate	accurate	

5. Does the response **demonstrate an effective application** of the relevant content and academic knowledge from the applicable RICA domain?

yes	**reasonably**	**no**
effective	effective	ineffective and inaccuracies

6. To what extent does the response **provide supporting examples, evidence, and rationale** based on the relevant content and academic knowledge from the applicable RICA domain?

strong	**adequate**	**limited or no**
support	support	support

Important Points

Some of the points your essay could have covered for Practice Topic 3 were as follows:

❑ There is a strong relationship between students' orthographic knowledge and reading achievement. When students have strong orthographic knowledge, their reading is easier and more fluent.

❑ Using the Error Guide for the Inventory, the teacher can identify the student's spelling level. Direction can then be planned, which is specific to the student's need.

❑ We know from Adams' research that success in one component of the reading process predicts success in the other components. The teacher can use assessment, instruction, and practice to help students to achieve success in spelling. This should, in turn, assist in students' attaining further success in reading.

❑ Instructional strategies such as webbing, word clusters, and graphic organizers may be used with flexible skill groups to provide practice, help students make connections, and, thus, build spelling ability.

Domain III

Practice Essay Topic 4

Use the following information to complete the given exercise.

A second-grade teacher is concerned about his students' understanding and appreciation of literature. He decides to select a different story each day to read to his class. The teacher also considers rereading some of the stories.

Examinee Task

Using your knowledge of reading, write a response in which you (1) discuss the benefits of reading a new story each day and (2) explain the benefits of rereading a story.

Your essay should be approximately 150 words in length.

You may use the space below to make notes. The notes will not be scored.

Practice Essay for Topic 4

RICA Practice Essay Evaluation Form

Use this checklist to evaluate your essay:

1. To what extent does this response reflect an **understanding of the relevant content** and academic knowledge from the applicable RICA domain?

thorough	**adequate**	**limited or no**
understanding	understanding	understanding

2. To what extent does this response fulfill the purpose of the assignment?

completely	**adequately**	**partially**
fulfills	fulfills	fulfills or fails to

3. To what extent does this essay **respond to the given task(s)?**

fully	**adequately**	**limited or inadequately**
responds	responds	responds

4. How **accurate** is the response?

very	**generally**	**inaccurate**
accurate	accurate	

5. Does the response **demonstrate an effective application** of the relevant content and academic knowledge from the applicable RICA domain?

yes	**reasonably**	**no**
effective	effective	ineffective and inaccuracies

6. To what extent does the response **provide supporting examples, evidence, and rationale** based on the relevant content and academic knowledge from the applicable RICA domain?

strong	**adequate**	**limited or no**
support	support	support

Important Points

Some of the points your essay could have covered for Practice Topic 4 were as follows:

- ❑ Increases exposure to good literature.
- ❑ Promotes story enjoyment and literature appreciation.
- ❑ Good for noting what the author does in the writing process so students may make similar choices for themselves.
- ❑ There are good reasons to reread a familiar story. Rereading helps to increase students' fluency level. Rereading is often used in shared reading, when the teacher is using the text to teach concepts.
- ❑ Rereading enhances vocabulary development and the love of reading.

Domain III

Practice Essay Topic 5

Use the following information to complete the given exercise.

Each week a second-grade teacher reads a different story aloud to her class. Before she gets to the end of the story, she asks students to tell her how they think the story will end.

Examinee Task

Using your knowledge of reading, write a response in which you (1) identify some of the benefits of her technique and (2) explain how this techniques works.

Your essay should be approximately 150 words in length.

You may use the space below to make notes. The notes will not be scored.

Practice Essay for Topic 5

RICA Practice Essay Evaluation Form

Use this checklist to evaluate your essay:

1. To what extent does this response reflect an **understanding of the relevant content** and academic knowledge from the applicable RICA domain?

thorough	**adequate**	**limited or no**
understanding	understanding	understanding

2. To what extent does this response fulfill the purpose of the assignment?

completely	**adequately**	**partially**
fulfills	fulfills	fulfills or fails to

3. To what extent does this essay **respond to the given task(s)?**

fully	**adequately**	**limited or inadequately**
responds	responds	responds

4. How **accurate** is the response?

very	**generally**	**inaccurate**
accurate	accurate	

5. Does the response demonstrate an effective application of the relevant content and academic knowledge from the applicable RICA domain?

yes	**reasonably**	**no**
effective	effective	ineffective and inaccuracies

6. To what extent does the response **provide supporting examples, evidence, and rationale** based on the relevant content and academic knowledge from the applicable RICA domain?

strong	**adequate**	**limited or no**
support	support	support

Important Points

Some of the points your essay could have covered for Practice Topic 5 were as follows:

- ❏ The teacher is utilizing **prediction** questions, among the best kind of open-ended questions.
- ❏ Readers describe what they think will happen in a story or predict an ending before they read it.
- ❏ They confirm, adjust, or disprove their predictions.
- ❏ Children use prior knowledge, past experiences, and what they see in the pictures.
- ❏ Older children use these factors in addition to what they already know about authors and literature.
- ❏ Prediction questions work equally well with nonfiction and sometimes stimulate children's interest in a topic.
- ❏ The higher order thinking skill prediction is similar to forming a hypothesis, and students must analyze data and make a reasonable prediction.

Domain IV

Practice Essay Topic 6

> **Use the following information to complete the given exercise.**
>
> Reading, writing, and spelling are interrelated.
>
> **Examinee Task**
>
> Explain why is it important for a teacher to understand the relationships between reading, writing, and spelling.

Your essay should be approximately 50 words in length.

You may use the space below to make notes. The notes will not be scored.

Practice Essay for Topic 6

RICA Practice Essay Evaluation Form

Use this checklist to evaluate your essay:

1. To what extent does this response reflect an **understanding of the relevant content** and academic knowledge from the applicable RICA domain?

thorough	**adequate**	**limited or no**
understanding	understanding	understanding

2. To what extent does this response fulfill the purpose of the **assignment?**

completely	**adequately**	**partially**
fulfills	fulfills	fulfills or fails to

3. To what extent does this essay **respond to the given task(s)?**

fully	**adequately**	**limited or inadequately**
responds	responds	responds

4. How **accurate** is the response?

very	**generally**	**inaccurate**
accurate	accurate	

5. Does the response demonstrate an effective application of the relevant content and academic knowledge from the applicable RICA domain?

yes	**reasonably**	**no**
effective	effective	ineffective and inaccuracies

6. To what extent does the response **provide supporting examples, evidence, and rationale** based on the relevant content and academic knowledge from the applicable RICA domain?

strong	**adequate**	**limited or no**
support	support	support

Important Points

Some of the points your essay could have covered for Practice Topic 6 were as follows:

- ❑ Phoneme awareness, word recognition, and spelling are all interrelated. They predict one another in the early stages of reading development.
- ❑ Spelling knowledge, which is poorly developed, inhibits writing and word recognition.
- ❑ The relationship is noted and supported by the research findings of Marilyn Adams that success in one component of the reading process predicts success in the other components.
- ❑ The accuracy, facility, and quality of spelling knowledge are a basis for predicting reading acquisition between grades K–2.
- ❑ The writing processes of prewriting, writing, and revising can be enhanced and reinforced through oral language experiences and reading.

Introduction to the Case Study

Based on Student Profile

The case-study essay follows six to eight pages of information about a student. The information given could include

- background information.
- samples and assessments.
- worksheets.
- teacher and parent comments and evaluations.

You will be given four pages and asked to write an essay of approximately 300 words to

- assess the reading performance.
- describe and prescribe instructional strategies and/or activities.
- explain "why" strategies would be effective.

The case-study essay is scored on a 1–4 scoring scale by two scorers, so the actual scores range from 2 to 8. Since the case study is weighted by a factor of three (score is multiplied by 3), the total points possible for the case study are 24. Although the case study can be time consuming, you can get a lot of points, so make sure to leave **at least 1 hour** to complete the review of the information and to write the essay.

Understanding the Scoring

Now let's take a careful look at the scoring system.

Case Study Scoring Guide

Score 4

You will receive a score of 4 if the response:

- reflects a thorough understanding of the relevant content and academic knowledge from the applicable RICA domains.
- fulfills the purpose of the assignment completely.
- responds fully to the given task(s).
- is very accurate.
- demonstrates an effective application of the relevant content and academic knowledge from the applicable RICA domains.
- provides strong supporting examples, evidence, and rationale based on the relevant content and academic knowledge from the applicable RICA domains.

Score 3

You will receive a score of 3 if the response:

- reflects an adequate understanding of the relevant content and academic knowledge from the applicable RICA domains.

- ❑ fulfills the purpose of the assignment adequately.
- ❑ responds adequately to the given task(s).
- ❑ is generally accurate.
- ❑ demonstrates a reasonably effective application of the relevant content and academic knowledge from the applicable RICA domains.
- ❑ provides adequate supporting examples, evidence, and rationale based on the relevant content and academic knowledge from the applicable RICA domains.

Score 2

You will receive a score of 2 if the response:

- ❑ reflects a limited understanding of the relevant content and academic knowledge from the applicable RICA domains.
- ❑ fulfills the purpose of the assignment only partially.
- ❑ responds in a limited way to the given task(s).
- ❑ is partially accurate, but may contain significant inaccuracies.
- ❑ demonstrates a limited or generally ineffective application of the relevant content and academic knowledge from the applicable RICA domains.
- ❑ provides limited supporting examples, evidence, and rationale based on the relevant content and academic knowledge from the applicable RICA domains.

Score 1

You will receive a score of 1 if the response:

- ❑ reflects little or no understanding of the relevant content and academic knowledge from the applicable RICA domains.
- ❑ fails to fulfill the purpose of the assignment.
- ❑ responds inadequately to the given task(s).
- ❑ is inaccurate.
- ❑ demonstrates an ineffective application of the relevant content and academic knowledge from the applicable RICA domains.
- ❑ provides little or no supporting examples, evidence, and rationale based on the relevant content and academic knowledge from the applicable RICA domains.

U

The response will receive a score of U for "unscorable" if it is:

- ❑ off task.
- ❑ unrelated to the assigned topic.
- ❑ illegible.
- ❑ not of sufficient length to score.
- ❑ written in a language other than English.

B

The response will receive a score of B if it is blank.

How to Respond to a Case Study

Some General Strategies

The following steps will get you started.

1. Read and mark the tasks given. That is, circle or underline what you are being asked to do. Remember, typically you will be asked to identify strengths and/or weaknesses, describe or recommend a strategy and/or activity, and explain how this strategy/activity will be effective.

2. Quickly jot down, in the area provided in the test booklet, pertinent facts and information needed to answer the question. You can make a list of individual words or jot down phrases. Do not attempt to make a complete formal outline of your answer. Time constraints limit the effectiveness of detailed formal outlines.

Some General Guidelines for Writing

Follow these guidelines in writing your case-study essay.

- ❏ Write in a clear, concise style.
- ❏ Identify the strengths, weaknesses, or needs; recommend a strategy or activity; and explain why this strategy would be effective.
- ❏ Answer all of the tasks given. It's easy to skip a part under the time pressure—for example, identifying three weaknesses, describing activities, but forgetting to explain why they will be effective.
- ❏ Refer back to the tasks to make sure that your answer is focused. Marking the tasks will help in maintaining focus.
- ❏ Specific assessments, activities, materials, and key words ("buzzwords") that are used in the field will often help display your knowledge of a subject.

Some Points for Checking Your Essay

Keep the following points in mind.

- ❏ Keep track of your time. Pace yourself. Make time to briefly scan your essay to make sure that you've answered the given tasks.
- ❏ Look for major errors in focus. Don't be overly concerned with minor spelling or grammar errors.
- ❏ Complete the case-study essay in the proper booklet.

The Approach

Plan to spend 1 hour working on the case study—analyzing and writing.

The Analysis

1. Divide the area provided for scratch work into three columns. Label one column **"strengths,"** one column **"weaknesses,"** and one column **"instructional strategies and activities."**

2. Read each piece of data in the case study. While reading each document, if you notice a strength, write it in the **strength** column. If you see a weakness, write it in the **weakness** column. If you see the same strength or weakness in other documents as you read, put a checkmark next to where you wrote it on your notes page.

3. After reviewing all the data given to you in the case study, look at your notes page for the strengths and weaknesses that came out the most times. Those should be the ones to focus on in your write up of the case study. You should also focus on skills that are more elementary or basic before you focus on skills that are more advanced. For example, if a student has trouble with short vowel sounds in single-syllable words and suffixes in multi-syllabic words, you should recommend working on the short vowels before working on multi-syllabic words. Put a star or checkmark next to the strengths and weaknesses on which you will be focusing.

4. Next to the strengths you will be building on and the weaknesses you will be remediating, in the column labeled **instructional strategies and activities,** list some instructional strategies and activities that would work on those specific identified strengths and weaknesses.

strengths	_weaknesses_	_instructional strategies and activities_

The Writing

1. When you write your analysis of the case study, first describe the student's strengths and cite the piece or pieces of data from the case study that led you to the conclusion that those were strengths.

2. Next, do the same for the weaknesses: Explain what the weaknesses are and cite the data that showed that they were weaknesses.

3. Finally, write your recommendations for instructional strategies and activities to meet the student's strengths and weaknesses. Describe what the strategy and/or activity is and how it works. Give your rationale for why you selected that specific strategy or activity for that student. You want to answer the questions, "What would you do about it?" and "How would you do it?"

Important Note: The more specific you can be, the better your score will be. If you can give names of specific programs or assessments that address the student's strengths or weaknesses, you should. It is also helpful to give the names of specific types of materials or titles of books to use as examples. If you are not sure that a specific program or assessment actually addresses the specific need, then don't mention it. In that case it is better to be more general than to be inaccurate.

A Sample Case Study

Case Study 1: Danny

This case study focuses on a student named Danny, who is in the seventh grade. The documents on the following pages describe Danny's performance during the middle of the school year. Using these materials, write a response in which you apply your knowledge of language arts assessment and instruction to analyze this case study. Your response should include three parts:

1. identify three of Danny's important reading strengths and/or needs at this point in the school year, citing evidence from the documents to support your observations;

2. describe two specific instructional strategies and/or activities designed to enhance Danny's literacy development by addressing the needs and/or building on the strengths you identified; and

3. explain how each strategy/activity you describe would promote Danny's reading proficiency.

Your response should be approximately 300 words in length.

You may use the space below to make notes. These notes will not be scored.

Word Recognition Assessment

Danny's reading teacher gave him a test to measure the recognition of words out of context. The test consists of graded word lists to get an idea of what grade level further testing should be done. Mispronunciations are written down next to the word. The teacher noted that Danny read the words slowly, sounding them out. The results of this assessment are on the following page.

San Diego Quick Assessment ~ Record Form

Name **Danny**   Grade **7**   Date **Feb. 4**

Directions: Begin with a list that is at least two or three sets below the student's grade level. Have the student read each word aloud in that list. Continue until the student makes three or more errors in a list.

Reading Levels: One error, independent level; two errors, instructional level; three errors, frustration level. When testing is completed, record the highest grade level in each of these categories in the spaces below.

Independent **3**   Instructional **3**   Frustration **4**

sound out words

Preprimer	Primer	Grade 1	Grade 2	Grade 3
see	you	road	our	city
play	come **can**	live	please	middle
me	not	thank	myself	moment
at	with	when	town	frightened
run	jump	bigger	earl	exclaimed
go	help	how	send	several
and	is	always	wide	lonely
look	work	night	believe	drew
can	are	spring	quietly	since
here	this	today	carefully	straight **start**

Grade 4	Grade 5	Grade 6	Grade 7
decided **decide**	scanty	bridge	amber
served **serve**	business	commercial	dominion
amazed	develop	abolish	sundry
silent	considered **consider**	trucker	capillary
wrecked **wreck**	discussed **discuss**	apparatus	impetuous
improved	behaved **behave**	elementary	blight
certainly **certain**	splendid	comment	wrest
entered **enter**	acquainted **account**	necessity	enumerate
realized	escaped	gallery	daunted
intercepted **interpt**	grim	relatively	condescend

Grade 8	Grade 9	Grade 10	Grade 11
capacious	conscientious	zany	galore
limitation	isolation	jerkin	rotunda
pretext	molecule	nausea	capitalism
intrigue	ritual	gratuitous	prevaricate
delusion	momentous	linear	visible
immaculate	vulnerable	inept	exonerate
ascent	kinship	legality	superannvate
acrid	conservatism	aspen	luxuriate
binocular	jaunty	amnesty	piebald
embankment	inventive	barometer	crunch

Informal Reading Assessment

Danny's reading teacher gave him an informal assessment of reading performance to assess the rate and accuracy with which a student reads aloud. For this assessment, Danny read aloud short, graded passages, and the teacher made notes about his performance. Following are the results of some of the passages he read. The teacher put a line through words that he misread, writing what he said above the printed word. After reading each passage, Danny was asked to retell what the paragraph was about, and he was able to do so with reasonable accuracy.

Tool I
ORAL READING TEST

No.4

cowboy
Three more cowboys tried their best to rope and
tie a calf as quickly[r] as Red, but none of them
came within ten seconds of his time. Then came
the long, thin cowboy. He was the last one to
enter the contest.

			1st Testing	2nd Testing	3rd Testing
Errors	Level				
1 (0-2)	(Indep.)		☒	☐	☐
3-4	Instr.		☐	☐	☐
5-6	Frust.		☐	☐	☐
Speed:	Fast		☐	☐	☐
	Avg.		☐	☐	☐
	(Slow)		☒	☐	☐
	V. Slow		☐	☐	☐

No.5

hill
High in the hills they came to a[r] wide ledge
[sc]
where trees grew among the rocks[rock]. Grass grew
in patches and the ground was covered with bits
of wood from trees blown over a long time ago
and dried by the sun. Down in the valley it was
already beginning to get dark.

			1st Testing	2nd Testing	3rd Testing
Errors	Level				
2 (0-2)	(Indep.)		☒	☐	☐
3-4	Instr.		☐	☐	☐
5-6	Frust.		☐	☐	☐
Speed:	Fast		☐	☐	☐
	Avg.		☐	☐	☐
	(Slow)		☒	☐	☐
	V. Slow		☐	☐	☐

			1st Testing	2nd Testing	3rd Testing
Errors	Level				
0-2	Indep.		☐	☐	☐
3-4	Instr.		☐	☐	☐
6 (5-6)	(Frust.)		☒	☐	☐
Speed:	Fast		☐	☐	☐
	Avg.		☐	☐	☐
	Slow		☐	☐	☐
	V. Slow		☒	☐	☐

No.6

subropan
Businessmen from suburban areas may travel to
helicopter [a]
work in helicopters, land on the roof of an office
building, and thus avoid city traffic jams. Families
can spend more time at summer homes and
cabin [r]
mountain cabins through the use of this
[sc]
marvelous craft. People on farms can reach city
shop
center quickly for medical service, shopping,
sales
entertainment, or sale of products.

			1st Testing	2nd Testing	3rd Testing
Errors	Level				
0-2	Indep.		☐	☐	☐
3-4	Instr.		☐	☐	☐
5-6	Frust.		☐	☐	☐
Speed:	Fast		☐	☐	☐
	Avg.		☐	☐	☐
	Slow		☐	☐	☐
	V. Slow		☐	☐	☐

Key
sc = self correct
r = repeated a word
⌢ = repeated a phrase

Fluency Assessment

Danny was timed on a fifth-grade level reading passage. He read aloud for 1 minute. The teacher recorded his performance on the following page. She put a line through the words he misread and wrote what he said above the printed words. He read a total of 111 words in 1 minute with 12 errors, so that he read 99 words correctly per minute.

Grade 5 Probe 3

        horizone   **use**
Where the horizon is hilly and uneven, it can be used as a sun calendar.   15

                   sc   **horazone**
A Native American group, the Hopi, use such a horizon calendar.   26

  observe
Observing from the same place each day, the Hopi take note of where the   40

   rise   **impatent**   **impatent**   **a**
sun rises and sets on important days. Each important day has the peak of   54

a hill or notch of a valley named after it-the peak or notch where the   71

   rise   **watch**
sun rises or sets on that day. The sun-watcher looks for the first glimpse   85

                                                          r
of the sun in the morning, and the sun's last gleam in the evening. He   100

                notch   **warn**
numbers the days with notches on a wooden stick, and warns the people   113

when an important day is coming. The time for planting corn or beans,   126

the time for the flute dance, the main harvest, and the winter-solstice   139

ceremony-all are marked on the distant horizon.   147

 Halfway around the world, Russian peasants track the sun in the same   159

way as the Hopi. In the Caucasus Mountains, village chiefs choose an   171

old man to watch for sunset each day. He sits on a bench and watches   186

the sun disappear behind the jagged mountain peaks. Using landmarks   196

on the horizon to keep track of the year is a very old practice used by   212

people everywhere.   214

 This method could be used in early times because it was so simple.   227

Nothing had to be built. All that was needed was a good view of the   241

horizon, with natural landmarks and a place to stand while watching   253

the sunrise and sunset.   257

Key   **sc** = self correct
         r = repeated a word
      ⌒ = repeated a phrase

Phonics Test

Danny's reading teacher gave him a phonics assessment in which he read multisyllabic words containing the most common phonograms and spelling patterns. The purpose was to determine which phonics elements he could read, and on which ones he needed to work. The results of the assessment are on the following three pages. When Danny misread a word, the teacher wrote what he said on the line next to it. The two pages after that contain the scoring matrix for the assessment.

California Reading & Literature Project: Focusing on Results, Pre K - 3

CALIFORNIA READING, PROFESSIONAL DEVELOPMENT INSTITUTE

California Language Arts Content Standards 1.1, 1.2

Reading		
CUNNINGHAM NAMES TEST		
BEGINNING-OF-YEAR NAME: **Danny** DATE: **1-31** CORRECT: **19** /25		

1. Jay Conway			14. Wendy Swain		
2. Tim Cornell	✓ **Carnell**		15. Glen Spencer		
3. Chuck Hoke	✓ **Hawk**		16. Fred Sherwood		
4. Yolanda Clark			17. Flo Thornton	✓ **Trenton**	
5. Kimberly Blake			18. Dee Skidmore		
6. Roberta Slade	**Robetta Slad**		19. Grace Brewster		
7. Homer Preston			20. Ned Westmoreland		
8. Gus Quincy			21. Ron Smitherman		
9. Cindy Sampson			22. Troy Whitlock	✓ **Whitelock**	
10. Chester Wright			23. Vance Middleton		
11. Ginger Yale			24. Zane Anderson		
12. Patrick Tweed			25. Bernard Pendergraph	**Bernerd** ✓	
13. Stanley Shaw					

California Reading & Literature Project: Focusing on Results, Pre K - 3

CALIFORNIA READING, PROFESSIONAL DEVELOPMENT INSTITUTE

SCORING MATRIX FOR THE NAMES TEST

Name: **Danny**   Date: **Feb. 5**

NAME	CONSONANTS	CONSONANTS BLENDS	CONSONANTS DIGRAPHS	SHORT VOWELS	LONG VOWELS	VOWEL DIAGRAPHS	CONTROLLED VOWELS	SCHWA
Jay Conway	J, C, w			o, on		ay	(or)	
Tim Cornell	T, C, n			i, im, e, ell			er	
Chuck Hoke	H	ck	Ch	u, uck	(o)oke			
Yolanda Clark	Y	Cl		a, and			ar, ark	o, a
Kimberly Blake	K, b, l	Bl		i, im	y, a, ake		(er)ert	o, a
Roberta Slade	R	Sl		o, ome	(a)ade		er	o
Homer Preston	H, n	Pr, st	e, est				er	
Gus Quincey	G, Qu, c			u, us, u, i, in	y			
Cindy Sampson	C, S, n	mp	Ch, Wr	i, ind, a, amp	y			o
Chester Wright				e, est	i, ight		er	
Ginger Yale	G, Y			i, in	a, ale		er	
Patrick Tweed	P, r	tr, ck, Tw		a, at, i, ick	e, eed			
Stanley Shaw		St, Sh		a, an	ey			
Wendy Swain	W, d	Sw		e, end	ai, ain, y	aw		
Glen Spencer	c	Gl, Sp		e, en			er	
Fred Sherwood	W	Fr, Sh		e, ed		oo, ood	er	
Flo Thornton	t	Fl, (Tn)		i, id	o		(or)orn	o, on
Dee Skidmore	D, m	Sk			ee, o, ore		er, ter	
Grace Brewster		Gr, Br, st		e, ed, est, a, and	a, ace	ew		
Ned Westmoreland	N, W, m, l		th	o, on, i, ith, a, an	o, ore		er	
Ron Smitherman	R	Sm	Wh	(it) o, ock			er	
Troy Whitlock	l	Tr				oy		
Vance Middleton	V, M			a, ance, i, id, iddle	a, ane		o, on	o
Zane Anderson	Z, s			A, And			er	o, on
Bernard Pendergraph	B, n, P	gr	ph	e, end, a, aph			er, ern, (ar)(ard)	o, on
	44/44	25/36	6/6	65/67	27/31	6/6	14/21	12/12

Qualitative Spelling Inventory

Danny's language arts teacher gave the class a qualitative spelling inventory of 25 words to examine the types of errors they made in spelling. The teacher then classified the students into particular developmental stages of spelling. Danny's spelling test and analysis of his errors on the Feature Guide are on the following two pages.

Spelling Test

Name **Danny**

1. speck
2. switch
3. throat
4. nirse ✓
5. scrap ✓
6. charge
7. phone
8. smugg ✓
9. point
10. squoret ✓
11. drawing
12. trapt ✓
13. waving
14. powerful
15. battle
16. fever
17. lesson
18. penies ✓
19. fraction
20. salier ✓
21. diestins ✓
22. confusion
23. discovery
24. resadint ✓
25. visable ✓

Feature Guide for Upper Elementary Spelling Inventory

Student's Name **Danny**   Teacher _____   Grade **7**   Date **02/04**   Total Points **44/58**

	EMERGENT LATE	LETTER NAME-ALPHABETIC EARLY MIDDLE LATE		WITHIN WORD PATTERN EARLY MIDDLE LATE			SYLLABLES AND AFFIXES EARLY MIDDLE LATE	DERIVATIONAL RELATIONS EARLY		
	Consonants Initial / Final	Short Vowels 6	Digraphs and Blends 13	Long Vowel Patterns 4	Other Vowel Patterns 6	Syllable Junctures, Consonant Doubling, Inflected Endings, Prefixes Suffixes 23	Bases and Roots 6	Word	Points
speck		e	sp ck					1 speck	
switch		i	sw tch					2 switch	
throat			thr	o-a				3 throat	
nurse					ur			4 nurse	
scrape			scr	a-e				5 scrape	
charge			ch		ar			6 charge	
phone			ph	o-e				7 phone	
smudge		u	sm dge					8 smudge	
point			nt		oi			9 point	
squirt			squ		ir			10 squirt	
drawing			dr		aw	ing		11 drawing	
trapped		a				pp ed		12 trapped	
waving						ing		13 waving	
powerful					ow	er ful		14 powerful	
battle		a				tt le		15 battle	
fever						ev er		16 fever	
lesson		e				ss on		17 lesson	
pennies						nn ies		18 pennies	
fraction						tion	frac	19 fraction	
sailor				at		or		20 sailor	
distance						ance	dis	21 distance	
confusion						con sion	fus	22 confusion	
discovery						dis ery	cov	23 discovery	
resident						ent	resid	24 resident	
visible						ble	vis	25 visible	
feature totals	6/6		12/13	2/4	4/6	19/23	3/6	15/25	44/58

Interest Survey

Danny's language arts teacher created an interest survey for her students to complete at the beginning of the year. Printed on the following page are Danny's responses to the survey.

Interest Survey

1. What do you like to do at home? <u>listen to rap music, draw, surf the internet,</u>
<u>play video grams</u>

2. What do you like to do with your friends? <u>Skateboard, play basketball, sports, have fun</u>

3. What is your favorite subject in school? <u>Art</u>

4. Do you like school? Why? Or Why not? <u>Sometimes, I get to be with my friends.</u>
<u>I don't like when I get in trouble or have to do hard work.</u>

5. What would you like to do better? <u>Get better grades</u>

6. Do you like to read? Why? Or Why not? <u>Not much. It's boring</u>

7. Do you read at home? <u>When I'm bored</u>

8. What kinds of things do you like to read? <u>Sci fi and adventure books</u>

Case Study 1: Danny

Your three columns of notes from Danny's profile might have looked something like this

strengths	_weaknesses_	_instructional strategies and activities_
comprehension strong	lacks fluency	repeated readings of familiar text
retells well	reads slowly	easy sci fiction, advent books
monitors for meaning	sounds out words	freq. 1-min. silent reading assessments
self corrects	comprehension	chart no. of words read, helps
	will suffer	motivation
motivated to do better	confused long vowels	work in groups, Readers Theater
	(e ending)	
lots of interests	R-controlled vowels	word sorts for long vowels
likes drawing		making words activities
video games		word walls, spelling lists, word hunts
		encourage to keep on self-monitering

Sample Essay

Danny has some reading strengths. His comprehension is relatively strong. When reading a passage at his reading level, he was able to retell it reasonably well, and he monitors his reading for meaning. On his oral reading and fluency assessments, he self-corrected when his reading didn't make sense, and he repeated words to check for meaning. He is motivated to do better. He wrote that he would like to get better grades on his interest survey.

Danny lacks fluency in his reading. On his fluency test he read 99 words correctly in a minute on a fifth-grade passage. On his oral reading test the teacher marked that he read at a slow rate. On the word recognition test, Danny sounded out the words instead of reading them as a whole. Although Danny's comprehension is good, without fluency it will suffer when he reads more demanding material. Since he will have to focus most of his attention on decoding, there will be little attention left for comprehension.

Another weakness Danny had was that he confused long vowels, especially ones with the silent "e" ending on the phonics test and fluency assessment. He had trouble spelling long vowel words on the qualitative spelling inventory. This puts him in the within word stage of reading.

An instructional strategy for fluency would be repeated readings of familiar text at Danny's independent reading level. The teacher should provide him with some easy science fiction and adventure books because those are the types of books he likes. He should have *frequent 1-minute silent reading assessments and graph the number of words read on a chart. This will motivate him because he wants to get better grades, and he can visually see his progress. He can also read Readers Theater scripts, which are easier to read than original text, and it is done in a group. Danny likes working in groups as indicated by his interest survey in which he wrote that he likes to spend time with his friends in school.*

Danny can work on long vowels through word sorts by sorting words with different long vowel spellings. He will learn long vowel spelling patterns by repeated exposure to them. He can also do making words activities in which he constructs smaller words from the letters in a larger word. He would be asked to build words that have different long vowel spelling patterns.

Danny should be encouraged to keep self-monitoring his reading for comprehension. When he misreads a word, the teacher can tell him and ask him to go back and reread in order to make sense.

Case Study 1: Danny

Evaluating the Essay

This is a strong case-study analysis because it addresses all parts of the prompt. Some of Danny's strengths were listed and then some of his weaknesses. The strengths and weaknesses described were taken from a list of several possible ones. The person who did this analysis chose what she thought were the most salient strengths and weaknesses. In an analysis of this size not every possible strength and weakness need to be listed. Danny's strengths were comprehension and retelling, using meaning cues, self-correcting, and motivation to read better. After each strength, the writer gave evidence from the data in the case study that led her to her conclusions. She listed which piece or pieces of data exhibited each strength. An analysis that wouldn't be as strong might not include the evidence to back the writer's conclusions.

The same was done with Danny's weaknesses. The weaknesses listed were fluency and long vowels. Again, these weaknesses were determined to be the most salient from a list of possible weaknesses. A strong essay lists at least two strengths and two weaknesses. The writer probably wouldn't be able to discuss more than that in the space given. An analysis that isn't as strong might just list one strength and weakness. A poor analysis might be missing either strengths or weaknesses. After each weakness, the writer gave evidence from the data that proved that these were weaknesses. For fluency, she cited the fluency test, oral reading test, and word recognition test. This shows that the writer can take data from several sources and extrapolate a conclusion. She is able to use multiple measures. An acceptable, but not strong, analysis might just cite one piece of data. For long vowels, the writer also used three pieces of data: the phonics assessment, the fluency test, and the qualitative spelling inventory. Keep in mind that every piece of data in the case study is there to provide information for the analysis and should be used in some way for a strong score. The writer even gave a rationale for why fluency is important. This shows that she understands the components of reading.

After listing Danny's strengths and weaknesses, the writer described instructional strategies for working on fluency, the instructional strategies for working on long vowels, and then strategies to build on Danny's strengths. In this way, she addressed both how to improve on his weaknesses and how to capitalize his strengths. An acceptable, but not strong, essay might only list instructional strategies for weaknesses.

The prompt asked for at least two methods or strategies that would assist in the student's reading development. This analysis is strong because it described four strategies for fluency and the rationale behind selecting those. The writer told why Danny, specifically, would benefit from them. Those strategies were repeated readings of familiar and interesting text, 1-minute fluency assessment practices, graphing the words read in 1 minute, and Reader's Theater. These four methods are all successful ways to work on fluency and were selected from many possible fluency strategies because the writer determined that they would be suitable for Danny's needs. The information about why these strategies would be compatible with Danny's interests and learning styles was taken from the data given in the case study. Three strategies were also listed for working on long vowels. They were word sorts, repeated exposure to words, presumably through reading, and making words. One strategy was listed for building on one of Danny's strengths: self-monitoring. An acceptable essay might have one strategy for working on fluency, one for working on long vowels, and a method for continuing to build on a strength. A poor essay might only describe one strategy in total, or might list two or three but not go into detail about how any of them would work or how any would benefit the student. It would merely be a list. This analysis was strong because it described several possible strategies that would work and didn't just list them. However, all the methods and strategies listed should actually be proven to be effective with the specific reading component being addressed. It is more important to be accurate than to have a long list.

A Thorough Analysis of Case Study 1: Danny

The following is a very thorough analysis of the case study. This thorough analysis is designed to show you many of the possible items that you could have mentioned in the case-study essay. It is also designed to help you understand some of the items to look for as you do your analysis. **Needless to say, in the time allotted (about 1 hour) you could not nearly complete this level of analysis.**

The Analysis

Overall, Danny is a poor reader. He is reading below grade level. He scored at third-grade level on the word recognition assessment, and his independent and instructional levels were at the fifth-grade level on the oral reading test. Weak readers recognize words in context more easily than out of context because they over rely on context in reading as a result of not having become proficient in word recognition strategies. Hence, Danny scored worse on the test in which he read words out of context than on the one in which he read leveled passages. On the upper elementary qualitative spelling inventory, Danny scored at the within word developmental stage of spelling.

Strengths

Some of the following strengths may be pointed out:

- Danny is motivated to do better as he indicated on his interest survey when he wrote that he would like to get better grades.
- Danny likes working in groups. On his interest survey, he listed several activities he likes to do with his friends, and he wrote that what he likes best about school is that he gets to be with his friends.
- Danny has lots of interests that he noted on the interest survey. He likes rap music, skateboarding, drawing, the Internet, video games, and sports.
- Danny wrote on his interest survey that he likes reading science fiction and adventure books.
- He is relatively strong in comprehension. On the oral reading test his teacher noted that he was able to retell what he read reasonably well.
- Danny self-corrected and repeated words on his oral reading test and fluency assessment. This indicates that he is reading for meaning, and he is trying to make sense out of what he is reading.

Recommendations Based on Strengths

Some of the following recommendations for activities and assignments can be made to build on Danny's strengths, so that he can start from where he is strong and move to his areas of need.

- Danny can work in groups on projects because he likes being with other students. He could be the illustrator of the group because he likes drawing.

- Danny can read books about rap music, skateboarding, videogames, and sports because he is interested in those topics. Have books about those topics in your classroom library, along with science fiction and adventure books, because those are his favorite types of books to read.

- Since Danny likes to surf the Internet, give him assignments to locate and read information on the Internet. Have him do a research project on rap music, skateboarding, videogames, or sports in which he finds information on the Internet. Since he likes to skateboard, play basketball, and engage in sports with his friends, he could complete a group project on those topics. Danny could be given the text of songs to read. Since he already knows the songs, he will be getting practice reading material that is familiar to him.

- Danny could draw pictures about what he has read because he likes drawing. This will build on his comprehension strengths because he is transferring the meaning of what he has read into a visual representation. This is using the comprehension strategy of visualization.

- Danny could write science fiction and adventure stories to practice his spelling skills and then illustrate them.

- Praise Danny when he self-corrects or rereads for meaning. When he misreads a word, prompt him by asking, "Did that make sense?" Or tell him "Go back and look at that again and make it make sense."

Weaknesses

Danny's assessments indicated four major weaknesses:

- Fluency
- Long vowels
- Word endings—suffixes and inflectional endings, especially "ed" for past tense and "s" for plurals
- R-controlled vowels

Fluency

Comprehension of the material read is the goal of reading. Reading instruction should focus on comprehension strategies. Fluency is one of the two building blocks of comprehension. Fluency is the ability to read with ease and automaticity. It is a combination of reading speed and accuracy. Although fluent reading is not an end in itself, it leads to better comprehension. Fluent readers are able to focus their attention on understanding the text. When students read fluently, they are not struggling to decode the words, so that their efforts can be concentrated on comprehension and making meaning. Nonfluent readers must focus their attention on decoding, thus leaving little attention free for comprehension. Although Danny's comprehension is adequate for what he is reading, he is reading at least two years below grade level. A student who reads haltingly and makes several reading errors is unlikely to have good comprehension of high demand text.

On his fluency test, Danny read 99 words correct per minute (wcpm). He made 12 errors on his reading passage. At the minimum, a seventh grader should be reading more than 120 wcpm with less than 6 errors. A person needs to read more than 140 wcpm in order to handle all of the cognitive demands of the text and to maximize comprehension. An average adult reads 200 wcpm.

On the oral reading test, the teacher marked that Danny read the fourth and fifth grade passages at a slow rate, and the sixth-grade passage at a very slow rate. Oral reading gives a good indication of the fluency with which a child is able to read.

On the word recognition test, the teacher noted that Danny sounded out the words instead of reading them fluently and rapidly.

For students who read more slowly than average, more practice is needed at their independent level so that they can gain fluency.

Recommendations for Working on Fluency

There are several strategies for working on fluency. Following are some of the ones that might be helpful to Danny.

- Repeated readings—Reading a familiar text many times for a variety of purposes. The material read should be at his independent reading level, which is text that he can read with an accuracy rate of 95% or more. He should not have to struggle with the decoding so that all of his effort can be expended into the fluency practice. His teacher should have books in the classroom library that are at Danny's independent reading level, which the oral reading test showed to be at fifth-grade level. On the interest survey, Danny wrote that he doesn't like school when the work is hard or when he gets in trouble. Therefore, if the reading material is too difficult, Danny will become frustrated and perhaps misbehave because he is "turned off" to the task.

The forms of repeated readings that might be especially effective for Danny would be choral reading, *Readers Theater,* partner reading, and reading to someone else because these are group activities, and Danny likes working in a group. *Readers Theater* would make the reading task appealing to Danny because it promotes cooperative interaction with his classmates, and the scripts appear less daunting than whole books, so reading wouldn't seem like hard work. In partner reading, Danny would be reading with a stronger reader who would read first to model fluent reading. Then Danny would read the same text aloud.

- Modeling—Read aloud to Danny so that he can hear examples of fluent reading.

- Tape assisted reading—Danny could get support by listening to the text read by a fluent reader on an audiotape or CD and follow along. He could record himself reading text that he knows well and reading unfamiliar text. He could then listen to his rate and be made aware of what fluent reading sounds like in contrast to nonfluent reading.

- Timed readings—Give Danny and other students 1 minute to read silently and have them count how many words they read in 1 minute. Once again, the material read should be familiar text at his independent level. It can be text about his interests such as music, skateboarding, sports, adventure, and science fiction. It would be effective for Danny to keep a running graph and chart the number of wcpm after each timed reading so that he can see his progress. This would be motivating to him because on his interest survey he wrote that he would like to get better grades. On the graph he would be able to see his ongoing progress toward improvement. After the first 1 minute timing, Danny could be timed on the same passage again to immediately see his progress between the first and second readings.

- Phrase reading—The text could be segmented into phrases by drawing a pencil line to at the end of each phrase. Danny could be told to read all the words between two pencil lines together in one breath.

  Practice phrasing and intonation by reading works with rhythm such as songs or poems. Since Danny likes rap music, he could read the lyrics to rap songs. That would work especially well because rap music is like talking to a beat with a very definite rhythm.

- Direct instruction—Ask Danny to read it quickly, make it sound like talking, or read the punctuation.

- Wide reading—Danny needs to read a lot in order to get enough practice to improve his fluency. He should do SSR and/or independent reading every day in school, and he should read at home every night. He could keep a reading log of what he reads and the number of pages read every day in school, and he could also have a home reading log.

Word Endings

Often non-native English speakers leave the endings off words because they don't have suffixes in their first languages that mark tenses, so they don't notice the "ed" endings. They are not familiar enough with the structure of English to realize that when they leave an "s" off the ending of a plural, it doesn't sound right.

Danny needs to work on the structure of language. He needs to get lots of practice hearing the endings of the words and distinguishing between words with suffixes and inflections and words without them both orally and in print.

On the qualitative spelling test, Danny did not write "ed" at the end of "trapped." He wrote "trapt." This shows that he needs to work on the structure of past tenses because he wrote what he heard and not what he should know about past tense.

On the word recognition test, every error that Danny made in the fourth- and fifth-grade tests was the omission of an ending.

On the oral reading test, Danny left the "s" off many plural nouns. In fact, that type of error comprised the majority of all his errors. Some examples of these errors were that he read "cowboy" instead of "cowboys," "hill" instead of "hills," and "cabin" instead of "cabins."

On the fluency assessment, Danny left off "ed" and "s." He read "use" instead of "used" and "notch" instead of "notches."

Recommendations for Working on Word Endings

- Direct instruction on suffixes and their meanings. Danny could practice putting suffixes onto base words. Give him definitions of the words to create, and he has to find the base and syllable that would make the words with the given meanings.

- Practice reading words with suffixes and breaking down words by syllables in reading and writing.

- Direct instruction on singulars and plurals.

- Tell Danny to look at the whole word. Uncover a word slowly, one part at a time, until he reads the whole word.

- Leave blanks in a selection in which Danny has to figure out which word goes in the blank (**cloze activities**). He needs to use the context of the other words in the sentences to figure out which structure of the word would make sense. The words that fit meaningfully in the blanks would be words with suffixes.

- Have Danny sort words into the categories of those that have suffixes and those that don't (**word sorts**). For example one column would be words without a suffix and words with "ed," or one column could be for singular words, and one could be for plurals. Then Danny could sort for several suffixes at a time. For example, one column could be for words that end with "ed," another column would be words that end with "ly," and a third column could be words that end with "ing."

- Have Danny record words with a specific suffix in a word study notebook (**word hunts**). When he finds more words with the targeted suffix in his reading, he will add them to the word study notebook.

- Have the teacher post words with a specific suffix on a word bank on the wall, and Danny will add to it (**word walls**).

- Have Danny build smaller words from the letters in a longer word (**making words**). The words that he builds will have some "ed" or "s" endings. Then he will sort the words he built by the endings.

- Have Danny play games such as concentration for practice. Danny will uncover two cards with words written on them from among an array of cards. If the cards consist of a base word on one card, and the same base word plus a suffix on the other card, then he has a match. If he reads the words on the cards correctly, he gets to keep them.

Confusion with Long Vowels

Danny's teacher gave the phonics test after she gave the word recognition test and oral reading test to find out the cause of his poor oral reading performance. She wanted to see whether it was due to a phonics problem and with which specific phonics elements he was having difficulty, so that she could target instruction to those needs. On the phonics test, he said "slad" instead of "Slade" and "hawk" instead of "Hoke."

On the spelling inventory, Danny wrote "scrap" instead of "scrape." This places him at the mid within word stage of spelling where students "use but confuse" long vowel patterns. On the fluency assessment, Danny read "horizone" with a /$\bar{o}$/ sound instead of "horizon" with a schwa sound.

The vowel pattern with which he is having the most difficulty is the long vowel with a silent "e" at the end, which puts him in the mid within word developmental stage of spelling.

Recommendations for Working on Long Vowel Patterns

- Put Danny in a small flexible group with other students working on the same patterns or who are in the mid within word stage because he likes working with others.

- Give Danny and/or his group spelling activities and games for practice from the mid within word stage using resources such as *Words Their Way*.

- Have Danny sort words into the columns of words with a short vowel sound and words of the long vowel sound for the same vowel, such as short "a" words and long "a" words (**word sorts**). Then he can sort all long vowel words together for words that have the same spelling pattern. So there would be a column for /$\bar{a}$/, /$\bar{e}$/, /$\bar{i}$/, /$\bar{o}$/, /$\bar{u}$/, and all the words in the /$\bar{a}$/ column would have the silent "e" at the end, and all the words in the columns for the other long vowels would have silent "e" at the end. He could also sort for different spelling patterns of the same vowel sound; for /$\bar{o}$/ he could have a column for the spelling with silent "e" at the end, for "oa," for "o," and so on.

- Have Danny record words with a specific long vowel in a word study notebook (**word hunts**). When he finds more words with the targeted spelling pattern in his reading, he will add them to the word study notebook.
- The teacher will post words with a specific long vowel spelling pattern on a word bank on the wall and Danny will add to it (**word walls**).
- Have Danny build smaller words from the letters in a longer word (**making words**). The words that he builds will have different spelling patterns for long vowels. Then he will sort the words he built by the spelling patterns.

R-Controlled Vowels

On the phonics tests, Danny misread the "er" in "Roberta" the "ar" in "Bernard," and the "or" in "Cornell" and "Thornton."

On the qualitative spelling test, Danny misspelled the "or" in "sailor," the "ur" in "nurse," and the "ir" in "squirt." He spelled all the "er" patterns correctly.

On the fluency test, Danny misread the "or" in "important."

On the oral reading test, Danny misread the "ur" in "suburban."

It appears that Danny is not having much trouble with the "er" pattern, but he is having some trouble with the other r-controlled vowels.

On the Basic Phonics Skills Tests, Qualitative Spelling Inventory, and phonics Names Test, r-controlled vowels is a more difficult skill to master than long vowel spelling patterns. The developmental spelling level for r-controlled vowels is more advanced than the one for long vowel spelling patterns. On the phonics tests, long vowel spelling patterns come before r-controlled vowels in the hierarchy of phonic elements to learn.

Recommendations for Working on R-Controlled Vowels

- Wait until Danny has learned long vowel patterns.
- When starting to work with Danny on r-controlled short vowels, have him distinguish between two at a time. He could start with "or" and "ar" because those are the two with which he is having the most difficulty. Since he does pretty well with "er," he does not need to work with that pattern until he is distinguishing among all five.
- Have Danny sort words into categories of different r-controlled vowels (**word sorts**). He would start with two vowels. For example one column would be "or" words, and one column would be "ar" words. Then he could do one for "ur" words and "ir" words, and he could follow with other combinations of two. Next Danny could sort for three r-controlled vowels, then four, and finally all five.
- Have Danny record words containing the various r-controlled vowels in a word study notebook (**word hunts**). When he finds more words with the targeted r-controlled vowels in his reading, he will add them to the word study notebook.
- Post words on the word wall with r-controlled vowels. Danny can add to it (**word walls**).
- Give Danny lists of words for spelling tests that are made up of words with r-controlled vowels (**spelling lists**). At first the list could have only two r-controlled vowels and then combinations of three, four, and all five.

A Case Study for Practice

Now try analyzing the following case study and writing an essay. Use the four lined pages that follow to write your essay. Limit your time to **1 hour** to complete this case study practice.

Case Study 2: Sam

This case study focuses on a first-grade student named Sam. The documents and information on the following pages describe Sam's reading performance during the middle of the school year. After reviewing the information and materials, write a response in which you apply your knowledge of language arts assessment and instruction to analyze this case study. Your response should include three parts:

1. identify strengths and weaknesses in Sam's reading ability at this point in the school year, citing evidence from the documents to support your observations;

2. describe at least two methods or instructional strategies and/or activities designed to assist Sam's reading development by addressing the strengths and weaknesses you identified; and

3. explain how each method, strategy, and/or activity you describe would work in promoting Sam's reading proficiency.

Your response should be approximately 300 words in length.

You may use the space below to make notes. These notes will not be scored.

Home Survey

Sam's teacher sent home a survey to be completed by the parents prior to parent-teacher conferences during the school year's first grading period. The survey was brought to the conference and discussed.

Home Survey

My Child as a Reader and Writer

Child's Name __Sam_____   Date __11/98_____

Please take a few minutes to answer the following questions about your child's reading and writing. Because you are your child's first teacher, we appreciate your insight into how your child learns.

Does you child like going to school? Why or why not? __Yes._____

What are your child's strengths? __He knows a lot about animals and tries hard.____

What goals do you have this school for your child? __He learns how to read._____

Does your child enjoy reading? __No. He likes me to read to him._____

What does your child like to read at home? __Science books._____

What types of books do you read at home? __Anything - school or library books.____

How often do you read at home? __We try each night._____

For how long? __15 minutes_____

How well do you think your child is reading? __He struggles._____

How does your child feel about his/her own reading? __He thinks it is hard._____

What does your child like to write at home? __He likes to draw._____

Does your child use his/her own or developmental spelling? __Yes._____

Does your child share his/her writing with anyone in the family? __sometimes._____

How well do you think your child is writing? __It's hard for him to get started._____

How does your child feel about his/her own writing? __It's not his favorite._____

What activities do you do together as a family? __Sports, movies, pets._____

What are your child's interests? __sports and animals._____

How do you think your child learns best? __with praise and a chance to be active.____

What else would you like me to know about your child? __His parents are divorced and there is shared custody._____

Signature __Sam's mom_____

Student Survey

Four months into the school year Sam's teacher sat down and asked Sam the questions on this survey. The teacher was attempting to learn more about Sam's attitude toward reading.

Myself as a Reader

Child's Name **Sam**

Do you enjoy reading? Why or why not? **No, It is hard.**

Are you a good reader? How do you know? **No, I am really slow and sound out words.**

What are your favorite books at school? **Animal books.**

What are your favorite books at home? **snake books.**

Who reads to you at home? **mom and sometimes dad.**

What is your favorite place to read? **In bed.**

Do you enjoy talking about books you have read? **No.**

How have you improved as a reader? **I try hard.**

What do you do when you come to a word you don't know? **Ask the teacher**

What is one thing you would like to do better in reading? **Sound out words and read hard books.**

Running Record

For this running record the teacher was assessing which level book Sam could read at an instructional level. The running record was completed in the fifth month of first grade. The benchmark level for first graders at the end of the year is level 16.

The teacher listened as Sam read the book to her. The teacher made marks for each word the student read on the running record form that follows. The teacher analyzed the running record and noted the cueing systems the student used while decoding words.

Notes were also taken as the student retold the story. See the last part of the running record form for information about the student's retelling of the story.

| BOOK EVALUATION |

Name: **Sam**

Date: **1-15-99**

Recorder: _____

LEVEL	ACC.	%SC rate
6	93%	1:56

Title: | **The Busy Mosquito** |

Phrasing and Fluency: _**X**_ word by word ___ in short phrases
___ in longer phrases ___ punctuation

		Word Count	**7**	**2**	Cues Used	
					E	SC
Page #	Sentence	112	E	SC	MSV	MSV
2	✓ musquit ✓ ✓ ✓ The mosquito buzzed the cow.	5	1		MS(V)	
	✓ ✓ ✓ "Buzz, buzz, buzz."	3				
	✓ oway _____/A ✓ ✓ ✓ "Go away, mosquito/" said the cow,	6	2		MS(V) MSV	
	✓ ✓ ✓ fell oway and the mosquito flew away.	5	2		MS(V) MS(V)	
4	✓ ✓ ✓ her The mosquito buzzed the horse.	5	1		MS(V)	
	✓ ✓ ✓ "Buzz, buzz, buzz."	3				
	✓ cut ✓ ✓ ✓ h-or-s ✓ "Go away, mosquito," said the horse,	6	1		(M)SV	
	✓ ✓ ✓ fell /SC and the mosquito flew/away.	5		1	MS(V)	(M)SV
6	✓ ✓ ✓ ✓ The mosquito buzzed the dog.	5				
	✓ ✓ ✓ "Buzz, buzz, buzz."	3				
	✓ ✓ ✓ ✓ ✓ ✓ "Go away, mosquito," said the dog,	6				
	✓ ✓ ✓ ✓ ✓ and the mosquito flew away.	5				
8	✓ ✓ ✓ ✓ ✓ The mosquito buzzed the cat.	5				
	✓ ✓ ✓ "Buzz, buzz, buzz."	3				

page 1

	✓ ✓ ✓ ✓ ✓ ✓ "Go away, mosquito," said the cat,	6			
	✓ ✓ ✓ ✓ ✓ and the mosquito flew away.	5			
10	✓ ✓ ✓ ✓ The mosquito buzzed me.	4			
	✓ ✓ ✓ "Buzz, buzz, buzz."	3			
	✓ ✓ ✓ ✓ ✓ "Go away, mosquito," I said.	5			
	✓ ✓ ✓ ✓ ✓ The mosquito did not go away.	6			
12	✓ ✓ ✓ ✓ I got a fly swatter. **SC**	5	1	M⑤V	Ⓜ SV
	✓ ✓ ✓ ✓ "Go away, mosquito," I said.	5			
	✓ ✓ ✓ ✓ ✓ and the mosquito flew away.	5			
	✓ ✓ ✓ "Buzz, buzz, buzz."	3			

RETELLING	**NOTES**
T: "Tell me in your own words what happened in the story" Initial retelling included:___characters___important details ___vocabulary/special phrases from the story___setting ___events in sequence ✓events out of sequence___ending *T: If initial retelling is incomplete, prompt: "Tell me more."* Added information about: : ✓characters___important details◄ ✓vocabulary/special phrases from the story ✓setting ___events in sequence___events out of sequence ✓ending	⎫ ⎬ **Needed to be prompted to retell.** ⎭ ✓

page 2

High Frequency Words

During the fifth month of first grade, the teacher assessed Sam's automatic reading of the 100 most frequently used words. By the end of the school year, first graders are expected to know the first 100 words automatically.

Fry's Sight Word Recording Sheet

Student: **Sam**   Fall (Winter) Spring

List 1		Pre	Post
1	the	✔	
2	of	✔	
3	and	✔	
4	a	✔	
5	to	✔	
6	in	✔	
7	is	✔	
8	you	—	
9	that	✔	
10	it	✔	
11	he	✔	
12	was	saw	
13	for	✔	
14	on	✔	
15	are	✔	
16	as	✔	
17	with	✔	
18	his	✔	
19	they	✔	
20	I	✔	
21	at	✔	
22	be	✔	
23	this	✔	
24	have	✔	
25	from	✔	
		23/25	/25

List 2		Pre	Post
26	or	✔	
27	one	on	
28	had	✔	
29	by	✔	
30	word	—	
31	but	✔	
32	not	✔	
33	what	wait	
34	all	✔	
35	were	—	
36	we	✔	
37	when	✔	
38	your	—	
39	can	✔	
40	said	sad	
41	there	✔	
42	use	us	
43	an	✔	
44	each	—	
45	which	—	
46	she	✔	
47	do	✔	
48	how	✔	
49	their	—	
50	if	✔	
		15/25	/25

List 3		Pre	Post
51	will	✔	
52	up	✔	
53	other	—	
54	about	—	
55	out	✔	
56	many	✔	
57	then	✔	
58	them	✔	
59	these	—	
60	so	✔	
61	some	som	
62	her	✔	
63	would	—	
64	make	mack	
65	like	✔	
66	him	—	
67	into	✔	
68	time	tim	
69	has	✔	
70	look	lock	
71	two	—	
72	more	—	
73	write	—	
74	go	✔	
75	see	✔	
		13/25	/25

List 4		Pre	Post
76	number	—	
77	no	on	
78	way	—	
79	could	—	
80	people	—	
81	my	✔	
82	than	✔	
83	first	fist	
84	water	—	
85	been	bean	
86	call	✔	
87	who	—	
88	oil	—	
89	mpw	—	
90	find	fand	
91	long	—	
92	down	—	
93	day	✔	
94	did	✔	
95	get	✔	
96	come	com	
97	made	mad	
98	may	✔	
99	part	—	
100	over	—	
		7/25	/25

Writing Sample

This is a writing sample taken from Sam's journal. In his guided reading lesson, after reading a book about making breakfast, Sam was to write a question and answer using words he had read in the book.

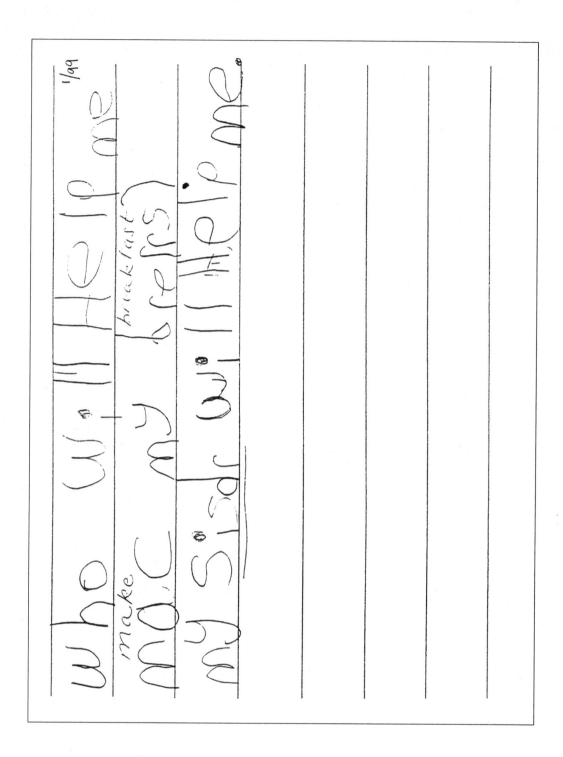

Teacher's Comments

Sam's teacher also made the following comments about his classroom work and behavior.

Sam is easily frustrated, especially when reading or writing.

Sam has a difficult time starting to write independently.

Sam loves science and animals.

Sam often loses things and forgets materials.

Sam responds best to praise and rewards.

Sam loves sports.

Write your case study essay on the following four pages. After you complete your case-study essay, use the Evaluation Form to evaluate your response.

RICA Practice Case Study Evaluation Form

Use this checklist to evaluate your essay:

1. To what extent does this response reflect an **understanding of the relevant content** and academic knowledge from the applicable RICA domain?

thorough	**adequate**	**limited**	**little or no**
understanding	understanding	understanding	understanding

2. To what extent does this response fulfill the purpose of the assignment?

completely	**adequately**	**partially**	**fails to fulfill**
fulfills	fulfills	fulfills	

3. To what extent does this essay **respond to the given task(s)?**

fully	**adequately**	**limited**	**inadequately**
responds	responds	responds	responds

4. How **accurate** is the response?

very	**generally**	**partially**	**inaccurate**
accurate	accurate	accurate	

5. Does the response **demonstrate an effective application** of the relevant content and academic knowledge from the applicable RICA domain?

yes	**reasonably**	**limited**	**no**
effective	effective	generally ineffective	inaccurate and ineffective

6. To what extent does the response **provide supporting examples, evidence, and rationale** based on the relevant content and academic knowledge from the applicable RICA domain?

strong	**adequate**	**limited**	**little or no**
support	support	support	support

Following is a sample essay for this case study followed by an evaluation of the essay.

Case Study 2: Sam

Sample Essay

Sam is a struggling reader, with some strengths. He is motivated to read better. On his student survey he said that he tries hard and he would like to learn how to sound out words and read hard books. He likes to be read to, and his mother reads to him regularly. He is interested in sports, animals, science, and drawing as noted in his home and student surveys and teacher comments.

Sam has little confidence in his reading ability. Mother and Sam noted that he doesn't like reading and he thinks it is hard. He is weak in writing. His mother indicated that it is hard for him to get started and he doesn't like writing. His writing sample had many errors, and his teacher wrote that he has a difficult time getting started.

107

Sam said that he asks the teacher when he comes to a word he doesn't know, and he would like to sound out words better. He needs to learn more sight words because he read 58 words correctly on the Sight Word Test. On his running record, he read word by word, further indicating that he is not recognizing words by sight. Sam could increase his sight word vocabulary by reading words on flashcards quickly. His teacher could give him a word ring with words to practice written on cards. He can play sight word identification games such as Concentration and My Pile, Your Pile where he identifies words on cards quickly.

On his running record, Sam read a Level 6 selection with 93% accuracy, so Level 6 is his instructional level. He should continue reading books, perhaps about science, sports, and animals, at level 6 while working on his weaknesses. The teacher should supply the class-room library with books on these topics, so Sam can read books about his interests. This will help boost his confidence because he will understand what he is reading. Sam relied on visual cues on his running record. He especially had trouble with vowel sounds. He could do word sorts with different vowel sounds to learn to distinguish between them. Sam should be encouraged to check for meaning, so that when he misreads a word, he can be prompted with a question such as "Did that make sense?" Since he has a difficult time getting motivated to write, he should write about sports, animals, and science. Because he is interested in these topics, he will have an easier time getting started. He likes to draw, so if he illustrates his story before he writes, he will also be motivated to write. Mother should continue reading to him.

Evaluating the Essay

This is a strong case-study analysis because it addresses all parts of the prompt. It listed Sam's reading strengths and weaknesses and described at least two methods or strategies that would assist in his reading development. Some of Sam's strengths were listed and then some of his weaknesses. Sam did not exhibit many reading strengths, so the writer took them from his interests. The strengths highlighted were that he is motivated to read better; his mother reads to him; and he is interested in sports, animals, science, and drawing. After each strength, the writer gave evidence from the data in the case study that led him to the conclusions that he made about it. He listed which piece or pieces of data exhibited each strength. An analysis that wouldn't be as strong may not include the evidence to back the writer's conclusions.

The same was done with Sam's weaknesses. The weaknesses described were taken from a list of several possible ones. The person who wrote this analysis chose what he thought were the most prominent weaknesses. That is, they were the ones that showed up in several pieces of data and/or are the most necessary to be mastered first in order to ensure future reading progress. The weaknesses listed were lack of confidence, writing, small sight word vocabulary, and decoding vowel sounds. A strong essay lists at least two strengths and two weaknesses. In this analysis, the writer described three strengths and four weaknesses. An analysis that isn't as strong may just list one strength and weakness. A poor analysis might be missing either strengths or weaknesses. After each weakness, the writer gave evidence from the data that proved that these were weaknesses. For lack of confidence, he cited the parent and student surveys. For writing, he cited the parent survey, writing sample, and teacher comments. For sight word vocabulary he used the student survey, sight word test, and running record. For decoding vowel sounds he cited the running record. The writer showed that he is able to use multiple measures to draw conclusions. An acceptable, but not strong, analysis might just cite one piece of data. Keep in mind that every piece of data in the case study is there to provide information for the analysis and should be used in some way for a strong score. The writer even showed that he knows about instructional levels. This shows that he knows about reading instruction.

The writer described instructional strategies for working on sight words, then instructional strategies for working on Sam's confidence, next strategies to work on vowels, and finally strategies to improve Sam's writing. In the strategies described, the writer addressed both how to improve on Sam's weaknesses and how to build on his strengths. An acceptable, but not strong, essay might only list instructional strategies for weaknesses without building on the strengths.

The prompt asked for at least two methods or strategies that would assist in the student's reading development. This analysis is strong because it described four strategies for sight word vocabulary. Those strategies were flashcards, word rings, word identification games, and reading books about topics in which he is interested at his instructional level. These four methods are all successful ways to build sight word vocabulary. Strategies for boosting Sam's confidence were to read and write about topics in which he is interested. His interests were determined from the parent and student surveys. The writer also made a connection between reading and writing about the topics of interest to Sam and motivation, which is one of his strengths. In doing this, the writer has shown how to work on a weakness by building on a strength, thereby, using strategies that address strengths **and** weaknesses. Two strategies were also listed for working on decoding vowel sounds. They were word sorts and checking for meaning.

The analysis ended with the writer's writing that Sam's mother should continue reading to him. This is an attempt to address a strength. The writer could have made it stronger by explaining why he is recommending that Sam's mother should continue reading to him. An acceptable essay might have one strategy for working on one weakness and one for working on another. A poor essay might only describe one strategy in total or might list two or three but not go into detail about how any of them would work or how any would benefit the student. It would merely be a list. This analysis was strong because it described several possible strategies that would work, and did not just list them. However, all the methods and strategies listed should actually be proven to be effective with the specific reading component being addressed. It is more important to be accurate than to have a long list.

REVIEW OF EXAM AREAS

The following section is designed to **give you a review of the important basic concepts** of reading instruction as it applies to the RICA test. It includes a review of the four domains and a glossary of important terms and concepts.

Read this section carefully. Make notes in the margins to help you understand the terms or concepts.

Reading Domains

The purpose of the RICA written and video assessment is to determine a teacher's knowledge and skills necessary for effective reading instruction. Teachers must demonstrate competency in the content for effective reading instruction. These competencies are described in the RICA Content Specifications in the RICA bulletin.

The goal of reading instruction as stated in the RICA bulletin is to "develop competent, thoughtful readers who are able to use, interpret, and appreciate all types of text."

Effective Reading Instruction as Noted in the Bulletin

- is based on the results of ongoing assessment.
- reflects knowledge of state and local reading standards for different grade levels.
- represents a balanced, comprehensive reading curriculum.
- is sensitive to the needs of all students.

The knowledge and abilities necessary for teachers to deliver this effective instruction are organized into four domains in the RICA.

Domain I: Planning and Organizing Reading Instruction Based on Ongoing Assessment

Domain II: Developing Phonological and Other Linguistic Processes Related to Reading

Domain III: Developing Reading Comprehension and Promoting Independent Reading

Domain IV: Supporting Reading Through Oral and Written Language Development

Questions to Focus Your Review

The following questions will be discussed in the Domain Review that follows. You should use the questions in each domain as a diagnostic test of your knowledge of the content areas. These questions can also be used as a review test and to reinforce your learning after completing the Domain Review.

Domain I

Planning and Organizing Reading Instruction Based on Ongoing Assessment

1. What are some of the tests to use for **ongoing** assessment to plan reading instruction?
2. What criteria are used to select the test or assessment to use?
3. How do you use the data from tests?
4. What are some ways you would use test results in relation to the Reading/Language Arts Standards?
5. What are some factors to consider in planning reading instruction?
6. What factors may be used in long-term planning?
7. What factors may be used in weekly/daily lesson plans?
8. What are some of the factors to consider when setting-up your classroom to manage, organize, and differentiate instruction in reading?

Domain II

Developing Phonological and Other Linguistic Processes Related to Reading

1. What is phonemic awareness, and what part does it play in learning to read?
2. What do teachers need to know concerning phonemic awareness?
3. What is the role of phonemic awareness in learning to read?
4. What instruction can be presented to assist in the development of phonemic awareness?
5. How can a teacher plan direct systematic, explicit, and implicit instruction in phonemic awareness?
6. What role do concepts about print and an understanding of how the letters, words, and sentences are represented in written language play in students learning to read?
7. What do we mean by systematic, explicit phonics and other word identification strategies?
8. What tasks must the teacher address to implement a systematic, explicit phonics program?
9. What must a teacher consider in planning spelling instruction?
10. What must a teacher consider in teaching students that spelling is an aspect of word knowledge?

Domain III

Developing Reading Comprehension and Promoting Independent Reading

1. How does a teacher assess reading comprehension? How does a teacher use the data from comprehension assessment?
2. How does a teacher assist students in increasing fluency?
3. How can a teacher facilitate student attainment of comprehension?
4. What are the levels of comprehension? How should these levels be taught?

5. What are comprehension strategies? How should these strategies be taught?

6. How can a teacher assess student literary response and analysis? How can this data be used?

7. How can a teacher assist students in making connections and responding to literature?

8. How can a teacher teach elements of literary analysis and criticism?

9. How can the teacher assess content area literacy, and how should data from the assessment be used?

10. How does a teacher plan instruction in different types of text—e.g., narrative, expository, and functional?

11. How can the teacher teach reading strategies for students to gain meaning from text in a variety of ways?

12. How does a teacher teach study skills?

13. What does a teacher need to know about individual students to assist in promoting independent reading?

14. How can a teacher promote independent student reading?

15. How can a teacher support at-home reading?

16. What does a teacher need to know to teach content area literacy/comprehension?

17. How can a teacher promote the reading of good books?

Domain IV

Supporting Reading Through Oral and Written Language Development

1. How can a teacher assess oral and written language?

2. How can the teacher support oral language development?

3. How can the teacher support written language development?

4. How can a teacher use explicit instruction to build on students' prior knowledge, to improve listening and speaking vocabulary, and to enhance vocabulary development?

5. What are conventions of the English language?

6. How can a teacher design instruction using the conventions of the English language to enhance literacy skills?

Some Important Notes from the RICA Bulletin

1. Two or more content areas are included in each Domain.

2. The order of the content areas and the order of the competency statements within each content area do not indicate relative importance or value.

3. Examples are included with many of the competencies. These examples are provided to help clarify the knowledge and abilities described in the particular competency.

4. The examples given with the competencies should be helpful but are not comprehensive.

5. The competencies pertain to the teaching of reading in English, even though many of the competencies may also be relevant to the teaching of reading in other languages.

6. Each competency refers to the provision of instruction to all students, including English language learners, speakers of non-mainstream English, and students with special needs.

7. Instruction should be characterized by a sensitivity to and respect for the culture and language of the students and should be based on students' developmental, linguistic, functional, and age-appropriate needs; that is, instruction should be provided in ways that meet the needs of the individual student.

8. The RICA is not designed to assess the candidate's writing ability. It is designed to assess the knowledge of the reading research and skills necessary for competent readers.

9. Candidates must communicate a clear understanding and knowledge of the necessary pedagogy and skills. The candidate should know the reading research and know how to apply the findings from the research in a classroom situation.

10. Candidates can obtain further information regarding the RICA through the RICA Registration Bulletin or by checking the website at http://www.rica.com.

The RICA Domains—A Closer Look

Domain I

Planning and Organizing Reading Instruction Based on Ongoing Assessment

Content Area 1: Conducting Ongoing Assessment of Reading Development

> Ongoing assessment of reading development refers to the use of multiple measures and the ongoing analysis of individual, small-group, and class progress in order to plan effective instruction and, when necessary, classroom interventions. All instruction should be based on information acquired through valid assessment procedures. Students must be able to recognize their own reading strengths and needs and be able to apply strategies for increasing their own reading competence. Teachers must be able to use and interpret a variety of informal and formal assessment tools and communicate assessment data effectively to students, parents, guardians, school personnel, and others.

1.1 **Principles of assessment.** The beginning teacher knows how to collect and use assessment data from multiple measures on an ongoing basis to inform instructional decisions. The teacher is able to select and administer informal reading assessments in all areas of reading and to analyze the results of both informal and formal reading assessments to plan reading instruction.

1.2 **Assessing reading levels.** The beginning teacher is able to use a variety of informal measures to determine students' independent, instructional, and frustration levels of reading. The teacher conducts these assessments throughout the school year and uses the results to select materials and plan and implement effective instruction for individuals and small and large groups in all areas of reading.

1.3 **Using and communicating assessment results.** The beginning teacher knows what evidence demonstrates that a student is performing below, at, or above expected levels of performance based on content standards and applies this information when interpreting and using assessment results. The teacher is able to recognize when a student needs additional help in one or more areas of reading, plans and implements timely interventions to address identified needs, and recognizes when a student may need additional help beyond the classroom. The teacher is able to communicate assessment results and reading progress to students, parents, guardians, school personnel, and others.

Questions for Review

1. **What are some of the tests to use for *ongoing* assessment to plan reading instruction?**

Your answers might include:

- Phonemic Awareness Survey such as the Yopp-Singer or the Rosner Phonemic Awareness Survey
- Alphabet Recognition Test, Letter Identification, Alphabetic Principle
- Phonics Survey such as Shefelbine's, Beginning Phonics Skills Test (BPST)
- Concepts of Print Survey such as Marie Clay's Concepts of Print Survey
- Sight/High Frequency Words such as the Dolch List or First Grade 100 Words
- Reading Comprehension such as text comprehension, retellings, or cloze test
- Running Records

- Spelling test such as Donald Bear's Qualitative Spelling Inventory
- Vocabulary tests

These are some of the available assessments; there are many more from which to choose. The California Reading Language Arts Framework is another source of assessment ideas.

2. What criteria are used to select the test or assessment to use?

Your answers might include:

- State and district Language Arts Standards
- Developmental level of students
- Skill level of students; identified skill needs
- District guidelines/assessments
- Grade level expectations

3. How do you use the data from tests?

Some uses of data might include:

- Target instruction to meet individual needs.
- Communicate; grade-level peers, parents, students, and administrators.
- Determine student reading level; independent, instructional, and frustration.
- Form flexible skill groups.
- Plan instruction, including intervention, to meet student needs.
- Plan materials, resources needed.

The California State reading Language Arts Standards can be viewed as the bar for determining whether a student's performance is at, below, or above grade level.

4. What are some ways you would use test results in relation to the Reading/Language Arts Standards?

Your answers might include:

- Record individual student progress toward mastery of standards.
- Plan reading groups to meet identified needs.
- Communicate with parents.
- Plan interventions for students who need additional help beyond.
- Communicate specific performance information based on Standards to students, parents, and school personnel.

Your answers should include a rationale for selecting data, description on how to use the data, and the context for collecting, analyzing, and presenting.

Content Area 2: Planning, Organizing, and Managing Reading Instruction

Planning, organizing, and managing reading instruction refer to teacher practices necessary for delivering an effective, balanced, comprehensive reading program. Students' reading development is supported by a well-planned and organized program that is based on content and performance standards in reading and is responsive to the needs of individual students. Students must develop as proficient readers in order to become effective learners and take advantage of the many lifelong benefits of reading. Teachers need to understand how to plan, organize, manage, and differentiate instruction to support all students' reading development.

2.1 **Factors involved in planning reading instruction.** The beginning teacher is able to plan instruction based on state and local content and performance standards in reading. The teacher knows the components of a balanced, comprehensive reading program (see Content Areas 1 and 3 through 13) and the interrelationships among these components. The teacher is able to do short and long-term planning in reading and develop reading lessons that reflect knowledge of the standards and understanding of a balanced, comprehensive reading program. The teacher reflects on his or her reading instruction and uses this and other professional development resources and activities to plan effective reading instruction.

2.2 **Organizing and managing reading instruction.** The beginning teacher understands that the goal of reading instruction is to develop reading competence in all students, including English language learners, speakers of non-mainstream English, and students with special needs, and the teacher knows how to manage, organize, and differentiate instruction in all areas of reading to accomplish this goal (e.g., by using flexible grouping, individualizing reading instruction, planning, implementing timely interventions, and providing differentiated and/or individualized instruction). The teacher knows how to select and use instructional materials and create a learning environment that promotes student reading (e.g., by organizing independent and instructional reading materials and effectively managing their use, by taking advantage of resources and equipment within the school and the larger educational community).

Questions for Review

5. **What are some factors to consider in planning reading instruction?**

Your answers might include some reference to the following:

- **Assessment data,** analysis, and findings
- **Instructional plan;** including assessment data, Standards, components of literacy, grouping, time/pacing, instructional strategies/possible interventions, student activities, individual student needs, text, materials and resources, technology, and other curriculum variables
- **Instruction;** direct Instruction and other instructional strategies
- **Meaningful practice**
- **Assessment**

6. **What factors may be used in long-term planning?**

7. **What factors may be used in weekly/daily lesson plans?**

Your answers might include:

Long-Term Planning	Weekly/Daily Plan
California State Standards	Results of ongoing assessment
District Standards	Developmental level of students
Text guidelines	Individual student needs
Grade level expectations	Text guidelines
District Pacing Guide	Site timeline/pacing

8. **What are some of the factors to consider when setting up your classroom to manage, organize, and differentiate instruction in reading?**

Your answer might include:

- State and District Standards
- Instructional materials, technology, and other resources available
- Groupings such as flexible, individualized, skill specific, and whole group
- Planning and implementing timely interventions
- Learning environment, print rich to support literacy, areas noted for specific literacy activities, centers, hands-on activities, and small group collaboration
- Providing differentiated and/or individualized instruction

Domain II

Developing Phonological and Other Linguistic Processes Related to Reading

Content Area 3: Phonemic Awareness

Phonemic awareness is the conscious awareness that words are made up of individual speech sounds (phonemes), and it is strongly related to reading achievement. To become effective readers, students must be able to perceive and produce the specific sounds of the English language and understand how the sound system works. Therefore, teachers must understand how and why phonemic awareness skills develop both before students are reading and as they are learning to read. Teachers need to know how to plan implicit and systematic, explicit instruction in phonemic awareness and how to choose a variety of materials and activities that provide clear examples for the identification, comparison, blending, substitution, deletion, and segmentation of sounds. Teachers need to analyze students' spoken language development in order to match instruction with the students' needs.

3.1 **Assessing phonemic awareness.** The beginning teacher knows how to assess students' auditory awareness, discrimination of sounds, and spoken language for the purpose of planning instruction in phonemic awareness that meets students' needs.

3.2 **The role of phonemic awareness.** The beginning teacher knows ways in which phonemic awareness is related to reading achievement both before students are reading and as they are learning to read. The teacher understands the instructional progression for helping students acquire phonemic awareness skills (i.e., words, syllables, onsets and rimes, and phonemes).

3.3 **Developing phonemic awareness.** The beginning teacher is able to promote students' understanding that words are made up of sounds. The teacher knows how to achieve this goal by delivering appropriate, motivating instruction, both implicitly and explicitly, in auditory awareness and discrimination of sounds, phoneme awareness (e.g., teaching students how to rhyme, blend, substitute, segment, and delete sounds in words), and word awareness (i.e., recognition of word boundaries). The teacher is able to select materials and activities for teaching phonemic awareness skills that are appropriate for students at different stages of reading development.

Questions for Review

1. **What is phonemic awareness and what part does it play in learning to read?**

Answers to the question should address some of the following:

- Phonemic awareness is the awareness of the sounds (phonemes) that make up spoken words.
- Phonemic awareness is the ability to hear, identify, and manipulate individual sounds.
- Phonemic awareness is more highly related to learning to read than general intelligence, reading readiness, or listening comprehension. (Stanovich)
- Phonemic awareness can be directly taught so that a beginning or poor reader can learn that words are composed of phonemics or speech sounds. (Adams)

Students must be able to perceive and produce the specific sounds of the English language and understand how the system works.

- Phonemic awareness can improve students' word reading and reading comprehension.
- Phonemic awareness helps students learn to spell. (See "Put Reading First/NIFL" for elaboration and further ideas.)

2. What do teachers need to know concerning phonemic awareness?

1. The English sound system, including the consonant and vowel phonemes of English.
2. How to assess student needs in auditory awareness, discrimination of sounds and spoken language— e.g., Phonemic Awareness Survey, Yopp-Singer.
3. How to plan systematic, explicit instruction.
4. How to choose materials and activities to assist in the understanding and the manipulation of sounds (phonological awareness).
5. A system for comparing speech sounds in other languages with the speech sounds in English—thus, contrasts can be made explicit for English language learners (ELL) when appropriate.

3. What is the role of phonemic awareness in learning to read?

A few possible answers are as follows:

- It is a predictor of success in learning to read (Adams).
- Phonemes, the smallest units in spoken language are identified, practiced, and manipulated. The phonemic awareness instructional progression includes words, syllables, onsets and rimes, and phonemes.

4. What instruction can be presented to assist in the development of phonemic awareness?

- Awareness that words are made up of sounds
- Awareness of the English sounds system, consonant and vowel phonemics in English
- Auditory awareness and discrimination of sounds, identifying and categorizing phonemes
- Word awareness (recognize word boundaries), syllable awareness
- Instruction and practice in phoneme awareness—for example, rhymes, blending sounds, substituting sounds, segmenting sounds in a word, deleting sounds
- Selection of appropriate materials and activities for teaching phonemic awareness skills

5. How can a teacher plan direct systematic, explicit, and implicit instruction in phonemic awareness?

- Instruction should be structured and planned using assessment data of student need in phonemic awareness developmental progression.
- Plan should address assessment data, Academic Standards, individual student needs, grouping, time, technology, text, materials and resources, district Standards and pacing guide, and other curriculum variables.
- Present direct, explicit instruction in phonemic awareness. Include a variety of lessons in phonemic awareness skills such as sound manipulation and identification, comparison blending, substitution and segmentation, onset and rimes.
- Focus instruction on only one or two types of phoneme manipulation at a time.
- Select activities and materials to make the connection between oral language and print (e.g. big books, songs, alliteration, and word play).
- Knowledge of instructional strategies for teaching phonemic awareness both before and during beginning reading.
- Provide meaningful practice in phonemic awareness skills.
- Plan ongoing assessment to demonstrate student progress toward mastery of State Standards.

Content Area 4: Concepts About Print

Concepts about print refer to an understanding of how letters, words, and sentences are represented in written language, and these concepts play a critical role in students' learning to read. Students need to understand that ideas can be represented in print forms and that print forms may have unique characteristics that differ from oral representations of those same ideas. Teachers need to know that if a student does not demonstrate understanding of concepts about print and the written language system, then these concepts must be explicitly taught.

4.1 **Assessing concepts about print.** The beginning teacher is able to assess students' understanding of concepts about print and knows how to use assessment results to plan appropriate instruction in this area.

4.2 **Concepts about print.** The beginning teacher knows the instructional progression of concepts about print (e.g., sentence, word, and letter representation; directionality; tracking of print; understanding that print carries meaning). The teacher is able to select appropriate materials and activities and to provide effective instruction in these concepts.

4.3 **Letter recognition.** The beginning teacher knows the importance of teaching upper- and lowercase letter recognition and is able to select, design, and use engaging materials and activities, including multi-sensory techniques (visual, auditory, kinesthetic, tactile) to help students recognize letter shapes and learn the names of letters.

Questions for Review

6. **What role do concepts about print and an understanding of how the letters, words, and sentences are represented in written language play in students learning to read?**

Answers to this question might include:

- An understanding of concepts of print is an essential element in learning to read. It is a predictor of success in reading (Adams).
- The role of concepts about print, such as left to right sequence and word identity, convey the critical knowledge that print represents language.
- Print is oral language or talking put on paper.

Therefore, concepts about print must be explicitly taught to students who demonstrate a need. To do this, teachers must perform some of the following:

- **Assess** student understanding of concepts about print and design instruction to meet any identified need. There are several surveys and observation tools to assess understanding and plan appropriate instruction.
- **Plan instruction** and **select appropriate materials** and activities in alignment with the **instructional progression of concepts about print** such as letter, word, State Standards, sentence representation, directionality, tracking of print, and understanding that print carries meaning.
- **Plan instruction** and select appropriate materials in **recognition of letters in print**, accompanied by practice both in and out of context. Recognition should include upper- and lowercase letters, shapes, and letter names.
- **Select and design engaging materials** and activities including multi-sensory techniques (visual, auditory, kinesthetic, and tactic).
- **Provide meaningful practice** in concept of print skills. Use multi-sensory techniques—e.g., visual, auditory, kinesthetic, and tactic.
- **Use ongoing assessment** to demonstrate progress toward mastery of Standards.

Content Area 5: Systematic, Explicit Phonics, and Other Word Identification Strategies

Systematic, explicit phonics, and other word identification strategies refer to an organized program in which letter-sound correspondences for letters and letter clusters are taught directly in a manner that gradually builds from basic elements to more complex patterns. Word identification strategies build on phoneme awareness and concepts about print. Skillful and strategic word identification plays a critical role in rapid, accurate decoding, reading fluency, and comprehension. Students must understand the alphabetic principle and conventions of written language so that they are able to apply these skills automatically when reading. Teachers must provide systematic, explicit instruction in phonics and other word identification strategies.

5.1 **Assessing phonics and other word identification strategies.** The beginning teacher is able to select and use a variety of appropriate informal and formal assessments to determine students' knowledge of and skills in applying phonics and other word identification strategies, including decoding tests, fluency checks (rate and accuracy), and sight word checks. The teacher is able to use this information to plan appropriate instruction.

5.2 **Explicit phonics instruction.** The beginning teacher knows that rapid, automatic decoding contributes to reading fluency and comprehension. The teacher is able to plan and implement systematic, explicit phonics instruction that is sequenced according to the increasing complexity of linguistic units. These units include phonemes, onsets and rimes, letters, letter combinations, syllables, and morphemes. The teacher is able to select published and teacher-developed instructional programs, materials, and activities that will be effective in the systematic, explicit teaching of phonics.

5.3 **Developing fluency.** The beginning teacher knows how to help students develop fluency and consolidate their word identification strategies through frequent opportunities to read and reread decodable texts and other texts written at their independent reading levels. The teacher is able to select appropriate texts for supporting students' development of reading fluency.

5.4 **Word identification strategies.** The beginning teacher is able to model and explicitly teach students to use word identification strategies in reading for meaning, including graphophonic cues, syllable division, and morphology (e.g., use of affixes and roots), and to use context cues (semantic and syntactic) to resolve ambiguity. The teacher is able to select materials for teaching decoding and word identification strategies and knows how to model self-correction strategies and provide positive, explicit, corrective feedback for word identification errors.

5.5 **Sight words.** The beginning teacher is able to provide opportunities for mastery of common, irregular sight words through multiple and varied reading and writing experiences. The teacher is able to select materials and activities to develop and reinforce students' knowledge of sight words.

5.6 **Terminology.** The beginning teacher knows the terminology and concepts of decoding and other word identification strategies (e.g., consonant blends, consonant digraphs, vowel patterns, syllable patterns, orthography, morphology) and knows how phonemes, onsets and rimes, syllables, and morphemes are represented in print.

Questions for Review

7. What do we mean by systematic, explicit phonics and other word identification strategies?

Answers might include the following:

- Organized program in which letter-sound correspondences both for letters and letter clusters are directly taught in a manner that builds from simple to complex in a gradual manner.
- Organization of instruction, which includes sound symbol relationship, decoding skills, and word attack skills.
- Dents are taught information that is sequenced according to organizational patterns, which are intrinsic to the English language. These include: concepts about print, letter recognition, sound symbol association, rapid fluent recognition of sounds, sight vocabulary, syllable patterns, and meaningful parts and fluent application of these skills to text.

8. What tasks must the teacher address to implement a systematic, explicit phonics program?

1. **Assess** phonics and other word identification strategies. Select and use formal and informal tools such as decoding tests, fluency tests, and sight word checks to collect data and analyze to plan instruction.

2. **Plan** instruction that is systematic, explicit, and sequenced according to the increasing complexity of linguistic units including sounds, phonemes, onsets and rimes, letters, letter combinations syllables, and morphemes.

3. **Select or design** resources materials and strategies for assessment and instruction. Resources include materials for teaching decoding, word identification strategies, and sight word mastery in multiple and varied reading and writing experiences.

4. **Explicitly** teach and model phonics, decoding, and other word identification strategies in reading for meaning. Positive explicit feedback for word identification errors is an essential strategy in this process.

5. Provide **fluency practice** in a variety of ways.

   - **Practice decoding** and word attack skills so they become **automatic** in reading text.

   - Provide **application** and practice decoding skills to fluency in decodable (controlled vocabulary) text and word recognition skills taught out of context.

   - Continue to **develop fluency** through the use of decodable texts and other texts written at the student's instructional level.

6. *Ongoing assessment* **to demonstrate student progress toward mastery of State Standards.**

To implement this systematic, explicit program, the teacher must possess the following:

- **Knowledge** of the terminology and concepts of phonics decoding and word attack skills (blends, digraphs, diphthongs, syllables, prefixes, and so on) are necessary for all teachers.

- **Knowledge of instructional strategies** and knowledge that the purpose of learning phonics is to recognize words fluently and to read for meaning (comprehension). Independent readers, motivated and comprehending what is read, is the goal of reading instruction.

Content Area 6: Spelling Instruction

Spelling maps sounds to print. Spelling knowledge and word identification skills are strongly related. Students' knowledge of orthographic (spelling) patterns contributes to their word recognition, vocabulary development, and written expression. Teachers need to know the stages of spelling and be able to provide meaningful spelling instruction that includes systematic, explicit teaching of orthographic patterns (e.g., sound-letter correspondence, syllable patterns), morphology, etymology, and high-frequency words.

6.1 **Assessing spelling.** The beginning teacher is able to analyze and interpret students' spelling to assess their stages of spelling development (pre-phonetic, phonetic, transitional, conventional) and to use that information to plan appropriate spelling instruction.

6.2 **Systematic spelling instruction.** The beginning teacher is able to use a systematic plan for spelling instruction that relates to students' stages of spelling development. The teacher knows how to select spelling words and use deliberate, multi-sensory techniques to teach and reinforce spelling patterns. The teacher knows how the etymology and morphology of words relate to orthographic patterns in English, knows high-frequency words that do and do not conform to regular spelling patterns, and is able to use this knowledge in planning and implementing systematic spelling instruction.

6.3 **Spelling instruction in context.** The beginning teacher knows how to teach spelling in context and provides students with opportunities to apply and assess their spelling skills across the curriculum. The teacher knows how to plan spelling instruction that supports students' reading development (e.g., phonics skills, knowledge of morphology, vocabulary development) and writing development (e.g., use of decoding skills as a strategy for proofreading their spelling). The teacher is able to identify spelling words that support and reinforce instruction in these areas.

Questions for Review

9. **What must a teacher consider in planning spelling instruction?**

Answers must include the following:

- The teacher must assess student's spelling level.
- Apply a systematic plan for spelling instruction.
- Provide many varied opportunities to practice spelling in context.

To perform these three steps, the teacher might use the following tasks:

1. **Assessment**—Analyze and interpret student's spelling to assess stages of spelling development e.g., pre-phonic, transitional, and correctional). The teacher should be guided by the child's spelling level and know the purpose and limitations of "inventive spelling." Plan developmentally appropriate spelling instruction to meet identified levels and needs.

2. **Systematic** spelling instruction that follows a logical scope and sequence and is logically connected to the phonics sequence used in reading. Orthographic patterns, high-frequency words, etymology, and morphology must be taught as an integral part in systematic, spelling instruction.

3. **Opportunities to practice spelling skills in context,** which support students' reading development. The teacher should use active, constructive learning activities that require children to think about the relationship between speech and print. Many opportunities to apply spelling skills in writing should be provided and encouraged.

10. What must a teacher consider in teaching students that spelling is an aspect of word knowledge?

- Knowledge of orthographic patterns enables word recognition and vocabulary development.

- The teacher must plan instructional strategies to promote generalizations of spelling study to writing, (e.g., personal proofreading checklists, incentives for accuracy, think-alouds, self-corrections strategies, and spelling patterns).

- Systematic and explicit phonics instruction significantly improves kindergarten and first-grade children's word recognition and spelling. It is most effective when it begins in kindergarten or first grade. (Put Reading First, NIFL.)

Domain III

Developing Reading Comprehension and Promoting Independent Reading

Content Area 7: Reading Comprehension

Reading comprehension refers to reading with understanding. Reading fluency and reading comprehension are necessary for learning in all content areas, sustaining interest in what is read, and deriving pleasure from reading. The end goal of reading instruction is to enable students to read with understanding and apply comprehension strategies to different types of texts for a variety of lifetime reading purposes. Effective readers produce evidence of comprehension by clarifying the ideas presented in text and connecting them to other sources, including their own background knowledge. Teachers need to be able to facilitate students' comprehension and provide them with explicit instruction and guided practice in comprehension strategies.

7.1 **Assessing reading comprehension.** The beginning teacher is able to use informal and formal procedures to assess students' comprehension of narrative and expository texts and their use of comprehension strategies. The teacher knows how to use this information to provide effective instruction in reading comprehension.

7.2 **Fluency and other factors affecting comprehension.** The beginning teacher understands factors affecting reading comprehension (e.g., reading rate and fluency, word recognition, prior knowledge and experiences, vocabulary) and knows how proficient readers read. The teacher is able to use this knowledge to plan and deliver effective instruction in reading comprehension.

7.3 **Facilitating comprehension.** The beginning teacher is able to facilitate comprehension at various stages of students' reading development (e.g., before students learn to read, as they are learning to read, and as they become proficient readers). The teacher is able to select and use a range of activities and strategies before, during, and after reading to enhance students' comprehension (e.g., developing background knowledge, encouraging predictions, questioning, conducting discussions).

7.4 **Different levels of comprehension.** The beginning teacher knows the levels of comprehension and is able to model and explicitly teach comprehension skills. These include (a) literal comprehension skills (e.g., identifying explicitly stated main ideas, details, sequence, cause-effect relationships, and patterns); (b) inferential comprehension skills (e.g., inferring main ideas, details, comparisons, cause-effect relationships not explicitly stated, drawing conclusions or generalizations from a text; predicting outcomes), and (c) evaluative comprehension skills (e.g., recognizing instances of bias and unsupported inferences in texts, detecting propaganda and faulty reasoning; distinguishing between facts and opinions; reacting to a text's content, characters, and use of language). The teacher is able to select materials (both narrative and expository texts) to support effective instruction in these areas.

7.5 **Comprehension strategies.** The beginning teacher is able to model and explicitly teach a range of strategies students can use to clarify the meaning of text (e.g., self-monitoring, rereading, note taking, outlining, summarizing, mapping, using learning logs). The teacher knows how to select materials and create opportunities for guided and independent practice using comprehension strategies.

Questions for Review

1. **How does a teacher assess reading comprehension? How does a teacher use the data from comprehension assessment?**

Possible answers might include the following:

- Informal assessments such as teacher observation and retelling, student's writing.
- Formal assessment such as end of unit or chapter comprehension test, Running Records, cloze type tests.

- Data from the assessment may be used to target instruction.
- Data from the assessment may be used to communicate to a variety of audiences such as the student, other teachers, administrators, and parents.

2. How does a teacher assist students in increasing fluency?

Possible answers might include the following:

- Ongoing fluency assessments to monitor fluency progress and determine independent reading level.
- Modeling fluent reading.
- Guided repeated oral reading with systematic and explicit guidance and feedback from the teacher.
- Independent silent or oral reading on student's independent reading level.
- Practice, practice, practice! Reread, reread, reread!

3. How can a teacher facilitate student attainment of comprehension?

Possible answers might include the following:

- Provide instructional activities such as direct and indirect vocabulary building and fluency activities to build comprehension skills.
- Teach, model, practice that text comprehension is both purposeful and active.
- Teach comprehension strategies and demonstrate their application throughout the reading—e.g., monitoring comprehension, using graphic and semantic organizers, answering questions, generating questions, recognizing story structure, visualizing, comparing and contrasting, previewing, predicting, retelling and summarizing, and using prior knowledge. (Put Reading First, NIFL.)
- Direct comprehension instruction, modeling, guided practice, student independent application of comprehension skill.
- Provide a repertoire of activities that foster connections between reading and writing.

4. What are the levels of comprehension? How should these levels be taught?

Possible answers might include the following:

- Levels of Comprehension
  1. **Literal Comprehension Skills**—These include clearly, explicitly identifying items such as main idea, sequence, patterns, cause and effect.
  2. **Inferential Comprehension Skills**—These include making inferences concerning items not explicitly stated such as comparisons, drawing conclusions, predicting, and cause/effect relationships not explicitly stated.
  3. **Evaluative Comprehension Skills**—These include critical reading such as recognizing unsupported inferences in text, distinguishing between facts and opinions, using of language and detecting propaganda and faulty reasoning.
     - Instruction in levels of comprehension should include the following:
     1. Direct, explicit instruction of skills
     2. Modeling of each level of comprehension skills
     3. Guided practice
     4. Independent practice
     5. Use of resources and materials and activities selected by the teacher to support effective instruction and practice in levels of comprehension

Skills and Strategies Represent Different Stages of Development. A skill becomes a strategy when the student can use it independently.

5. What are comprehension strategies? How should these strategies be taught?

Possible answers might include the following:

- Comprehension strategies are activities that we use to gain meaning or understanding from text and to clarify text. These include strategies such as reread, retell, self-monitor, reorganize text (outline, note-taking, summarize), predict answer and generate questions, compare and contrast, use graphic and semantic organizers, monitor comprehension, recognize story structure, use prior knowledge and visualization.
- To teach these strategies, the teacher should do the following:

1. **Assess** student understanding of the strategy.
2. **Plan** instruction to meet identified needs.
3. The plan should include instructional strategies for direct instruction, modeling, guided practice, and independent practice. In addition, the plan should **include** possible resources and materials to be used in instruction and practice.
4. **Instruct** students using direct instruction and modeling.
5. Provide **practice** in both guided and independent settings.
6. **Assess** to monitor for mastery of skills.

Content Area 8: Literary Response and Analysis

Literature provides readers with unique opportunities to reflect on their own experiences, investigate further ranges of human experience, gain access to unfamiliar worlds, and develop their own imaginative capacities. Students who are fully engaged in literature find a rich medium in which to explore language. Teachers need to provide explicit instruction and guided practice in responding to literature and analyzing literary text structures and elements.

8.1 **Assessing literary response and analysis.** The beginning teacher is able to assess students' responses to literature (e.g., making personal connections, analyzing text, providing evidence from text to support their responses) and use that information to plan appropriate instruction in these areas.

8.2 **Responding to literature.** The beginning teacher is able to select literature from a range of eras, perspectives, and cultures and provides students with frequent opportunities to listen to and read high-quality literature for different purposes. The teacher knows how to use a range of instructional approaches and activities for helping students apply comprehension strategies when reading literature and for developing students' responses to literature (e.g., using guided reading, reading logs, and discussions about literature; encouraging students to connect elements in a text to other sources, including other texts, their experiences, and their background knowledge).

8.3 **Literary analysis.** The beginning teacher knows and can teach elements of literary analysis and criticism (e.g., describing and analyzing story elements, recognizing features of different literary genres, determining mood and theme, analyzing the use of figurative language, analyzing ways in which a literary work reflects the traditions and perspectives of a particular people or time period). The teacher is able to select literature that provides clear examples of these elements and that matches students' instructional needs and reading interests.

Questions for Review

6. How can a teacher assess student literary response and analysis? How can this data be used?

Possible answers might include the use of the following:

- Teacher observation and assessment of personal connections in essays and reading logs and analysis of text in response to teacher questions, observation of student participation in literature circles.
- Data from assessment can be used to target instruction and to communicate with students, parents, and/or school personnel.

7. How can a teacher assist students in making connections and responding to literature?

Possible answers might include the following:

- The teacher can engage students in reading or listening to high-quality literature.
- Students should be engaged in activities and strategies to clarify and understand text.
- Student responses to text, linked with prior knowledge, might include such activities as reading logs, literature circles, *Reader's Theater,* essays, cross curricular discussions, and writings.
- Engaging students in response activities, which include book reports, identifying main problem in the story, semantic webs, trait charts, and analyzing different types of literature.

8. How can a teacher teach elements of literary analysis and criticism?

Possible answers might include the following:

- The teacher can **assess** student knowledge of elements of literary analysis and criticism such as: historical fiction, biographies, autobiographies, poetry, plays, realistic fiction, multicultural literature, fact, and fantasy.
- Using the data from the assessment, the teacher can **plan** direct instruction, modeling, guided practice, and independent practice.
- The teacher can **plan resources,** materials, and student groupings to use in instruction, which will assist in meeting identified student needs and interests. Elements of literary analysis and criticism include such elements as analyzing the use of figurative language, genre, story elements, mood, theme, and time period.
- **Instruction** in elements of literary analysis should be direct instruction, teacher modeling, and guided practice.

Students should be involved in a variety of activities for **independent practice.**

- **Ongoing assessment** to monitor progress and determine mastery of skills should be implemented after sufficient independent practice.

Content Area 9: Content Area Literacy

Content-area literacy refers to the ability to learn through reading. Learning in all content areas is supported by strong reading comprehension strategies and study skills. Students need to know how to apply a variety of reading comprehension strategies to different types of texts, analyze the structures and features of expository (informational) texts, and select and vary their reading strategies for different texts and purposes. Teachers need to model and provide explicit instruction in these skills and strategies and provide students with frequent opportunities for guided and independent practice using them.

9.1 **Assessing content-area literacy.** The beginning teacher is able to assess students' comprehension in content-area reading and use that information to provide effective instruction.

9.2 **Different types of texts and purposes for reading.** The beginning teacher knows and is able to teach students about different types and functions of text and the skills and strategies required for reading and comprehending different types of texts. The teacher is able to select texts that provide clear examples of common text structures (i.e., cause/effect, comparison/contrast, problem/solution) and knows how to model and explicitly teach students to use text structures to improve their comprehension and memory of expository texts. The teacher is able to model and teach reading strategies for different reading purposes (e.g., skimming, scanning, and in-depth reading)

9.3 **Study skills.** The beginning teacher is able to model and explicitly teach study skills for locating and retrieving information from reference materials and content-area texts, for retaining and using information, and for test taking.

Questions for Review

9. How can the teacher assess content area literacy and how should data from the assessment be used?

Possible answers might include the following:

- **Teacher observation and anecdotal records** during instruction in content areas such as math, science, and social studies.
- **Chapter or unit text tests** are assessments to use in content area comprehension and literacy.
- **Student work** in content areas can be analyzed to determine literacy or understanding in that content area.
- **Rubrics** can be used across content areas.

Data from content area literacy assessments can be used to do the following:

- Target instruction to meet individual student needs.
- Communicate with students, parents, and school personnel.
- Plan skill instruction across the curriculum—e.g., preview (comprehension strategy) that is applicable in math, science, social studies, and other content areas.
- Plan study skills applicable to a variety of content areas—such as note-taking, outlining, skimming, and mapping.

10. How does a teacher plan instruction in different types of text, e.g., narrative, expository, and functional?

Possible answers might include the following:

- **Assess** student knowledge of skills to be taught in the identified type of text—narrative, expository, or functional text.
- **Plan** skill instruction to meet identified need, e.g., in problem/solution skill. Select materials, resource texts to support instruction and clarify skill. Planning should include several curricular elements such as grouping, technology, and scheduling.
- **Instruct** in skills using a variety of instructional strategies. Direct instruction in skills should be used with teacher modeling and opportunities for guided practice.
- **Practice** in the skill should be meaningfully linked to the type of text. Students should be involved in a variety of opportunities to practice the identified skill.
- **Ongoing assessment** to monitor student progress toward skill mastery and to target instruction.

11. How can the teacher teach reading strategies for students to gain meaning from text in a variety of ways?

Possible answers might include the following:

- **Reading for different purposes** to gain meaning and clarify text can be taught in a direct manner, modeled by the teacher and practiced by students in guided practice activities.
- These strategies can be **applied and practiced** across curricular areas and include such skills as browsing, previewing, skimming, and in-depth reading.

12. How does a teacher teach study skills?

Possible answers might include the following:

- **Assess** student knowledge of study skill to be assessed. Use data to plan instruction.
- **Plan** instruction to meet identified need such as research skills, using reference materials, organizing information, and relating information to content area text and tests. Planning should include curriculum elements such as direct instruction strategies, teacher modeling, materials and resources, technology, scheduling, and student activities.
- **Instruction** should include direct instruction supported by teacher modeling and guided practice.
- **Practice** should include locating and retrieving information from a variety of sources including the Internet, reference sources, and texts. In addition, students practice using and retaining information for test taking.

Content Area 10: Student Independent Reading

> Independent reading plays a critical role in promoting students' familiarity with language patterns, increasing fluency and vocabulary, broadening knowledge in content areas, and motivating further reading for information and pleasure. Independent reading improves reading performance. To become effective readers, students should be encouraged to read as frequently, broadly, and thoughtfully as possible. Teachers need to understand the importance of independent reading and know how to encourage and guide students in their independent reading.

10.1 **Encouraging independent reading.** The beginning teacher is able to determine each student's reading interests and preferences, survey the quantity and quality of students' reading, consider each student's independent reading level, and use that information to promote extensive independent reading. The teacher promotes student reading that extends beyond the core curriculum by providing daily opportunities for self-selected reading and frequent opportunities for sharing what is read. The teacher knows how to guide students in selecting independent reading materials and how to motivate students to read independently by regularly reading aloud to students from high-quality texts, providing access to a variety of reading materials, and suggesting texts that match student interests.

10.2 **Supporting at-home reading.** The beginning teacher is able to use a variety of strategies to motivate students to read at home. The teacher encourages and provides support for parents or guardians to read to their children, in English and/or in the primary languages of English language learners, and/or to use additional strategies to promote literacy in the home. The teacher is able to select and organize, for various purposes, a range of reading materials at different levels in English and, when available, in the primary language(s) of the students in the classroom.

Questions for Review

13. What does a teacher need to know about individual students to assist in promoting independent reading?

Answers might include the following:

- Using surveys, observation anecdotal, and other qualitative data collection tools, the teacher collects reading preference and interest information regarding each student.
- The teacher needs to know the independent reading level of each student and the quantity and quality of each student's reading.

14. How can a teacher promote independent student reading?

Answers might include the following:

- The teacher modeling the enjoyment of reading during daily read-alouds is one of the best ways to promote student independent reading.
- The teacher should encourage independent reading by having a classroom library with a variety of reading materials including a variety of levels and a variety of genre.
- The teacher should provide in-school opportunities for independent reading on a daily basis and assign reading in a variety of content areas both in school and at home.
- Students are engaged in many reading activities including shared reading, oral reading, and repeated reading of favorite text.

15. How can a teacher support at-home reading?

Answers might include the following:

- The teacher can organize a variety of materials on different reading levels and, if possible, in the student's primary language to be used in homework assignments.
- The teacher can use a variety of motivational and support strategies to engage parents and students in literacy activities at home.

- The heart of the literacy activities should involve parents/guardians reading to their child in English or in their primary language.

16. What does a teacher need to know to teach content area literacy/comprehension?

Possible answers include the following:

- **Assessment strategies** to determine student comprehension in content areas. Assessment could be informal observation and discussion of student reading or formal tests created by the teacher or pulled from the text.

  - **Recognition and understanding** of different types of texts and purposes for reading. This includes the structures of narrative, expository, and poetic text.

  - Provide examples and explicitly teach **common text structures**—e.g., cause/effect.

  - Model and teach reading **strategies for different reading purposes**—e.g., skimming, scanning, and in-depth reading.

  - **Study skills** to explicitly teach students how to

    1. locate and retrieve information from reference sources and content area text.

    2. retain and use information for text taking.

17. How can a teacher promote the reading of good books?

A few ideas are as follows:

- Provide a wide variety of reading materials, fiction and non-fiction organized by level of difficulty.
- Guide and motivate students to select reading materials from high-quality texts on a daily basis. Keep records to assist in motivation.
- Read aloud to students on a daily basis, encourage home monitoring of independent reading.
- Promote shared reading, oral reading, and repeated reading of favorite text.

Domain IV

Supporting Reading Through Oral and Written Language Development

Content Area 11: Relationships Among Reading, Writing, and Oral Language

An effective, comprehensive language arts program increases students' language facility through relevant daily opportunities to relate listening, speaking, reading, and writing. Reading is supported by effective writing, listening, and speaking instruction, and the goal of language arts instruction is to fully develop students' communication skills. Students must be able to connect reading, writing, listening, and speaking tasks to their experiences, intentions, and purposes. Teachers need to be aware of the interdependent nature of reading, writing, listening, and speaking and be able to use interrelated instruction in the four areas to promote reading proficiency.

11.1 **Assessing oral and written language.** The beginning teacher is able to informally assess students' oral and written language and use that information when planning reading instruction.

11.2 **Oral language development.** The beginning teacher knows how to provide formal and informal oral language opportunities across the curriculum that enhance students' development as readers (e.g., through language play, group discussions, questioning, and sharing information). The teacher helps students make connections between their oral language and reading and writing.

11.3 **Written language development.** The beginning teacher is able to provide purposeful writing opportunities across the curriculum to enhance students' reading development. The teacher explicitly teaches the transfer of skills from oral language to written language. The teacher provides instruction in which reading, writing, and oral language are interrelated.

11.4 **Supporting English language learners.** The beginning teacher is able to interrelate the elements of language arts instruction to support the reading development of English language learners (e.g., using preview-review, visual aids, charts, real objects, word organizers, graphic organizers, and outlining). The teacher knows general ways in which the writing systems of other languages might differ from English (e.g., that not all writing systems are alphabetic, that English is less regular phonetically than some other alphabetic languages). The teacher understands factors and processes involved in transferring literacy competencies from one language to another (e.g., positive and negative transfer) and uses knowledge of language similarities and differences to promote transfer of language skills (e.g., through scaffolding strategies, modeling, and explicit instruction).

Questions for Review

1. **How can a teacher assess oral and written language?**

Answers might include the following:

- The teacher might use informal assessments including teacher observation during retellings, oral sharing and other oral activities, writing samples, portfolios, and rubrics to assess oral and written language.
- The teacher analyzes the data and uses the results to plan instruction targeted to meet individual needs.

2. **How can the teacher support oral language development?**

Answers might include the following:

- The teacher models oral language throughout the day in all content areas.
- The teacher provides a variety of formal and informal opportunities for oral language practice across the curriculum; these might include show and tell, brainstorming, group discussions, and story telling.

- Students are involved in oral language activities in a variety of settings and in different groups such as whole class, small group, and pairs.
- Structured discussions, games, language play, questioning, and sharing, and many other activities are used to practice oral language.
- The teacher uses experience charts, chart stories, big books, read-alouds, and guided writing to demonstrate the connections between oral language and reading and writing.

3. How can the teacher support written language development?

Answers might include the following:

- The teacher gives direct instruction and guided practice in the writing process.
- The teacher uses a variety of activities such as experience stories and charts to demonstrate how oral language can be written to enhance communication.
- The teacher uses a variety of activities such as experience stories and charts to demonstrate or model that oral language can be recorded in written language.
- The teacher provides a variety of experiences for meaningful written reflection in all content areas.
- The teacher uses direct instruction and guided practice to instruct in writing for a variety of purposes and writing to a variety of audiences. Students are provided many opportunities for meaningful independent practice in writing for a variety of purposes and to a variety of audiences.
- The teacher uses direct instruction to demonstrate that reading is visual language input, and writing is visual language output. In addition, listening is oral language input; speaking is oral language output.

Content Area 12: Vocabulary Development

Vocabulary constitutes the building block of language. Vocabulary knowledge plays a critical role in reading comprehension, and readers learn most vocabulary through wide reading. Students need to know how to use a range of strategies, including those involving word analysis, context, and syntax, that promote reading fluency and enable independent comprehension, interpretation, and application of words contained in narrative and expository text. Upon entering school, students have a listening and speaking vocabulary that forms the foundation for vocabulary and comprehension instruction. Teachers need to build upon this foundation by providing explicit instruction in vocabulary development and in determining the meaning and accurate use of unfamiliar words encountered through listening and reading.

12.1 **Assessing vocabulary knowledge.** The beginning teacher is able to informally assess students' vocabulary knowledge in relation to specific reading needs and texts and is able to use that information to plan appropriate vocabulary instruction.

12.2 **Increasing vocabulary knowledge.** The beginning teacher knows how to provide opportunities for students to increase their vocabulary by listening to and reading a variety of texts and encourages students to apply their vocabulary knowledge in new contexts. The teacher is able to select vocabulary words on the basis of appropriate criteria (e.g., words that are related to each other, words needed to comprehend a reading selection). The teacher knows how to select appropriate instructional materials (e.g., read-aloud materials that promote vocabulary development and lay the foundation for complex language structures) and is able to teach vocabulary using a range of instructional activities (e.g., word sorts, word banks, classification, semantic mapping).

12.3 **Strategies for gaining and extending meanings of words.** The beginning teacher is able to model and explicitly teach students a variety of strategies for gaining meaning from unfamiliar words, such as using word analysis (e.g., decoding, prefixes and suffixes, base words, roots), context, and syntax. The teacher knows how to select and use materials and activities that help students extend their understanding of words, including words with multiple meanings. The teacher is able to provide instruction in the use of reference materials that can help clarify the meaning of words (e.g., dictionary, thesaurus, glossary, and technological sources).

Questions for Review

4. How can a teacher use explicit instruction to build on students' prior knowledge, to improve listening and speaking vocabulary, and to enhance vocabulary development?

Answers to the question should include the following:

- Use formal and informal tools to assess reading and speaking vocabulary.

- Provide a variety of activities to build vocabulary skills. These would include listening to and reading a variety of texts, playing vocabulary games, word sorts, semantic mapping, classification, word banks, and many other activities.

- Use direct, explicit instruction to teach a variety of strategies for gaining meaning from unfamiliar words such as word analysis, decoding, prefixes, suffixes, roots, context, syntax, and root words.

- Use a variety of materials and resources to extend vocabulary and understanding of words.

- Direct instruction in vocabulary and in strategies to attain vocabulary knowledge is essential for all students. It is critical for ELL students to acquire vocabulary. Pre-teaching vocabulary/concepts is a scaffolding strategy that teachers must use on a consistent basis.

- Provide many opportunities for read-alouds and independent reading in the classroom. This independent reading will help to build the vocabulary knowledge of all students.

Content Area 13: Structure of the English Language

Structure of the English language refers to established rules for the use of the language. Students' knowledge of the structure of English promotes their reading fluency, listening, and reading comprehension, and oral and written expression. Students must be able to recognize, when listening or reading, and apply, when speaking or writing, English language conventions and structures. Teachers need a basic knowledge of English conventions and the structure of English language (sentence structure, grammar, punctuation, capitalization, spelling, syntax, and semantics) and must be able to provide instruction in these areas to enhance students' literacy skills.

13.1 **Assessing English language structures.** The beginning teacher is able to analyze students' oral and written language to determine their understanding and use of English language structures and conventions and knows how to use this information to plan appropriate instruction.

13.2 **Differences between written and oral English.** The beginning teacher is able to help students understand similarities and differences between language structures used in spoken and written English. The teacher knows how to use explicit instruction and guided practice to teach written-language structures to all students. The teacher uses a range of approaches and activities to develop students' facility in comprehending and using academic language (e.g., oral language development activities to build knowledge of academic language and familiarize students with grammatical structures they will encounter in written text).

13.3 **Applying knowledge of the English language to improve reading.** The beginning teacher has a basic knowledge of English syntax and semantics and is able to use this knowledge to improve students' reading competence (e.g., by teaching students to group words into meaningful phrases to increase reading fluency and comprehension, by teaching students to analyze how punctuation affects a text's meaning). The beginning teacher knows how to help students interpret and apply English grammar and language conventions in authentic reading, writing, listening, and speaking contexts. The teacher is able to help students consolidate their knowledge of English grammar and improve their fluency and comprehension by providing frequent opportunities to listen to, read, and reread materials that provide clear examples of specific English grammatical structures and conventions.

Questions for Review

5. How can a teacher design instruction using the conventions of the English language to enhance literacy skills?

Answers to this might include the following:

- Assess students' oral and written language to determine level of understanding of conventions.
- Plan instruction to meet identified needs in conventions. (Note grade level standards.)
- Use direct, explicit instruction and guided practice to learn written language structures.
- Use a variety of activities to practice and enhance knowledge of academic language and grammatical structures.
- Provide opportunities for students to apply their knowledge of English grammar and the structure of English language to reading, writing, and speaking in daily language activities.

Glossary of Terms and Concepts and Reading Assessments

Terms and Concepts

Affix   A bound (nonword) morpheme that changes the meaning or function of a root or stem to which it is attached, as the prefix ad- and suffix -ing in *adjoining*.

Alphabetic Principle   The assumption underlying alphabetic writing systems that each speech sound or phoneme of a language should have its own distinctive graphic representation.

Analytic Phonics   A whole-to-part approach to word study in which the student is first taught a number of sight words and then relevant phonic generalizations, which are subsequently applied to other words; deductive phonics.

Auditory Blending   The ability to fuse discrete phonemes into recognizable spoken words.

Auditory Discrimination   The ability to hear phonetic likenesses and differences in phonemes and words.

Auditory Processing   The full range of mental activity involved in reacting to auditory stimuli, especially sounds, and in considering their meanings in relation to past experience and to their future use.

Automaticity   The ability to recognize a word (or series of words) in text effortlessly and rapidly.

Basal Reading Program   A collection of student texts and workbooks, teacher's manuals, and supplemental materials for development of reading and sometimes writing instruction, used chiefly in the elementary and middle school grades.

Blend   To combine the sounds represented by letters to pronounce a word; sound out.

Comprehension   Comprehension, "the essence of reading," is often taken to mean reading comprehension in the literacy literature unless restricted specifically or by inference from its content.

Concepts to Print   Familiarity with writing and print conventions, such as left to right, top to bottom sequence of reading; the use of spaces to denote words; the idea that print represents words. An important predictor of learning to read.

Consonant   A speech sound made by partial or complete closure of part of the vocal tract, which obstructs air flow and causes audible friction in varying amounts.

Consonant Digraph   A combination of two consonant letters representing a single speech sound, as *th* for /th/ in that, or gh for /f/ in rough.

Context Clue   Information from the immediate textual setting that helps identify a word or word group, as by words, phrases, sentence illustrations, syntax, typography, etc.

Cueing System   Any of the various sources of information that might aid identification of a word unrecognized at first glance, as phonics, structural analysis, and semantic and syntactical information.

Curriculum-Based Assessment   The appraisal of student progress by using materials and procedures directly from the curriculum taught.

Decode   To analyze spoken or graphic symbols of a familiar language to ascertain their intended meaning. **Note:** To learn to read, one must learn the conventional code in which something is written in order to decode the written message. In reading practice, the term is used primarily to refer to word identification rather than to identification of higher units of meaning.

Decoding   A series of strategies used selectively by readers to recognize and read written words. The reader locates cues (e.g., letter-sound correspondences) in a word that reveals enough about it to help in pronouncing it and attaching meaning to it.

Diagnosis   The act, process, or result of identifying the nature of a disorder or disability through observation and examination. **Note:** Technically, diagnosis means only the identification and labeling of a disorder. As the term is used in education, however, it often includes the planning of instruction and an assessment of the strengths and weaknesses of the student.

Diagnostic Teaching   The use of the results of student performance on current tasks to plan future learning activities; instruction in which diagnosis and instruction are fused into a single ongoing process.

Diagnostic Test   A test used to analyze strengths and weaknesses in content-oriented skills. **Note:** Diagnostic tests may permit comparison among several subabilities of the same individuals and sometimes comparisons of strong and weak points of a group or class. Available instruments for the diagnosis of read difficulties vary widely in the thoroughness of analysis they permit and in the specific procedures followed.

Digraph   Two letters that represent one speech sound, as *ch* for /ch/ in *chin* or *ea* for /e/ in *bread*.

Diphthong   A vowel sound produced when the tongue moves or glides from one vowel sound toward another vowel or semivowel sound in the same syllable, as /i/ in *buy* and vowel sounds in *boy*, and *bough*.

Dyslexia   A development reading disability, presumably congenital and often hereditary, that may vary in degree from mild to severe. **Note:** Dyslexia originally called word blindness, occurs in persons who have adequate vision, hearing, intelligence, and general language functioning. Dyslexics frequently have difficulty in spelling and in acquiring a second language, suggesting that dyslexia is part of a broad type of language disability. Difficulties with phonology are typical of most.

Emergent Literacy   Development of the association of print with meaning that begins early in a child's life and continues until the child reaches the stage of conventional reading and writing, "the reading and writing concepts and behaviors of young children that precede and develop into conventional literacy."

Encode   To change a message into, as encode oral language into writing, encode an idea into words, or encode physical law into mathematical symbols.

Etymology   The study of the history of words.

Explicit Instruction   The intentional design and delivery of information by the teacher to the students. It begins with (1) the teacher's modeling or demonstration of the skill or strategy; (2) a structured and substantial opportunity for students to practice and apply newly taught skills and knowledge under the teacher's direction and guidance; and (3) an opportunity for feedback.

Fluency   The clear, easy, and quick written or spoken expression of ideas; freedom from word-identification problems that might hinder comprehension in silent reading or the expression of ideas in oral reading; automaticity.

Fluent Reader   A reader whose performance exceeds normal expectation with respect to age and ability; independent reader.

Frustration Reading Level   A readability or grade level of material that is too difficult to be read successfully by a student even with normal classroom instruction and support.

Genre   A term used to classify literary works, such as novel, mystery, historical fiction, biography, short story, poem.

Graded Word List   A list of words ranked by grade level, reader level, or other level of difficulty of complexity, often used to assess competence in word identification, word-meaning knowledge, and spelling.

Grapheme   A written or printed representation of a phoneme as *b* for /b/ or *oy* for /oi/ in boy.

Grapheme-Phoneme Correspondence   The relationship between a grapheme and the phoneme(s) it represents; letter-sound correspondence, as c representing /k/ in cat and /s/ in cent.

Graphic Organizer   A visual representation of facts and concepts from a text and their relationships within an organized frame. Graphic organizers are effective tools for thinking and learning. They help teachers and students represent abstract or implicit information in more concrete form, depict the relationships among facts and concepts, aid in organizing and elaborating ideas, relate new information with prior knowledge, and effectively store and retrieve information.

Guided Reading   Reading instruction in which the teacher provides the structure and purpose for reading and for responding to the material read.

High Frequency Word   A word that appears many more times than most other words in spoken or written language.

Informal Reading Inventory (IRI)   The use of a graded series of passages of increasing difficulty to determine students' strengths, weaknesses, and strategies in word identification and comprehension.

Interactive Writing   A shared writing experience used to assist emergent readers in learning to read and write. With help from the teacher, students dictate sentences about a shared experience, such as a story, movie, or event. The teacher stretches each word orally so that students can distinguish its sounds and letters as they use chart paper to write the letter while repeating the sound. After each word has been completed, the teacher and students reread it. The students take turns writing letters to complete the words and sentences. The completed charts are posted on the wall so that the students can reread them or rely on them for standard spelling.

Inventive Spelling   Spelling of sounds processed phonologically (a child's attempt to map speech to print).

Learning Center or Station   A location within a classroom in which students are presented with instructional materials, specific directions, clearly defined objectives, and opportunities for self-evaluation.

Metacognition   Awareness and knowledge of one's mental processes such that one can monitor, regulate, and direct them to a desired end; self-mediation.

Minimally Contrasting Pairs   Words that differ only in initial or medial or final sounds (e.g., pest/best, scrapple/scrabble, cat/cap).

Mnemonic   Having to do with memory, especially with strategies to improve memorizing.

Morpheme   A meaningful linguistic unit that cannot be divided into smaller meaningful elements, as the word book, or that is a component of a word, as s in books.

Morphology   The study of structure and forms of words including derivation, inflection, and compounding.

Nonphonetic Word   In teaching practice, a word whose pronunciation may not be accurately predicated from its spelling.

Nonsense Syllable   A pronounceable combination of graphic characters, usually trigrams, that do not make a word, as kak, vor, mek, pronounced as English spellings.

Orthographic   Pertains to orthography, the art or study of correct spelling according to established usage.

Orthography   The way a language is written (encoded).

Peer Editing   A form of collaborative learning in which students work with their peers in editing a piece of writing.

Phoneme   A minimal sound unit of speech that, when contrasted with another phoneme, affects the meaning of words in a language, as /b/ in book contrasts with /t/ in took, /k/ in cook, /h/ in hook.

Phoneme Grapheme Correspondence   The relationship between a phoneme and its graphemic representation(s), as /s/, spelled s in sit, c in city, ss in grass.

Phonemic Awareness or Phoneme Awareness   Phonemic awareness is the awareness of the sounds (phonemes) that make up spoken words. Such awareness does not appear when young children learn to talk; the ability is not necessary for speaking and understanding spoken language. However, phonemic awareness is important to understand the code of alphabetic languages and letters (and letter sounds). Having phonemic awareness provides some understanding of the notion that words are made up of phonemes. This insight is not always easily achieved. Phonemes are abstract units, and when one pronounces a word one does not produce a series of discrete phonemes; rather phonemes are folded into one another and are pronounced as a blend. Altogether most young children have no difficulty segmenting words into syllables; many find it very difficult to segment at the phoneme level.

Phonic Analysis   In teaching practice, the identification of words by their sounds.

Phonics   A way of teaching, reading, and spelling that stresses symbol-sound relationships, used especially in beginning instruction.

Phonogram   A graphic character or symbol that can represent a phonetic sound, phoneme, or word.

Phonological Awareness   A broader term than phonemic awareness; refers to language sensitivity and ability to manipulate language at the levels of syllables, rhymes, and individual speech sounds.

Phonology   The permissible part of arrangements of speech sounds in forming morphemes and words; the rules for producing the phonemes in words.

Prefix   An affix attached before a base word or root, as re- in reprint.

Preprimer   In a basal reading program, a booklet used before the first reader to introduce students to features in texts and books and sometimes to introduce specific characters found later in a series.

Prereading   Referring to activities designed to develop needed attitudes and skills before formal instruction in reading.

Prewriting   The initial creative and planning stage of writing, prior to drafting, in which the writer formulates ideas, gathers information, and considers ways in which to organize a piece of writing.

Primary language   The first language a child learns to speak.

Primer   A beginning book for the teaching of reading; specifically, the first formal textbook in a basal reading program, usually preceded by a readiness book and one or more preprimers.

Print Awareness   In emergent literacy, a learner's growing recognition of conventions and characteristics of a written language.

Print-Rich Environment   An environment in which students are provided many opportunities to interact with print, and an abundance and variety of printed materials are available and accessible. Students have many opportunities to read and be read to. In such an environment reading and writing are modeled by the teacher and used for a wide variety of authentic everyday purposes.

R-Controlled Vowel Sound   The modified sound of a vowel immediately preceding /r/ in the same syllable, as in care, never, sir, or curse, etc.

Recognition Vocabulary   The number of different words known without word analysis, words understood quickly and easily; sight vocabulary.

Rhyme   Correspondence of ending sounds of words or lines of verse.

Rime   A vowel and any of the following consonants of a syllable, as /ook/ in book or brook, /ik/ in strike, and /a/ in play.

Scaffolding   The temporary support, guidance, or assistance provided to a student on a new or complex task. For example, students work in partnership with a more advanced peer or adult who scaffolds the task by engaging in appropriate instructional interactions designed to model, assist, or provide necessary information. The interactions should eventually lead to independence.

Semantics   The study of meaning in language, as the analysis of the meanings of words, phrases, sentences, discourse, and whole texts.

Sight Word   A word that is immediately recognized as a whole and does not require word analysis for identification. A word taught as a whole.

Sound Out   The application of phonics skills in reproducing the sound(s) represented by a letter or letter group in a word.

Story Frame/Map   A graphic organizer of major events and ideas from a story to help guide students' thinking and heighten their awareness of the structure of stories. The teacher can model this process by filling out a chart on an overhead while reading. Or students can complete a chart individually or in groups after a story is read, illustrating or noting characters, setting, compare/ contrast, problem/solution, climax, conflict, and so forth.

Structural Analysis   The identification of word-meaning elements, as re and read in reread, to help understand the meaning of a word as a whole, morphemic analysis.

Suffix   An affix attached to the end of a base, root, or stem that changes meaning or grammatical function of the word, as -en added for ox to form oxen.

Syllabication   The division of words into syllables.

Syllable   In phonology, a minimal unit of sequential speech sounds composed of vowel sound or a vowel-consonant combination, as /a/, /ba/, /ab/, /bab/, etc.

Syntax   **1.** The study of how sentences are formed and of the grammatical rules that govern their formation. **2.** The pattern or structure of word order in sentence, clauses, and phrases. Syntax examines the various ways that words combine to create meaning. The direct teaching of syntactic patterns is critical for comprehension of higher-level texts as well as for good writing.

Synthetic Method   A way of teaching beginning reading by starting with word parts or elements, as sounds, or syllables, and late combining them into words.

Visual Discrimination   **1.** The process of perceiving similarities and differences in stimuli by sight. **2.** The ability to engage in such a process.

Vowel   A voiced speech sound made without stoppage or friction of the air flow as it passes through the vocal tract.

Web   A graphic organizer used to involve students in thinking about and planning what they will study, learn, read about, or write about within a larger topic. A teacher may begin with a brainstorming discussion of topics related to a particular theme and then represent subtopics through the use of a web drawn on the board. Webbing can be used to encourage students to consider what they know about each subtopic or what they want to know.

Word Play   A child's manipulation of sounds and words for language exploration and practice or for pleasure (using alliteration, creating rhymes, singing songs, clapping syllables, and so forth).

Reading Assessments

Formal and informal reading assessments are used with students in grades K–8 to target areas of strength and weakness, monitor student reading development, and aid the teacher in planning reading instruction.

Alphabet Knowledge   Identify letters, form letters.

Concepts about Print   Tests important concepts about books including the front/back of book, print tells the story, concept of letters, words, sentences, and that spaces have a purpose.

High Frequency Word Recognition   Measures word recognition out of context. In general, proficient readers can read words in and out of context and poor readers over-rely on context for decoding. Also assists teacher in determining a level to start testing in Oral Reading Inventories.

Phonemic Awareness   Estimates level of phonemic awareness in students.

Phonics Test   Tests phonics skills that are needed in reading.

Oral Reading Inventory   Graded passages that give an indication of the fluency with which a student is able to read. Also evaluated is accuracy, reading rate, reading level, and comprehension level.

Spelling Inventory   Through examination of words spelled correctly and incorrectly, a student's skills can be classified into developmental spelling stages. In this way, skills are examined that directly tie to reading. Assists in planning appropriate spelling and reading instruction.

PART III

TWO FULL-LENGTH PRACTICE TESTS

Practice, Review, Analyze, and Practice

This section contains two full-length simulation RICA Written Examinations. The practice tests are followed by complete answers, explanations, sample essays, and analysis techniques. The format, levels of difficulty, question structures, and number of questions are similar to those on the actual RICA Written Exam. **The actual RICA is copyrighted and may not be duplicated, so these questions are not taken directly from the actual tests.**

When taking these exams, try to simulate the test conditions. Remember, the total testing time for each practice test is 4 hours. Although you may divide your time between the two sections in any way you want, be sure that you budget your time effectively to finish all of the sections. Try to spend about 1 to 1½ minutes on each multiple-choice question, about 15 minutes each for written Assignments A and B, about 25 minutes each for written Assignments C and D, and about 1 hour for written Assignment E, the case study.

On the actual RICA test you will be given:

1. a **Test Booklet** with all the questions (multiple-choice and essay assignments);
2. an **Answer Document** to record your multiple-choice answers and Assignments A-D responses; and
3. a **Case Study Response Booklet** to record your response to the case study (Assignment E).

   Note: On the actual RICA you will NOT be tearing out any pages as your answers and essay will be written in separate documents or booklets.

Practice Test 1 Answer Document

Multiple-Choice Answer Sheets

1 Ⓐ Ⓑ Ⓒ Ⓓ		36 Ⓐ Ⓑ Ⓒ Ⓓ
2 Ⓐ Ⓑ Ⓒ Ⓓ		37 Ⓐ Ⓑ Ⓒ Ⓓ
3 Ⓐ Ⓑ Ⓒ Ⓓ		38 Ⓐ Ⓑ Ⓒ Ⓓ
4 Ⓐ Ⓑ Ⓒ Ⓓ		39 Ⓐ Ⓑ Ⓒ Ⓓ
5 Ⓐ Ⓑ Ⓒ Ⓓ		40 Ⓐ Ⓑ Ⓒ Ⓓ
6 Ⓐ Ⓑ Ⓒ Ⓓ		41 Ⓐ Ⓑ Ⓒ Ⓓ
7 Ⓐ Ⓑ Ⓒ Ⓓ		42 Ⓐ Ⓑ Ⓒ Ⓓ
8 Ⓐ Ⓑ Ⓒ Ⓓ		43 Ⓐ Ⓑ Ⓒ Ⓓ
9 Ⓐ Ⓑ Ⓒ Ⓓ		44 Ⓐ Ⓑ Ⓒ Ⓓ
10 Ⓐ Ⓑ Ⓒ Ⓓ		45 Ⓐ Ⓑ Ⓒ Ⓓ
11 Ⓐ Ⓑ Ⓒ Ⓓ		46 Ⓐ Ⓑ Ⓒ Ⓓ
12 Ⓐ Ⓑ Ⓒ Ⓓ		47 Ⓐ Ⓑ Ⓒ Ⓓ
13 Ⓐ Ⓑ Ⓒ Ⓓ		48 Ⓐ Ⓑ Ⓒ Ⓓ
14 Ⓐ Ⓑ Ⓒ Ⓓ		49 Ⓐ Ⓑ Ⓒ Ⓓ
15 Ⓐ Ⓑ Ⓒ Ⓓ		50 Ⓐ Ⓑ Ⓒ Ⓓ
16 Ⓐ Ⓑ Ⓒ Ⓓ		51 Ⓐ Ⓑ Ⓒ Ⓓ
17 Ⓐ Ⓑ Ⓒ Ⓓ		52 Ⓐ Ⓑ Ⓒ Ⓓ
18 Ⓐ Ⓑ Ⓒ Ⓓ		53 Ⓐ Ⓑ Ⓒ Ⓓ
19 Ⓐ Ⓑ Ⓒ Ⓓ		54 Ⓐ Ⓑ Ⓒ Ⓓ
20 Ⓐ Ⓑ Ⓒ Ⓓ		55 Ⓐ Ⓑ Ⓒ Ⓓ
21 Ⓐ Ⓑ Ⓒ Ⓓ		56 Ⓐ Ⓑ Ⓒ Ⓓ
22 Ⓐ Ⓑ Ⓒ Ⓓ		57 Ⓐ Ⓑ Ⓒ Ⓓ
23 Ⓐ Ⓑ Ⓒ Ⓓ		58 Ⓐ Ⓑ Ⓒ Ⓓ
24 Ⓐ Ⓑ Ⓒ Ⓓ		59 Ⓐ Ⓑ Ⓒ Ⓓ
25 Ⓐ Ⓑ Ⓒ Ⓓ		60 Ⓐ Ⓑ Ⓒ Ⓓ
26 Ⓐ Ⓑ Ⓒ Ⓓ		61 Ⓐ Ⓑ Ⓒ Ⓓ
27 Ⓐ Ⓑ Ⓒ Ⓓ		62 Ⓐ Ⓑ Ⓒ Ⓓ
28 Ⓐ Ⓑ Ⓒ Ⓓ		63 Ⓐ Ⓑ Ⓒ Ⓓ
29 Ⓐ Ⓑ Ⓒ Ⓓ		64 Ⓐ Ⓑ Ⓒ Ⓓ
30 Ⓐ Ⓑ Ⓒ Ⓓ		65 Ⓐ Ⓑ Ⓒ Ⓓ
31 Ⓐ Ⓑ Ⓒ Ⓓ		66 Ⓐ Ⓑ Ⓒ Ⓓ
32 Ⓐ Ⓑ Ⓒ Ⓓ		67 Ⓐ Ⓑ Ⓒ Ⓓ
33 Ⓐ Ⓑ Ⓒ Ⓓ		68 Ⓐ Ⓑ Ⓒ Ⓓ
34 Ⓐ Ⓑ Ⓒ Ⓓ		69 Ⓐ Ⓑ Ⓒ Ⓓ
35 Ⓐ Ⓑ Ⓒ Ⓓ		70 Ⓐ Ⓑ Ⓒ Ⓓ

CUT HERE

Note: On the actual RICA you will NOT be tearing out any pages as your answers and essay will be written in separate documents or booklets.

Assignment A

_____

_____

_____

_____

_____

_____

_____

_____

_____

_____

_____

_____

_____

_____

_____

_____

_____

_____

_____

_____

_____

_____

_____

_____

CUT HERE

CUT HERE

Assignment B

_____

_____

_____

_____

_____

_____

_____

_____

_____

_____

_____

_____

_____

_____

_____

_____

_____

_____

_____

_____

_____

_____

CUT HERE

CUT HERE

Assignment C

CUT HERE

Assignment D

CUT HERE

Practice Test 1 Case Study Response Booklet

Assignment E

CUT HERE

CUT HERE

Practice Test 1

General Directions

The RICA test is composed of two sections: a multiple-choice question section, which contains 70 multiple-choice questions, and an open-ended assignment section. This assignment section contains five assignments, A to E, requiring written responses. The weight of each section toward the total examination score is approximately 50%. Therefore, your performance on both sections is equally important.

The directions for each section appear immediately before that section. The multiple-choice questions and the open-ended assignments may be worked on or completed in any order that you choose. On the actual RICA test you will be given a checklist to help you keep track of the sections you have completed. Plan your time carefully to make sure that you can complete the entire test within the time allotted.

For security reasons, you may not take notes or remove any of the test materials from the room. Since no scratch paper is allowed, you may use the margins of this test booklet for your scratch work. Keep in mind that only the responses recorded in your Answer Document and your Case Study Response booklet will be scored.

Following the last open-ended assignment (E) you will see the words "End of Test." You may go back and review your answers at any time during the testing session if time permits. When you are sure you have answered all the multiple-choice questions, completed all the assignments, and properly recorded all of your responses in your Answer Document and Case Study Response Booklet, let the proctor know by raising your hand. At that time, your test materials will be collected, and you will be allowed to leave.

If you have any questions when you are taking the actual RICA test, be sure to ask them before beginning the test.

GO ON TO THE NEXT PAGE

Directions for Section I: Multiple-Choice Questions

Questions 1 to 70

This section is composed of seventy multiple-choice questions. Each of the questions is followed by four answer choices. You should read each question carefully and choose the **one** best answer. Make sure that you record each answer on page 1 or 2 of the Answer Document in the space that corresponds to the question number. Completely fill in the circle having the same letter as the answer you have chosen. *Use only a No. 2 lead pencil.*

Sample Question:

1. Which of the following cities is farthest south?

   A. Los Angeles
   B. Sacramento
   C. San Diego
   D. San Francisco

The correct answer to this question is **C.** You would indicate that on the Answer Document as follows:

1

You should try to answer all the questions. If you have some knowledge about a question, try to answer it. You will not be penalized for guessing.

DO NOT GO ON UNTIL YOU ARE TOLD TO DO SO.

1. A second-grade student skips over five or more words per page that he doesn't know while reading. Which of the following would be the best action that the teacher should consider?

   A. The teacher should select simpler material for the child and give strategies to decipher unknown words.
   B. The teacher should provide direct instruction in vocabulary building.
   C. The teacher can do more shared reading to help the child with word recognition skills.
   D. The teacher needs to present the new words before she has the children begin reading.

2. A first-grade teacher notices that one of her students is struggling with reading. He is in the lowest achieving reading group, and the teacher has tried some strategies to improve his reading, but he seems to not make any progress. The next steps the teacher should take in working with this student are:

   A. assess his reading and target instruction to meet identified skill needs followed by keeping anecdotal records and communicating with parents.
   B. request the help of any specialists, such as the reading specialist, resource specialist, or counselor, at her school to make a joint decision on how to best help the student.
   C. send home more homework for the child to practice reading skills with his parents.
   D. read more often with the child to encourage him and increase his confidence level, have the child do additional work with volunteers or peer tutors, and provide reading time with more capable students.

3. A fourth-grade student is able to read fluently but is unable to identify the main idea of what he has read. The teacher notices the difficulties that this student is having, individually assesses his comprehension, and tries to help him connect his experiences to what he is reading through discussions before, during, and after reading. There are some additional activities that might help this student bring meaning to the text he has read. Some suggested activities to help this student could include:

   A. making word banks, computer reading programs, and contextual analysis.
   B. reading response logs, adjusting reading rate, and owning books.
   C. word games, book sharing, and teacher modeling of how to connect text to experiences.
   D. paraphrasing text, summarizing and retelling, and graphic organizers.

4. A first-grade teacher is using the reading program adopted by her school district. The program includes decodable texts. The instructional advantage of using this type of book with beginning readers is that:

   A. controlled language patterns enable beginning readers to practice a skill and apply their knowledge of words.
   B. decodable texts can provide beginning readers with a controlled vocabulary that will enable them to read more books.
   C. books with controlled vocabulary that are predictable, can replace other literature in a reading program.
   D. decodable texts allow the school to accumulate more books in primary classrooms.

GO ON TO THE NEXT PAGE

5. Mr. Vasquez is planning phonemic awareness instruction for his kindergarten class. He gives each student the Yopp-Singer assessment. He then uses the test data to determine student needs and to form groups. When planning instruction groups, Mr. Vasquez should be primarily concerned with:

A. creating flexible skill groups and providing differentiated instruction.

B. balancing his phonemic awareness groups.

C. considering the classroom behavior of each student.

D. seeking outside intervention for students below grade-level standards.

6. Which of the following is a true statement about reading assessments?

A. All student reading assessments should include a formal test that measures comprehension.

B. The best use of standardized tests is to aid the classroom teacher in preparing a diagnostic profile on each student.

C. Using both formal and informal assessments will provide the classroom teacher with the most information about a student's reading level.

D. Teacher observation isn't a valid assessment measure and is not usually included as part of a reading assessment battery.

7. Mr. Tonning gives each of his sixth-grade students the same grade-level reading assessment at the beginning and middle of each school year. He then ranks his students' performance and determines who is reading at the grade-level standard benchmark, and who is reading above and below that mark. Mr. Tonning will use this data in a variety of ways. Mr. Tonning is least likely to use the results to:

A. plan interventions for students below grade level.

B. communicate to students, parents, and school personnel performance information regarding progress on the same assessment instrument, which is based on standards.

C. plan reading groups based on student needs.

D. interpret use of the three cueing systems and concepts about print and use them to report student achievement on the standards-based report card.

8. Which of the following statements is *not* a true statement about Informal Reading Assessments that determine a student's reading level?

A. Informal reading inventories base scores on percentages of correct word identification and correct comprehension responses.

B. Informal reading inventories can determine whether a student can read at a frustration, independent, or instructional level on a particular graded passage.

C. Informal reading assessments can aid the classroom teacher in instructional planning.

D. Informal reading assessments can provide information on teaching strategies to use in daily reading instruction.

9. A first-grade teacher has 20 students with varying abilities in reading. How should the teacher group the students for reading instruction?

A. The teacher should create small groups that remain constant throughout the school year to enable students to form bonds that further their reading progress.

B. Primary classes should have children grouped for reading throughout the day. The teacher can often use the same groups for all instruction.

C. Grouping is an effective practice, but the groups should remain flexible. The teacher should regroup students as a result of frequent assessment of their skill needs.

D. Research has proven that children do best in whole group instruction. This type of grouping provides for higher and lower ability children.

10. Which of the following gives the best reason that daily and ongoing observation of students is a powerful assessment tool for teachers?

A. Observing the student is helpful in planning instruction.

B. Student observation is extremely helpful in assisting the teacher to communicate to other professionals, administrators, and parents on student reading levels.

C. Daily observation provides the teacher with information on what students can and cannot do in authentic situations.

D. Student observation is one type of assessment that the teacher can collect on each student within the classroom.

11. Ms. Ramirez notices many of her eighth-grade students making spelling errors. She wants to gain more specific understanding of her students' spelling needs. In order to understand her students' spelling strengths and weaknesses and plan remediation in this problem area, Ms. Ramirez is most likely to begin by:

A. giving direct instruction in spelling, complete with weekly pre-tests and post-tests.

B. administering a comprehensive spelling assessment and analyzing student writing.

C. assigning extra spelling homework to go along with her comprehensive spelling program.

D. examining spelling in student journals, essays, and reports on a regular basis and taking anecdotal records.

12. When organizing reading instruction within the classroom, which of the following choices include the most effective opportunities to create flexible groupings?

A. shared reading, teacher read-alouds, and interactive writing

B. guided instruction, independent reading, and flexible spelling groups

C. morning message, peer tutoring, and writer's workshop

D. *Reader's Theater,* literature circles, and partner reading

13. What instruction should a teacher include in her guided or small-group reading lesson?

A. having the students take turns reading aloud so that each one gets a turn

B. previewing the text in order to tap into students' background knowledge

C. instruction of systematic, sequential spelling

D. practice sheets that reinforce skill instruction

14. A second-grade teacher is preparing a general reading plan for the week and a specific lesson plan for each day. Approximately how much time per day should she dedicate specifically for reading/language arts instruction?

A. under ½ hour

B. ½–1 hour

C. 1–1½ hours

D. 2 or more hours

15. A second-grade teacher listens to her students read orally in a small guided reading group. She notices that one of her students is continually struggling with fluency and often is unable to recognize grade-level words. What intervention strategies would best provide for the needs of this student?

A. The teacher should teach word identification strategies such as phonics and high frequency sight vocabulary. In addition, the teacher should provide very simple text for this student to become an independent reader.

B. The teacher needs to concentrate on using related workbook pages in word recognition skills for this student to become an automatic reader.

C. The teacher should increase time for read-alouds, which would provide this reader with more exposure to good literature. This would also result in the added benefit of increasing the student's vocabulary.

D. The teacher should give time for sustained, silent reading, which increases fluency when the student is reading books that are on his reading level.

16. Which of the following strategies would a primary teacher be *least* likely to instruct her students to use when they come to an unknown word in their reading?

A. Use phonetic clues.

B. Read parts of the word that you know.

C. Use the rest of the words in the sentence to help unlock the word.

D. Skip the word and go on to read the rest of the sentence.

GO ON TO THE NEXT PAGE

17. When assessing a kindergarten student's performance in May, the teacher notes that the student is able to name the letters of the alphabet and has mastered print concepts. However, the student is unable to identify rhyming words. What does this tell the teacher about the student?

    A. The student has completed most of the requirements of kindergarten and will be successful in first-grade reading.

    B. The student has not mastered a phonemic awareness skill (that is, rhyming words) that should be mastered by the end of kindergarten.

    C. The student will not be able to perform at grade level in first grade.

    D. The student needs direct instruction and practice in phonemic letter recognition skills.

18. When evaluating a student's reading, a primary teacher notes that when reading text orally, the student continually omits the silent "e" and reads:

    hat for hate   tap for tape   cop for cope

    What instructional implications does this behavior suggest?

    A. The student is performing poorly in spelling, and the teacher needs to focus on teaching silent "e" endings to the student.

    B. The teacher needs to focus the student's attention on making sense of what she is reading.

    C. The teacher needs to have the students reread the passage to clarify meaning.

    D. The student would benefit from more explicit skills instruction with attention to vowel sounds.

19. Which of the following choices are the best predictors of learning to read in first grade?

    A. mental age, family income, IQ

    B. perceptual/motor skills, mental age, parental education

    C. letter knowledge, knowledge about print, linguistic awareness

    D. hours of television watching, preferred modalities, favorite songs

20. The rule system in a language for producing phonemes in words is called:

    A. morphology.

    B. phonology.

    C. topology.

    D. phonics.

21. A third-grade student is confusing consonant pairs when writing in her daily journal. She writes *JUNCL* for jungle, *EFRYONE* for everyone, and *CARROD* for carrot. Which is an appropriate instructional strategy for this student?

    A. The teacher should assign related workbook pages from their reading series to improve this student's errors.

    B. The student would benefit from worthwhile practice in sound blending to make meaning of words.

    C. The teacher needs to instruct the student in articulating phonemes.

    D. The student needs to add similar words to her spelling lists and study them.

22. During daily writing, a third-grade student continually confuses long vowel sounds and writes; *hiev* for hive, *bote* for boat, *trea* for tree. The instructional strategies the teacher should use to meet the student's identified need are:

    A. more independent reading, additional homework with long vowel sounds, and frequent assessment.

    B. complete crossword puzzles, read independently to encounter more similar vocabulary, and complete word hunts.

    C. add weekly spelling words using the *look, see, say* method; picture sorts; vocabulary hunts.

    D. direct instruction in long vowel patterns, word sorts, and the use of word study notebooks and other activities to practice vowel patterns.

23. A third-grade teacher discovers that her students are unaware of some "spelling rules," so she teaches the rules to her students and has the students memorize them. What is a disadvantage of teaching these "rules" to students?

  A. There are so many spelling rules that students cannot possibly remember and apply all of them.

  B. The spelling rules are too numerous to remember, and most of them do not apply most of the time.

  C. Good readers know the spelling rules intrinsically and are able to apply them most of the time.

  D. Memorization of the spelling rules will not provide transference of the skills needed to be a good speller.

24. What are the instructional implications for a primary student who reads the word, "yell" as "will"?

  A. The student needs added practice with phonemes and letter names.

  B. Some examples of activities that would benefit the student are picture sorts and spelling puzzles.

  C. Maintenance of critical word skills is imperative to this student's progress.

  D. The ability to distinguish between letters and sounds is apparent, and the child should be moved to the next level.

25. Which of the following is an example of a phonological awareness task?

  A. listening to teacher-read stories
  B. phoneme segmentation
  C. student worksheets
  D. syntax identification

26. Some effective ways to teach letter recognition to kindergarten students includes the use of:

  A. a pocket chart, reciting nursery rhymes, and singing songs.

  B. magnetic letter play, creating alphabet books, and calling students' attention to individual letters that the teacher writes in morning message.

  C. clapping syllables, word segmentation, and matching letters to sounds.

  D. alphabet-sound charts, the use of sound boxes, and modeling stretching words when writing.

27. A teacher prepares a lesson using a series of boxes that correspond to the number of sounds that are heard in a word. For example, a kindergarten teacher provides her students with the following boxes along with round, plastic markers.

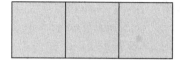

Next, the teacher then pronounces the word, "c-a-t" slowly, stretching the word into its sounds. Finally, she asks the students in her reading group to move their plastic markers into the boxes as she says the sounds in the word. Why is this an effective lesson for these students?

  A. These students are learning to isolate the sounds in a word that is spoken.

  B. These students are "playing with language," which research has shown is an essential precursor to reading.

  C. The teacher is guiding these students in an activity that develops their oral language and has proven to be an indicator of early reading success.

  D. The teacher understands that similar activities help students to develop an interest in language and how it works and will help them develop into proficient readers.

28. Which of the following strategies is most effective in the teaching of spelling to children?

  A. memorizing lists of words that are related to reading material
  B. looking at spelling patterns and vocabulary items
  C. taking a spelling test every week
  D. spelling words aloud

GO ON TO THE NEXT PAGE

29. A fourth-grade teacher is working with Tony, a student who is trying to decode the word *upsetting*. Read the passage printed below and use it to answer the following question about their conversation.

Teacher:	Can you read this word?
Student:	Yes. It's *upsing*.
Teacher:	Does *upsing* make sense?
Student:	No. I guess not.
Teacher:	You've read part of the word. Try again.
Student:	Oh! It's *upping*.
Teacher:	You've read the first syllable and the last syllable. Now I want you to focus on the middle part of the word. Can you try the word again?
Student:	*up-set-ting*.
Teacher:	You just read all of the syllables in the word. Try to put them together quickly to read the word.
Student:	*upsetting, upsetting*. I got it. The word is *upsetting*!
Teacher:	Great job! You figured out the word *upsetting*.

Based on the preceding conversation, this student would most clearly benefit from:

   A. participating in an organized, effective phonics program.
   B. paying attention to structure and syntactic cues.
   C. explicit instruction and guided practice decoding multisyllabic words.
   D. systematic instruction in decoding prefixes and suffixes.

30. Which of the following is the best reason for including meaningful spelling instruction as a component of language arts instruction?

   A. It reduces reading anxiety.
   B. It enhances reading/writing proficiency.
   C. It enables the student to read independently.
   D. It gives self-confidence to the student.

31. Which of the following are examples of phoneme manipulation tasks?

   A. syllable-splitting tasks
   B. sorting words by categories
   C. adding extra sounds to a word or word part
   D. spelling words on a pretest

32. What is the benefit of knowing how to break apart or segment words like "pancake"—i.e. pan cake— for a kindergarten or first-grade student?

   A. Children must be conscious of syllables and word origin to be proficient readers.
   B. The capacity to recognize individual phonemes is a strong predictor of reading success.
   C. The skill of breaking apart or segmenting words greatly assists children in playing word games like Scrabble.
   D. The ability to spell is linked directly to reading successfully.

33. In the context of writing, a first-grade student writes the word "family" as "famale." What can the teacher learn about the student?

   A. the child already knows how to read
   B. the letter reversals the child made show that the child will become a remedial reader and might have dyslexia
   C. the stage of the child's knowledge of phonetic spelling and phonological awareness
   D. children must learn correct spelling before learning to read

34. A teacher uses a Big Book to do a Shared Reading with her students. What are the advantages to using this strategy?

   A. The children can hear good quality literature, which fosters good reading, good listening skills, and better study skills.
   B. Kids can self-select their books and read independently.
   C. Word attack skills can be taught in context.
   D. The teacher can directly instruct concepts of print, such as title, author, left/right direct print, and table of contents.

35. The most important advantage of using invented spelling activities in the primary classroom is that:

A. children are able to move through the stages of the writing process even though they still can't spell in the conventional manner.

B. the teacher is developing phonemic awareness and furthering the child's understanding of the alphabetic principle.

C. the teacher is encouraging the students to become independent spellers and encouraging an active interest in correct spelling.

D. it is a good way to explain the developmental processes of spelling to parents.

36. A fifth-grade teacher asks his students to break into groups and each read a different passage from the same story in their respective groups. They are to discuss their passage in their group and then report the important story elements back to the whole class. What would be the primary reason a teacher would use this type of technique?

A. The teacher can cover more material in a shorter period of time.

B. The students can gain a deeper understanding of their passage and have the opportunity for more clarity by interacting with peers.

C. The teacher can evaluate each student's reading ability.

D. Cooperative learning can be a powerful instructional strategy.

37. The best instructional reason for a teacher to encourage independent reading at home is:

A. parents need to be included in the learning process.

B. the more a student reads, the better he/she becomes at reading.

C. students need to be assigned more homework in early grades.

D. reading at home helps the student to develop reading more smoothly.

38. A third-grade teacher continually has her students read silently in class and then quizzes them on what they have read. Which of the following is the greatest disadvantage in her approach?

A. The students will not become proficient at reading because the teacher is emphasizing comprehension techniques.

B. The teacher will defeat the purpose of self-selected silent reading, which is to motivate students to read for pleasure and practice the skill of reading.

C. The teacher will take too much time away from the period devoted to self-selected reading.

D. This will lead to reading failure.

39. During the reading period in a fourth-grade classroom, the teacher reads a difficult short piece of nonfiction to the class. After completing the passage, the teacher retells what she has read to the class and then evaluates her own comprehension. Immediately after, she rereads the piece, retells it again, and subsequently evaluates her own comprehension. The students witness that the teacher's understanding is increased after the second reading. What reading strategy is the teacher demonstrating to her students?

A. Rereading is a very effective reading strategy.

B. The demonstration of this strategy provides a model for what students may do when they have difficulty understanding vocabulary in a passage.

C. The teacher is helping her students prepare for state testing by reviewing material twice.

D. Modeling a reading technique for students is an optimum way to teach.

GO ON TO THE NEXT PAGE

40. The teacher leads a fifth-grade class in composing the following chart:

OUR "SURVEY" STRATEGIES

What to examine:	Pages when strategies are used:
• heading	
• captions	
• graphs	
• photos	
• maps	

Together as a class, they decide on what should be listed under the first column. The teacher explains that the class will fill out the second column after they finish reading the articles that she will pass out. Next, the teacher passes out articles from the newspaper and magazines to previously formed cooperative groups. The students are to read the selections within their groups and note on the chart when they use the strategies that are listed. What reading skill or strategy are these students practicing?

A. The students are receiving practice with comprehension strategies.
B. This lesson has been carefully planned so that each student is able to participate within the lesson.
C. The students are applying surveying strategies.
D. Students are being taught how to increase their comprehension.

41. A third-grade teacher puts the following chart headings (in the shaded part) on the board before reading a new story to her class:

Character	Is a.	Description of Appearance	Behavior: nice/mean/angry
Mandy	young lion	small, scraggly	very sweet, helpful
Samba	mother lion	strong, protective	angry when her cub is threatened

After reading, the students respond to the story by naming the characters while the teacher writes them on the chart. Next, they complete the rest of the chart. The best activity that the teacher could assign to his students would be to:

A. write their own story.
B. write character descriptions.
C. read the story again.
D. copy the chart.

42. A first-grade teacher decides to reread a story to her class instead of selecting a new story. Which of the following is the greatest benefit of this technique?

    A. Rereading a book promotes good listening skills.

    B. Rereading is a valuable technique that leads to more enjoyment of literature for the students.

    C. Reading a selection/book over again engages the student in a familiar text, enhancing their comprehension and building confidence.

    D. The rereading of a story is a delightful technique to use with young children.

43. A fifth-grade teacher notices that some of her students are unable to read fluently. The best strategy to use in her classroom with those students would be to:

    A. use books for reading in which the students can correctly read all the words.

    B. require shared reading.

    C. encourage repeated reading of familiar text.

    D. choose books that are on the students' reading levels.

GO ON TO THE NEXT PAGE

Use the information below to answer the three questions that follow.

Ms. Montell and her kindergarten students have been studying many books in the *Curious George* series, including *Curious George Rides a Bike*. Each day, she sends a "*Curious George* suitcase" home with a different student. In this suitcase, students will find a copy of *Curious George Rides a Bike*, a *Curious George* stuffed animal, a set of instructions, and a journal. Students are asked to read the book aloud with their parents. Students are then asked to dictate a story to their families while an adult records in the class journal labeled "Adventures with *Curious George.*" The kindergarteners will then illustrate a picture to go with the writing.

44. In the classroom, Ms. Montell asks students to brainstorm events from *Curious George Rides a Bike.* She records the events on sentence strips and asks students to organize them in a pocket chart. This strategy is likely to be particularly useful in helping Ms. Montell evaluate student ability to:

   A. apply inferential knowledge about the story in context.
   B. identify cause-effect relationships and patterns and sequence them in proper order.
   C. identify story grammar and story developments in order of when they appear in the text.
   D. determine main ideas from the story and organize them in sequential order.

45. When the students return the suitcase to the classroom the following day, Ms. Montell is most likely to ask her students to:

   A. read the journal aloud. Fellow students are asked to comment on their favorite parts from the writing and illustrations.
   B. ask the student to correct spelling and grammatical errors. The students are asked to publish the writing into a class book.
   C. read other *Curious George* stories. Ask students to retell the story in paragraph form.
   D. place the journal in the class library. Well-behaved students will be able to read the *Adventures of Curious George* as a reward for finishing their work.

46. Ms. Montell most likely chose to send this "*Curious George* suitcase" home because she wanted to:

   A. motivate students while encouraging and providing support for families to read at home with their children.
   B. enjoy reading and writing while practicing a written topic that will be on the next district–wide literacy assessment.
   C. acknowledge that parents are busy and give them tools to work with their students at home.
   D. motivate students while building literal, inferential, and evaluative comprehension skills in a nonthreatening home environment.

47. Teachers often ask students to predict what will happen in a text they are about to read. Which of the following is the best explanation of why this is a valuable technique?

    A. Student's ability to predict story happenings often is a predictor of reading success.

    B. The teacher's ability to ask thought provoking questions will lead the students to become more proficient readers.

    C. Prediction questions often stimulate student's interest in the text, encourage thinking, and give opportunities to share background knowledge.

    D. This technique encourages the student to take risks.

48. A first-grade teacher frequently assesses her students' reading to determine reading levels and to select guided reading books. When listening to one of her students read an unknown text, the teacher notices that the student is able to read all the words in the text without making any errors, but when asked to recall the story, the student is unable to do so with any detail. What does this information tell the teacher about the student's reading ability?

    A. This information tells the teacher that she is selecting books for the student at an independent reading level.

    B. The student is able to comprehend text at a very high level and the teacher needs to select more difficult text for the student to read.

    C. The student is able to decode the text but does not comprehend what she is reading.

    D. The student should be reading with other students who are reading on her level and needs to be further challenged.

49. During small group reading, the teacher notices that one of her third-grade students is struggling with understanding the story and is unable to make logical predictions about the story. After determining that the text is correctly matched to the child's reading ability, what strategies should the teacher use with this student?

    A. The teacher needs to emphasize decoding strategies with this student to further his understanding or comprehension of the story.

    B. The teacher should continually assess the student to determine the instructional reading level of the student and be sure that the text isn't too difficult.

    C. The student should be encouraged to do more silent reading with suitable text that matches his ability.

    D. The teacher should reread the story with the student and model the use of comprehension strategies such as predicting, questioning, and summing up.

50. A first-grade student is capable of fluently reading a grade-level story. However, when asked by the teacher to recall details about the story just read, she is unable to recall specific information and often answers, "I liked the story." What are some instructional implications for this student?

    A. The student needs direct instruction in comprehension skills which should be followed with guided and independent practice of the comprehension skills.

    B. The student needs to be given more structured situations for writing about stories so that she can better express herself.

    C. Instructional suggestions would include cooperative groups and paired learning.

    D. The teacher needs to structure her day to include opportunities for student interaction.

GO ON TO THE NEXT PAGE

51. A new first-grade teacher correctly understands that she needs to spend time during her instructional day teaching her students to focus on reading words automatically but thinks that she does not need to spend any time in teaching students understanding of the text. Is this a correct assumption?

    A. Yes, most of the day in a first-grade classroom the teacher needs to focus on phonics, decoding skills, and correctly reading words to order to enable the students to read texts accurately.

    B. No, all students beginning in the early grades need to be taught that reading is about making sense of text in addition to decoding the words.

    C. Yes, this teacher understands what she needs to spend the most time on within her instructional day.

    D. No, this teacher has not included writing as part of her instructional day.

52. Which of the following questioning techniques is *ineffective?*

    A. When a student responds correctly, ask him to explain his answer.

    B. If the student doesn't understand the question, rephrase it or break it down into parts.

    C. Give all students time to think before answering a question instead of calling on the first ones to raise their hands.

    D. If a student gives an incorrect answer, immediately call on another student.

53. A first-grade teacher puts the following diagram on the board after reading a selection for the grade-level text with a guided reading group. What is the purpose of using this graphic organizer?

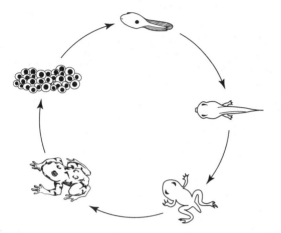

   A. This type of diagram can clarify for students what the text is trying to represent.
   B. Charts enable a teacher to promote an artistic understanding for students.
   C. This type of chart can compare and contrast the information that is presented within the text.
   D. Students are able to apply their understanding.

GO ON TO THE NEXT PAGE

54. Mr. Farley reads aloud the book *The Three Little Pigs,* a story in which a wolf tries to destroy the home of three pigs. The next day, Mr. Farley reads aloud *The True Story of the Three Little Pigs,* in which the wolf explains how he was framed by the pigs. The teacher leads a discussion comparing the two stories. This discussion is most likely to promote students' reading proficiency by:

A. guiding students to compare stories and determine a character's perspective and/or bias.

B. helping students self-monitor and identify common themes in related stories.

C. guiding students to distinguish fact versus opinion in similar stories.

D. helping students to use evaluative comprehension skills to determine the mood and theme in literary analysis.

55. Which of the following elements is *not* a factor in fluent reading?

A. accuracy in decoding words

B. processing text automatically

C. self-monitoring

D. expressive reading

56. Students from Mr. Ghali's class have been reading *Alexander and the Wind-Up Mouse.* Upon completion, they are asked to work with a partner to fill in this graphic organizer.

Title and Author:
Main Characters:
Problem:
Main Events:
Outcome:

Completing this story map is most likely to promote student reading proficiency by:

A. fostering students' ability to use reciprocal teaching strategies when working with a partner.

B. enhancing students' ability to identify cause and effect in story grammar.

C. helping students use Bloom's Taxonomy to organize literary details in the text frame.

D. guiding students to think about the structure of the text and how story elements relate to each other.

GO ON TO THE NEXT PAGE

57. A first-grade teacher is teaching a class with students from diverse cultural and ethnic backgrounds. As she prepares her reading lessons, her greatest concern should be:

   A. to make sure that her lessons include pictures or realia for the English Language Learner.

   B. to be aware of making connections from new information to existing knowledge.

   C. to be sensitive to the different languages that each child speaks.

   D. to consider and plan strategies to meet the instructional needs of each child.

58. A fourth-grade teacher has been assigned to teach an added class at her school. The class is made up of 30 students, many of whom are English Language Learners from different cultural backgrounds. When the teacher is selecting reading material for her classroom, she should:

   A. be sure to select reading material that is sensitive to each culture in her class.

   B. include reading material on many reading levels to reach all her students' abilities.

   C. continue to use the same material that she used with her previous fourth-grade class and use the materials other classes are using at her grade level.

   D. use the same reading material that the other fourth-grade classes are using and include culturally sensitive material.

59. After teaching a story in the text, a fifth-grade teacher uses upper grade student volunteers who are fluent readers to record the story on cassettes. He plans to use the tapes with his English Language Learners who can listen to the story another time at a listening station. What is an instructional advantage to using this strategy?

   A. This strategy involves eliciting student prior knowledge as it relates to the content.

   B. This approach helps the ELL student to build fluency and comprehension by hearing the story an additional time.

   C. An advantage of using taped stories would be to enrich the language output of ELL students.

   D. The advantage to this approach enables the ELL student to increase vocabulary enrichment.

60. A fifth-grade teacher is incorporating vocabulary building into her lessons. The most effective methods to build vocabulary are:

   A. encouraging wide reading and providing effective, language-rich instructional activities.

   B. studying organized word lists (i.e., synonym lists, etc.) and bringing in guest readers for read-alouds.

   C. discussing story elements after reading a story aloud and inviting story predictions.

   D. planning interactive read-alouds and incorporate sustained, silent reading into your school day.

61. An effective technique for teachers to promote children's oral language development is to have students:

   A. participate in group discussion about stories.

   B. listen to and participate in family conversations.

   C. watch television.

   D. give oral class reports.

62. A third-grade teacher asks her students to create "idiom posters." Each student is to choose the idiom he or she would like to illustrate on his or her poster from a list posted at the front of the classroom. What is the primary purpose for the teacher to assign this project to her students?

   A. This teacher knows that this is a fun way for her students to learn new vocabulary.

   B. The teacher understands that many children, especially ELL students, have difficulty learning figurative sayings, and this is a way to expose her students to these expressions.

   C. Learning this concept will help the students use more vivid language in their writing.

   D. This type of instruction will aid the students in unlocking their background knowledge.

63. Mrs. Ng has numerous ELL students in her fifth-grade class. She gives pairs of students a piece of paper folded in half and one sentence from the following sheet.

It rained cats and dogs.
He walks with his head in the clouds.
She was walking on air.
She had a frog in her throat.
He spilled the beans.
He has a heart of gold.

Students are asked to write the sentence on both sides of the folded paper. On one side they draw the literal definition, and on the other they draw an idiomatic illustration. Afterward, students will share their illustrations with the class, and then the student idioms will be displayed on the walls.

The primary objective for Ms. Ng is to:

A. shelter instruction so that her second language learners will read as well as her native English speakers.

B. illustrate idioms to bolster concepts about print for second language learners.

C. scaffold using graphic organizers to help meet the needs of all students.

D. support her vocabulary instruction with pictures to convey the true meaning of the sentence.

64. A first-grade teacher asks her students to illustrate an activity that they did with their families during the summer break. She then circulates throughout the room asking her students to tell her about their drawing. She writes what students have told her on their drawing. The drawings are posted throughout the classroom. Over the course of the next few weeks, the students read together what their classmates did over the summer. Why might the teacher do this?

A. This is a purposeful writing opportunity to help students understand that oral language and written language are interrelated and that we can write what we say.

B. This teacher is providing a meaningful opportunity for students to share their experiences.

C. This experience is giving students a first experience with writing.

D. This teacher is fostering the students' self-confidence by allowing them to share their experiences and artistic abilities.

65. A second-grade teacher provides time for her students to write in journals everyday. After the students make a written entry, often accompanied by an illustration, in their journal, the teacher responds in writing by writing a comment or a question. Why is this a good activity to do with ELL students?

A. This kind of activity provides the teacher with an opportunity to provide new vocabulary for an ELL student.

B. This type of journal gives the teacher an opportunity to model correct writing, questioning, and communication for the ELL student.

C. This activity allows the ELL student to have access to the teacher and provides the teacher with insight into the student's strengths and weaknesses.

D. This is an excellent way for the teacher to provide additional instruction to her ELL students.

66. In a third-grade classroom, the teacher actively involves her students in dancing and singing activities, pantomiming, book discussions, interaction about the classroom pet, and preparing puppet shows. The students get bonus points for reading a favorite poem to classroom visitors or to other students on the playground. The teacher and students also value dramatic play. Many students in this classroom are second language learners. Why might the classroom activities assist these students in developing oral language proficiency?

A. These students have daily opportunities to create understandings, form new meanings, and support interpersonal relationships through talk.

B. These activities promote reading and writing acquisition for these students.

C. Language acquisition and reading ability occur simultaneously in students who can read in their primary language.

D. Productive uses of language create a message.

67. Students in a first-grade classroom are given pictures to sort into categories during literacy center time. Why is this an effective technique to build vocabulary?

A. This technique is effective because words can be challenging for many students.

B. This is an effective technique because words with multiple meanings can be confusing.

C. This technique can be effective because building vocabulary is a precursor to reading acquisition.

D. This technique expands on children's natural tendency to sort and classify and assists in building vocabulary and the understanding of words.

68. A teacher uses an Informal Reading Inventory to assess a bilingual eighth-grade student who is having difficulty with reading. The teacher has noticed that this student does not participate in whole group discussions but seems to possess adequate oral language skills in English. After administering the IRI, she determines that he makes frequent errors on words with the *–ed* ending but determines that he understands "past tense," and these errors do not affect his reading comprehension. She also notes that he has recurrent errors with multisyllabic words that seem to impede his comprehension. The teacher notices that on the IRI, he does not recognize frequently occurring word patterns or common prefixes and suffixes in multisyllabic words. What would be the most effective intervention for this student?

A. This teacher can provide lessons on prefixes, suffixes, and roots to promote this student's ability to analyze and understand new words.

B. The teacher decides that the best intervention for this student is to model strategies for figuring out new words, such as using the dictionary and word searches.

C. The teacher determines that she will provide opportunities for this student that will promote self-selected reading, and in this way, will increase this student's vocabulary.

D. The teacher can provide more instruction in developing vocabulary and model strategies for unlocking new words.

69. What is a simple definition of *scaffolding* in the context of language and literacy development?

A. Scaffolding is a temporary means of support to assist students with more complex tasks in reading, writing, thinking, and understanding until they are ready to proceed at a higher level on their own.

B. Scaffolding is a technique used with students that provides needed instruction to complete literacy tasks.

C. Scaffolding in the context of language and literacy development provide students with the needed skills in order to function within a classroom.

D. Scaffolding is a means to assess ELL students to function within the regular classroom and achieve proficiency in quickly developing reading and reading comprehension skills.

70. Why might having a struggling fifth grade reader write a text for younger students provide an effective learning activity for that fifth-grade student?

    A.   This is a good technique to balance reading and writing skills.

    B.   Student written text is a highly motivating technique because it provides a real-life purpose for writing.

    C.   This is a good opportunity to use cross-age tutors.

    D.   Word-work can be created from that text and provide meaningful learning opportunities for the older student.

END OF SECTION I

Proceed to Section II of the test.

Directions for Section II: Open-Ended Assignments

Assignments A to E

This section of the test consists of four focused educational problems and instructional tasks and one case study. You are required to prepare a written response for each of these assignments and record each in the appropriate area provided in the Written Response Sheet in the Answer Document or, for the case study, in the Case Study Response Booklet.

Before you begin to write your response to an assignment, read the assignment carefully. Take some time to plan and organize your response. Blank space is provided in this test booklet following each assignment so that you can make notes, write an outline, or do any prewriting necessary. *Your final responses, however, must be written on the appropriate page(s) of the Answer Document. The case study must be written in the Case Study Response Booklet.*

The evaluation of your written responses will be based on how well the responses demonstrate knowledge and skills important for effective delivery of a balanced, comprehensive reading program. Make sure that you address all aspects of each given assignment. The evaluation criteria will include your attention to: fulfilling the purpose; effectively applying relevant content and academic knowledge; and supporting your response with appropriate evidence, examples, and rationales.

Considering that the complete RICA is 100% and that the multiple-choice section is weighted 50%, each of the individual assignments will be weighted approximately as follows:

Assignment A	5%
Assignment B	5%
Assignment C	10%
Assignment D	10%
Assignment E	20%
Total	50%

The assignments are intended to assess knowledge and skills of reading instruction and, although writing ability is not directly assessed, your responses must be written clearly enough to allow for a valid judgment of your knowledge and skills. As you plan your responses, keep in mind that the audience is composed of educators knowledgeable about reading instruction. Each written response should conform to the conventions of edited American English.

Your responses to the assignments should be your original work. They should be written in your own words and not copied or paraphrased from some other work. Citations, however, may be used when appropriate.

To maintain your anonymity during the scoring process of the written assignments, the multiple-choice section of the Answer Document containing your name will be removed from your written responses. Do not write your name on any other portion of the Answer Document and do not separate any of the sheets from the document.

You may work on the assignments in any order you choose, but be sure to record your final responses in the appropriate locations, as listed in the directions for each individual assignment.

Assignment A

Record your written response to Assignment A on the Assignment A Response Sheet on page 3 of the Answer Document. The length of your response is limited to the lined space available on the Assignment A Response Sheet.

Use the information here to complete the exercise that follows.

A first-grade teacher administers a phonics survey to his class at the beginning of the school year.

Examinee Task

Write a response in which you describe how a first-grade teacher would use the data from a phonics survey administered at the beginning of the school year.

Remember to record your final response on the **ASSIGNMENT A RESPONSE SHEET**
on page 3 of the Answer Document.

**(On the actual RICA test you will be warned NOT TO REMOVE THIS OR ANY OTHER PAGE,
or any portion of any page, from the test booklet.)**

You may use the space below to make notes. These notes will not be scored.

GO ON TO THE NEXT PAGE

Assignment B

Record your written response to Assignment B on the Assignment B Response Sheet on page 5 of the Answer Document. The length of your response is limited to the lined space available on the Assignment B Response Sheet.

Use the information here to complete the exercise that follows.

A kindergarten teacher is working with language experience in the beginning of the school year. She knows that her students are from diverse cultural, ethnic, and language backgrounds and have varying abilities and foundations in oral language.

<u>Examinee Task</u>

Describe three instructional strategies the teacher would use to develop and enhance the oral language ability of all students. Briefly explain why these strategies would be effective in assisting students in developing oral language.

Remember to record your final response on the **ASSIGNMENT B RESPONSE SHEET**
on page 5 of the Answer Document.

**(On the actual RICA test you will be warned NOT TO REMOVE THIS OR ANY OTHER PAGE,
or any portion of any page, from the test booklet.)**

You may use the space below to make notes. These notes will not be scored.

Assignment C

Record your written response to Assignment C on the Assignment C Response Sheet on pages 7 and 8 of the Answer Document. The length of your response is limited to the lined space available on the Assignment C Response Sheet.

Use the information here to complete the exercise that follows.

A first-grade teacher notices that a student is struggling with reading grade-level text. The student is able to retell what she has read but is decoding slowly, sound by sound, and seems confused when encountering long vowel patterns in text. What should the teacher do to address the problem?

<u>Examinee Task</u>

Using your knowledge of reading, write a response in which you: (1) describe how the teacher would identify the specific decoding need of the student; (2) state an instructional strategy and student activity to address the identified need; and (3) explain why the above process would be effective in addressing the problem.

Remember to record your final response on the **ASSIGNMENT C RESPONSE SHEET**
on pages 7 and 8 of the Answer Document.

**(On the actual RICA test you will be warned NOT TO REMOVE THIS OR ANY OTHER PAGE,
or any portion of any page, from the test booklet.)**

You may use the space below to make notes. These notes will not be scored.

GO ON TO THE NEXT PAGE

Assignment D

Record your written response to Assignment D on the **Assignment D Response Sheet** on pages 9 and 10 of the Answer Document. The length of your response is limited to the lined space available on the Assignment D Response Sheet.

Use the information here to complete the exercise that follows.

In analyzing a fluency assessment and retelling, which she had administered to her third- grade students, a teacher notes that Jane is carelessly reading the words and not applying knowledge of prefixes and suffixes when encountering multi-syllabic words.

Examinee Task

Using your knowledge of reading comprehension and the need for understanding multi-syllabic words, write a response in which you: (1) discuss one reading comprehension need identified by the teacher; (2) describe one instructional strategy and one student activity to address the student need; and (3) explain why the instructional strategy and student activity you describe would be effective for this purpose.

Remember to record your final response on the **ASSIGNMENT D RESPONSE SHEET**
on pages 9 and 10 of the Answer Document.

**(On the actual RICA test you will be warned NOT TO REMOVE THIS OR ANY OTHER PAGE,
or any portion of any page, from the test booklet.)**

You may use the space below to make notes. These notes will not be scored.

Assignment E

Case Study

Record your written response to the case study in the Case Study Response Booklet. Your response is limited to the lined space available in the Case Study Response Booklet.

> The following case study gives information about a second grade student named Brianna. Brianna is 7 years old, and her primary language is English. After carefully reading and reviewing the information on the following pages, write an analysis in which you apply your knowledge of reading assessment and instruction. Your response should include three parts:
>
> **1.** identify the strengths and weaknesses in Brianna's reading;
>
> **2.** describe at least two methods or strategies that would assist her reading development; and
>
> **3.** explain how these methods or strategies would work.

Remember to record your final response in the **CASE STUDY RESPONSE BOOKLET.**

(On the actual RICA test you will be warned NOT TO REMOVE THIS OR ANY OTHER PAGE, or any portion of any page, from the test booklet.)

You may use the space below to make notes. These notes will not be scored.

Reading Attitude Survey

Brianna's teacher, Ms. Smith, first recorded Brianna's answers on a Reading Attitude Survey. Ms. Smith read the survey questions and let Brianna respond orally. The survey follows.

Reading Attitude Survey

Name **Brianna**   Date **9/20/95**

Directions: Make one check for each of your choices.

☑ I like reading a lot.   ☐ Reading is O.K.   ☐ I'd rather do other things.

What kinds of books do you like to read?

☐ realistic fiction   ☑ picture books   ☐ poetry   ☐ true facts

☐ fantasy   ☐ folktales and fables   ☐ myths   ☐ mysteries

☐ historical fiction   ☐ biographies (about real people)   ☐ plays

☐ science fiction   ☐ _____ (write any other kind you like here)

How do you choose something to read?

☐ I listen to a friend   ☑ I look to see if it's easy enough

☑ I look at the front cover   ☐ I look to see if it's hard enough

☐ if it's part of a series I like   ☐ I read the back cover or jacket flap

☐ I read the first few pages   ☑ follow my teacher's suggestion

☐ if I liked other books by that author

When do you prefer to read?

☐ in my spare time   ☑ at home   ☑ as part of my class work

How do you like to read?

☐ with friend   ☐ with kids who read about the same as I do

☑ by myself   ☑ with my teacher in the group

GO ON TO THE NEXT PAGE

Family Survey

The following family survey was completed by her mother. The survey was mailed to her mother and was completed at home.

Family Survey

Date **9/20/95**

Dear Family

  Please take several minutes to help me learn more about your child as a reader and writer by responding to the questions below.

Sincerely,

Ms. Smith

Child's Name _Brianna_   **Family Member's Name** _Kathy (mother)_

1. What are some of your child's favorite activities at home? **Brianna likes reading, arts and crafts, and doing activities with her family. She is an accomplished gymnast.**

2. What kinds of books does your child look at or read at home? Which books are your child's favorites? **She is beginning to read chapter books. She likes the "Henry and Mudge" series.**

3. What kind of drawing or writing does your child do outside of school? **She writes stories and illustrates them.**

4. In what everyday situations does your child read something other than books (for example, food packages, catalogs, posters)? **She will read recipe directions to me. She also will read signs when we go somewhere.**

5. In what ways do you and other family members share reading and writing with your child? **We read stories to Brianna every night.**

6. What are your hopes for your child's reading and writing studies this year? **I hope that Brianna will read more "smoothly" this year.**

GO ON TO THE NEXT PAGE

Running Record

For the running record, Brianna read a story from an anthology, her school's adopted reading textbook for second grade. She had seen the story previously in her guided reading group but had not seen it lately. Her teacher, Ms. Smith, listened to her read the text and marked her responses on the running record that follows. Ms. Smith analyzed her running record and noted the cueing systems she used for decoding words.

RUNNING RECORD OF READING BEHAVIOUR

Name: **Brianna**   Age: **7.6**   Date: **3/27/96**

Title/Text: **Moon Mouse**   Emergent ☐   Early ☐   Fluency ☐   Seen ☐   Unseen ☐

Error Rate (ER) = $\frac{\text{Running Words } (138)}{\text{Errors } \quad 7}$ = 1:**19**   % Accuracy (ACC) = **94%**

Self-Correction Rate = $\frac{\text{(E) + (SC)}}{\text{(SC)}} = \frac{(7) + (3)}{(3)}$ = 1:**2.5**

(Percent Accuracy Chart on back of this sheet)

Easy ☐
Instructional ☐
Too Challenging ☐

M	Meaning (Semantic)
S	Structure (Syntactic)
V	Visual (Graphophonic)

Analysis of Errors: Using primarily meaning and structure cues and mostly ignoring visual cues. Is reading text again to check for meaning.

Summary:

Brianna read slowly, about 53 words per minute. She is beginning to monitor & cross-check her reading. She is starting to use some phrasing and expression.

Page #		# of E	# of SC	Analysis E	Analysis SC
	✓ ✓ ✓ ✓ ✓✓ ✓ One night Mother Mouse call to her baby. ✓ ✓ ✓ "Come, Arthur," she said ✓ ✓ ✓ ✓ ✓ ✓ ✓ ✓ **st**✓ "Now that you are old enough, you may stay ✓ ✓ ✓ ✓ ✓ ✓ ✓ ✓ up after dark. Let us look up at the night sky." ✓ ✓ ✓ ✓ ✓ ✓ ✓ Arthur ran happily to the door of the next ✓ ✓ ✓ ✓ ✓ ✓ ✓ and looked out. The black sky was all around **dark-ness** ✓ ✓ ✓ ✓ ✓ ⌐him┐Darkness was everywhere. The night was ✓ ✓ **cold**✓ ⌐still and┐cool. ✓ **called** ✓ ✓ **coldness** ✓✓ ✓ Arthur⌐could┐feel the coolness on his little ✓ ⌐**called** **sc**✓✓ ✓ ✓ ✓ ✓ nose.┐He could┐feel it on his whiskers and his ✓ ✓ ✓ round little ears		1 2 1		Ⓜ Ⓢ V Ⓜ Ⓢ V Ⓜ Ⓢ V Ⓜ Ⓢ V	Ⓜ Ⓢ Ⓥ

GO ON TO THE NEXT PAGE

Page #	**Moon Mouse**	# of E	# of SC	Analysis E	Analysis SC
	✓ ✓ ✓ ✓ ✓ night's✓ sc ✓ ✓ "So this is what the night is like!" he said	1		Ⓜ S Ⓥ	M Ⓢ V
	happy-happy sc happily.	1		Ⓜ S V	M Ⓢ Ⓥ
	✓✓ ✓ ✓ ✓ ✓ "It is wonderful!" Arthur looked up. There				
	✓ ✓ darkness ✓ ✓ ✓ ✓ in the blackness was something big and round	1		Ⓜ Ⓢ V	
	✓ ✓ and shining.				
	✓ ✓ ✓ ✓ ex-expression "Look!" he cried in excitement.	1		Ⓜ S V	
	✓ ✓ ✓ "Oh, look! Look!"				
	✓ ✓ ✓ Mother Mouse smiled.				
	It's - ✓ ✓ ✓ ✓ ✓ "It is only the moon," she said.	2		Ⓜ S V Ⓜ Ⓢ V	
	✓✓✓ ✓ ✓ ✓ ✓ "It is the big, round, yellow moon."				
	TOTALS	7	3	M-10 S-6 V-1	M-1 S-3 V-2

ERROR RATE		% ACCURACY
0:		100
1:200		99.5
1:100		99
1:50	**Easy**	98
1:35		97
1:25		96
1:20		95
1:17		94
1:14	**Instructional**	93
1:12.4		92
1:11.75		91
1:10		90
1:8		87.5
1:6		83
1:5	**Too**	80
1:4	**Challenging**	75
1:3		66
1:2		50

Story Discussion

Following the completion of the running record, Brianna discussed the story with her teacher. Brianna was able to retell the story she had just read with some accuracy. She remembered many details. The teacher then asked Brianna questions about the story. Brianna could answer almost all of the questions that her teacher asked her related to the story.

GO ON TO THE NEXT PAGE

Additional Reading and Summary

Brianna was asked to read another short story silently. Afterward, she was asked to write about the story. Brianna's writing about the short story actually told the story quite well and gave some good details. She did seem to have trouble spelling a few of the words. Although she appeared to read the story slowly, she seemed to enjoy the reading and the chance to write about it.

Teacher's Comments

Ms. Smith also made the following comments about Brianna's classroom work and behavior.

Brianna is an outstanding student. She is a hard worker and completes her assignments on time.

She enjoys reading in class and usually volunteers to read aloud.

Brianna has many friends in class and her group appears to be the top students and the most motivated.

Brianna takes advantage of her spare time in class using our reading corner.

Brianna also seems to enjoy writing, and although she still needs work on her spelling, her writing is very good. She also has outstanding penmanship.

End of Test

Answers and Explanations for Practice Test 1

Answer Key and Charts for Practice Test I

Multiple-Choice Questions

1.	A (Domain 1)	36.	B (Domain 2)
2.	A (Domain 1)	37.	B (Domain 3)
3.	D (Domain 1)	38.	B (Domain 3)
4.	A (Domain 1)	39.	A (Domain 3)
5.	A (Domain 1)	40.	C (Domain 3)
6.	C (Domain 1)	41.	B (Domain 3)
7.	D (Domain 1)	42.	C (Domain 3)
8.	D (Domain 1)	43.	C (Domain 3)
9.	C (Domain 1)	44.	D (Domain 3)
10.	C (Domain 1)	45.	A (Domain 4)
11.	B (Domain 1)	46.	A (Domain 3)
12.	D (Domain 1)	47.	C (Domain 3)
13.	B (Domain 1)	48.	C (Domain 1)
14.	D (Domain 1)	49.	D (Domain 3)
15.	A (Domain 2)	50.	A (Domain 3)
16.	D (Domain 2)	51.	B (Domain 3)
17.	B (Domain 2)	52.	D (Domain 3)
18.	D (Domain 2)	53.	A (Domain 3)
19.	C (Domain 2)	54.	A (Domain 3)
20.	B (Domain 2)	55.	C (Domain 2)
21.	C (Domain 2)	56.	D (Domain 3)
22.	D (Domain 2)	57.	D (Domain 4)
23.	D (Domain 2)	58.	B (Domain 4)
24.	A (Domain 2)	59.	B (Domain 4)
25.	B (Domain 2)	60.	A (Domain 4)
26.	B (Domain 2)	61.	A (Domain 4)
27.	A (Domain 2)	62.	B (Domain 4)
28.	B (Domain 2)	63.	D (Domain 4)
29.	C (Domain 2)	64.	A (Domain 4)
30.	B (Domain 2)	65.	B (Domain 4)
31.	C (Domain 2)	66.	A (Domain 4)
32.	B (Domain 2)	67.	D (Domain 4)
33.	C (Domain 2)	68.	A (Domain 4)
34.	D (Domain 2)	69.	A (Domain 4)
35.	B (Domain 2)	70.	B (Domain 4)

Practice Test 1 Explanations

Section I: Multiple Choice

1. A. Because the student is skipping over so many words per page, the teacher needs to select reading that is simpler or closer to the student's reading level. In addition, the teacher can do some direct instruction of strategies to figure out unknown words, but it is not helpful for students to skip words that they don't know. (Domain 1)

2. A. The first level of intervention is the classroom with a powerful program that is rich in language instruction. Teachers need to realize the importance of early and continuous assessment of reading as a tool for targeting instruction and planning interventions. (Domain 1)

3. D. Some graphic organizers that would be helpful to this student could include Venn Diagrams that compare and contrast different text elements, story maps, or K – W – L charts. These graphic organizers could help this student bring meaning to the text. In Choice A, word banks would not help this student with his reading difficulties, although contextual analysis and computer reading programs might assist him. Similarly, Choices B and C do not adequately address understanding main ideas and assessing comprehension. (Domain 1)

4. A. Decodable text with controlled vocabulary provides meaningful practice for beginning readers. The books should be aligned with the phonic element that is being taught. They present the phonic element of focus at least 12 times in the book. Decodable readers should be reread many times to develop automaticity and fluency with the identified phonic element. (Domain 1)

5. A. When organizing and planning phonemic awareness instruction, it is important that the teacher use data to plan flexible groups to meet identified student skill needs and provide differentiated and /or individualized instruction. Mr. Vasquez may consider behavior and balancing his groups, Choices B and C, but these are not the key factors. Choice D is incorrect because it suggests going outside the classroom rather than placing the child in his/her appropriate group. (Domain 1)

6. C. Choice C is the best answer to this question and is a *true* statement. The other choices are not correct. For example, in Choice A, it would be unlikely that you would test very early readers formally in comprehension. In Choice B, one of the disadvantages of most standardized tests is that they provide only very general reading information that is not diagnostic. Teacher observation, Choice D, provides important student information and *should* be included as an assessment when collecting multiple data on student reading achievement. (Domain 1)

7. D. Choices A, B, and C are all ways of using test results to measure student performance in relation to the standards. Concepts about print are generally mastered in the early grades and would not be assessed or reported on the report card by Mr. Tonning. (Domain 1)

8. D. Choices A, B, and C are all *true* statements about informal reading assessments that determine a student's reading level. Therefore, Choice D would be the correct answer because it is *not* true. Informal reading assessments do not provide information on strategies to use in daily instruction. (Domain 1)

9. C. In order to provide for the individual differences of all students, every classroom should provide a balance in types of grouping. Some examples of grouping types are whole groups, small groups, pairs of students, or single students. Grouping should always be flexible when teaching reading. It is not effective for teachers to always teach all reading instruction to a whole group. (Domain 1)

10. C. Choice C would be the best answer to this question. Although Choice A is also correct, it is not the best choice. Choice B is not a true statement, and Choice D does not address the question. (Domain 1)

11. B. The question specifically asks about determining student spelling needs. It is best to use multiple assessments when analyzing student performance to determine instructional needs. Choices A and D do not adequately address both understanding spelling strengths and planning intervention strategies. Choice C, assigning extra homework, is neither a good practice, nor is it an appropriate assessment tool. (Domain 1)

12. D. Choice D provides learning opportunities in which flexible groups might be created. The opportunities in Choice A would all be conducted in a whole group setting, and Choices B and C do not provide all correct opportunities. (Domain 1)

13. B. Previewing the text in order to tap into students' background knowledge is an instruction that a teacher should include in her guided or small-group reading lesson. (Domain 1)

14. D. A second-grade teacher should dedicate at least two hours per day for reading/language arts instruction. (Domain 1)

15. A. Marilyn Adams's research suggests that there is a firm base for the position that a balance between systematic word recognition instruction and the insurance of reading meaningful text produces superior achievement. There is also ample documentation that repeated readings of text develops young reader's fluency. Repeated reading must be at the independent level, beginning with decodable text. It is important that the text is matched to the reader. When reading text that is too difficult, instruction in word strategies cannot take place. The teacher must also include writing activities that reinforce word recognition. A child's ability to make visual discriminations between words has a positive effect on her reading. (Domain 2)

16. D. It is important to instruct children to use multiple strategies to help understand a word when they come to an unknown word in their reading. (Domain 2)

17. B. The greatest predictors of a child's success in beginning to read are a mastery of the alphabetic principle, phonemic awareness, and concepts of print. The Reading Program Advisory, Teaching Reading, states that phonemic awareness skills such as rhyming, clapping syllables, substituting sounds, and blending phonemes are end-of-kindergarten skills that virtually every kindergartner must have. (Domain 2)

18. D. The student needs explicit skills instruction with attention to vowel sounds. Activities could include word sorting. Also, *Words Their Way* by Donald Bear provides many ideas for phonics and word instruction such as word sorting and games with words. Additional strategies for practicing vowel sounds can be found in Patricia Cunningham's books, *Phonics We Use*, *Making Words*, and *Classrooms That Work*. (Domain 2)

19. C. These three indices—letter knowledge, knowledge about print, and linguistic awareness—best predict reading success in first grade. Linguistic awareness includes knowledge of words, syllables, and phonemes. (Domain 2)

20. B. Phonology is the rule system within a language by which phonemes are sequenced, patterned, and uttered to represent meaning—the rules of producing phonemes in words. (Domain 2)

21. C. The errors that this student is making show a lack of discrimination between two very similar consonant sounds. There are nine pairs of consonants (in English) that differ in only that one of the pair is quiet (unvoiced), and the other is heard (voiced). The nine pairs of consonants are

/p/, /b/ pet, bet

/t/, /d/ tip, dip

/k/, /g/ cake, gate

/f/, /v/ fast, vast

/th/, /th/ thin, this

/s/, /z/ cease, seize

/sh/, /zh/ attention, measure

/ch/, /j/ hatch, Madge

/wh/, /w/ when, was

Some activities that would help this child with this skill include the following:

- articulating phonemes
- looking in a mirror, feeling the throat while articulating the sounds
- read/spell contrasting pairs of words establishing the distinctions
  (Domain 2)

22. D. In this stage of spelling, the student is using, but confusing, long vowel patterns. The student is aware of how long vowels are represented but is using them incorrectly. The most generic activities for children in this stage are word sorts and working in a word study notebook. A sequence the teacher might follow when working with this skill is to:

- focus on the spelling patterns of one long vowel.
- compare and contrast short and long vowels.
- collect words that have the long vowel sound.

(Domain 2)

23. D. Good spellers have knowledge of patterns. They do not need to memorize rules that more often than not do not apply. Students need direct instruction in spelling patterns, morphology, and orthography. Then students need meaningful practice including word analyzing activities, discovering spelling structures, sorting words, sentence completion exercises, **and** discriminating between word similarities and differences. (Domain 2)

24. A. This is a common response in a beginning reader and demonstrates the need and importance for explicit teaching in distinguishing between letter names and letter sounds. The student is in an early alphabetic stage of reading. Phonemes are single speech sounds. (Domain 2)

25. B. Phoneme segmentation is an example of a phonological awareness task. Other examples are phoneme deletion, word to word matching, blending, sound isolation, phoneme counting, deleted phonemes, odd word out, and sound to sound matching. (Domain 2)

26. B. This answer includes some effective ways to provide letter recognition instruction. The ability to recognize and name the letters of the alphabet and understand that each letter makes a certain sound has been correlated to success in beginning reading. It is important that the teacher should make this instruction interesting and include letter recognition instruction that is in meaningful contexts. Additionally, students need to be assessed in letter recognition in the early grades. (Domain 2)

27. A. Three of the answer choices contain many misleading statements. Remember to be sure that you understand what the question is asking. Choice A is the correct answer because it states the objective of this lesson. These boxes, known as "Elkonian Boxes," help students understand that a word can be segmented into sounds and that those sounds can be isolated and reconnected. Choice B suggests that this activity is a way to demonstrate how to play with language, but Choice B isn't the best answer. In Choice C, this activity wouldn't be the best one to develop oral language and so is an incorrect choice. (Domain 2)

28. B. In addition to many other meaningful activities in which teachers guide children in word study, looking at spelling patterns and vocabulary is probably the most effective in teaching spelling. (Domain 2)

29. C. At first glance, Choice D might seem correct. However, Tony is having difficulty reading the whole word. He actually read the prefix and suffix correctly. Although Choices A and B are important for word identification, they may not remediate Tony's specific decoding problem. (Domain 2)

30. B. Meaningful spelling instruction enhances reading/writing instruction. Learning about spelling is an important factor in a child's development of morphemic development. Writing and reading are interdependent skills. (Domain 2)

31. C. Phoneme manipulative tasks, such as "saying *pill* without the *P*," reordering phonemes in a syllable, or adding extra phonemes to a word or syllable, correlate with reading achievement. (Domain 2)

32. B. The ability to segment sounds in words is the backbone of decoding—the child focuses on hearing sounds in sequence and blending them together. (Domain 2)

33. C. Conventional spelling follows developmental stages and the encouragement of invented spelling when writing develops phonemic awareness and promotes the understanding of the alphabetical principle. The teacher can focus on what the student *knows* in this example. (Domain 2)

34. D. The teacher is providing direct instruction through modeling. Students can hear the text while following along with their eyes. Even though the emphasis is on enjoyment, one or two teaching points, such as awareness to conventions of print, can be emphasized in subsequent readings. (Domain 2)

35. B. The most important advantage of using invented spelling activities in the primary classroom is that the teacher is developing phonemic awareness and furthering the child's understanding of the alphabetic principle. In addition, early writing activities promote and enhance a child's interest in learning about words and improve linguistic readiness for reading. Encouraging children to write complements instruction in reading. (Domain 2)

36. B. This technique allows students to read material among peers. It can help students of lower reading ability absorb the grade level's curriculum with their peers. It also allows for small discussion groups where each student can have the opportunity to interact affording a deeper understanding of the material. (Domain 2)

37. B. The goal of every reading program is to create life-long readers who enjoy reading and can read independently. Those who can read will probably read more. The student who reads more will be more educated. (Domain 3)

38. B. The teacher's approach puts emphasis on reading comprehension and limits what the teacher can learn about the other students' reading abilities. Since the student will not be demonstrating other reading abilities, such as pronunciation, the teacher will not be able to help students become more proficient in these important abilities. (Domain 3)

39. A. Research consistently shows that rereading is one of the best strategies for struggling readers, although it is rarely taught. Choice A is correct because this teacher is demonstrating firsthand how to increase comprehension by rereading. Choice B is incorrect because the teacher is not modeling how students deal with understanding vocabulary. Choice D is a correct statement but is not the best answer. Choice C is not a relevant answer. (Domain 3)

40. C. When students are able to concentrate on the information that is necessary, they can be more discriminating when reading. The correct answer is Choice C; these students are practicing "surveying" techniques. Even though Choices A and D also mention "comprehension," they are not the best answers. Choice B is not a reading skill or strategy. (Domain 3)

41. B. This chart is providing the students with character descriptions. A good follow-up activity would be to take the information from the chart and use it as a basis for writing descriptions about the characters. Choices A, C, and D would not be the best follow-up activities because they do not ask the students to use the information gained from charting. (Domain 3)

42. C. One of the most important strategies the teacher can use is reading aloud to her students, often rereading a favorite story. The teacher is also building vocabulary and literature appreciation, exposing students to literary level language and author's styles. Rereading aloud is one of the most important strategies for building attitude, giving motivation, and instilling the love of reading in her students. (Domain 3)

43. C. A result of rereading a passage is that the reader becomes more fluent. Some good ways to incorporate repeated reading within the classroom is to conduct *Readers Theater,* have students listen to taped stories, do partner reading, and read series books. (Domain 3)

44. D. The question asks about literal, rather than inferential comprehension, Choice A. Although Choices B, C, and D all mention sequencing, the activity does not help students identify cause-effect relationships or story grammar. Therefore, Choices B and C are also wrong. (Domain 3)

45. A. Choice B is wrong because it focuses on conventions, rather than ideas, in a piece of writing completed at home with parents. Choice C is incorrect because it is asking kindergarteners to read and write in paragraphs without teacher support. Although it would be appropriate to place the journal in the class library, such a motivating piece of writing should not be reserved only for fast workers and well-behaved students. Choice A is correct because it celebrates the student writing and helps make the connection between reading, writing, and oral language. (Domain 4)

46. A. Choice C does not address the importance of self-motivation in reading. Choice D is a possible answer, but we cannot assume that students will be working on all types of comprehension. Choice B is incorrect because it suggests that a teacher would send home something that would be on a formal assessment test. (Domain 3)

47. C. Prediction questions are among the best higher level thinking questions that a teacher can utilize. The teacher can use them before she starts reading a story or when the students are already involved in the story. (Domain 3)

48. C. The student has the ability to decode the text, but not comprehend. Note: Reading = Decoding + Comprehension. The goal of all beginning reading programs should be that all students can comprehend grade-level material. The teacher should be sure that the student is given an opportunity to discuss the meaning of any words he might not understand, use strategies such as "literature circles" that promote discussion of text, support the reader by tapping into any prior knowledge as it relates to the story, discuss the pictures before reading the story, and give clues to the story line beforehand.

If a student is able to decode but not comprehend, then the student is not able to enjoy and understand written language. The knowledge and active application of certain reading strategies is necessary for comprehension. (Domain 1)

49. D. Choice D suggests that the student is correctly matched to the text but is not applying comprehension strategies to understand the text. Choice A, decoding strategies would not help this student with comprehension. Choice B, assessment, is something that should be ongoing in the classroom. Choice C is also something that should be going on in the classroom; however, it does not address the problem of comprehension strategies. (Domain 3)

50. A. The student needs direct instruction in comprehension skills followed by practice. A significant number of poor readers enter school with poor verbal abilities. To be a successful reader, children need to possess both of the essential kinds of knowledge required for good reading comprehension—phonological and oral language skills. Even if they can learn adequate reading skills, they will continue to be hampered by weak verbal skills. These children will require special support in their growth of reading skills if they are to become successful readers. (Domain 3)

51. B. Teachers should not emphasize word decoding at the expense of teaching comprehension. Comprehension skills along with decoding skills should start in the early primary grades. (Domain 3)

52. D. The types of questions that are asked by the teacher can influence a student's comprehension and so the correct answer is Choice D. Choice D is an **ineffective** technique to use within the classroom when questioning the students while the other three choices are more effective. Note that the word "ineffective" is bold in the question. This is to call your attention to that word. (Domain 3)

53. A. This chart will help students understand the order of the concept presented by the text. Charting information is helpful to all readers, especially the ELL students. Graphic organizers such as story maps and Venn Diagrams are frequently used in primary grades to improve comprehension. They help clarify information that is presented. (Domain 3)

54. A. Choice B is incomplete since it does not mention perspective or bias. Since the stories are clearly fiction, determining fact versus opinion is not relevant, eliminate Choice C. (Domain 3)

55. C. Even though self-monitoring may indicate that a student is becoming a competent reader and should be encouraged, it is not a part of fluency and, therefore, the correct answer is Choice C. The other answers **are** important parts of being able to read fluently. Be sure that you notice if a word is bold, underlined, or italicized within a question to give it emphasis. (Domain 2)

56. D. This activity will not help develop reciprocal teaching strategies. Choice B could be a possible answer because it addresseses cause and effect, but it does not address other aspects of story structure. However, Choice D is more complete. Bloom's Taxonomy is incorrectly used in Choice C. (Domain 3)

57. D. Because the students are from diverse cultural and ethnic backgrounds, the needs of each student can vary tremendously. The teacher must be careful in planning her strategies to make sure that they meet the needs of each child. (Domain 4)

58. B. In a balanced comprehensive reading program, the teacher must provide reading materials to meet the reading level of all students in the class. (Domain 4)

59. B. Building fluency and comprehension is an instructional advantage. The teacher might also record her lesson while she teaches and plays it for ELL students additional times. The students can listen to the lesson again, increasing their understanding. (Domain 4)

60. A. The best way to build a vocabulary is by reading.

"Written language places greater demands on children's vocabulary knowledge than does their everyday spoken language. A rapidly growing vocabulary is crucial to growth in reading. The proportion of difficult words in a text is the single most powerful predictor of text difficulty, and a reader's general vocabulary knowledge is the single best predictor of how well that reader can understand text."—California Reading Advisory, *Teaching Reading*. (Domain 4)

61. A. Oral language development is strongly linked to reading comprehension. Children can benefit from in-depth conversation, in which they strengthen their understanding and share their opinions. Choice B could also promote children's oral language but is not always controllable by the teacher. Choices C and D do not promote children's oral language development. (Domain 4)

62. B. Even though Choice A is a correct statement, the best answer to this question is Choice B because idioms use figurative language and are often confusing to students, especially those who are learning English as a second language. Choice C might be true but is not the primary reason lower primary teachers introduce idiom posters. Choice D is not an accurate statement. (Domain 4)

63. D. The majority of instructional strategies helpful for ELL students are also beneficial for all students. Choice A is incorrect because the answer assumes that all ELLs perform at a lower level than native English speakers. Choice B at first appears correct because idioms are mentioned. However, idioms are not part of concepts about print. Choice C also appears correct. If you read the question carefully, a graphic organizer is not used in this question. The reader may have been misled due to the graphic nature of the grid. (Domain 4)

64. A. This is a relevant opportunity to relate speaking, reading, and writing. Choices B, C, and D are correct statements but are not the best answer. (Domain 4)

65. B. This activity provides the student with a reading and writing activity on his level in which the teacher can provide targeted assistance in literacy development. It might also provide new vocabulary, access to the teacher, and additional instruction as suggested in Choices A, C, and D, but the best answer would be Choice B. (Domain 4)

66. A. When students are learning a second language, oral language development is key. The activities in this classroom allow students to work and play together and, therefore, their conversations are based on concrete, relevant topics of interest. Additionally, these formal and informal opportunities allow these students to clarify their own understandings about language. (Domain 4)

67. D. Expanding on a child's natural tendency to sort and classify is an effective technique to assist in vocabulary building. Additionally, picture and word sorts can help expand a student's grasp of simple concepts. (Domain 4)

68. A. The teacher has determined that this student's inability to read multisyllabic words is due to his lack of knowledge about English root words, suffixes, and prefixes. Strengthening this student's skills is these areas will address not only word formation, but also aid in building his vocabulary. Choices B, C, and D are not the best answers, although they contain some true information. (Domain 4)

69. A. Scaffolding can help students function beyond the level that they could if unassisted. Activities that provide scaffolding have built-in teacher or peer assistance. (Domain 4)

70. B. Student written text is a technique that is excellent in motivating struggling readers. (Domain 4)

Section II: Open-Ended Questions

Sample Essays and Evaluations

Domain I/Assignment A

Sample Essay

Data from this entry-level survey can be used in a variety of ways.

First, the teacher could use the data to inform his systematic phonics instruction. He would provide targeted and direct instruction and practice in the phonics elements identified in the survey. Data could be shared with other teachers on his team. They may decide to form flexible skill groups among several classes.

The teacher may share this data with the student and parent during a beginning of the year conference. This would provide an understanding of where the student is in phonics skill attainment. Data could also be shared with administrators and/or coaches. This data demonstrates a beginning point for targeting phonics/decoding instruction.

Evaluating the Essay

The essay fulfills the task by identifying several ways to use the data. The data (information) must be communicated to several individuals or groups. The writer describes the recipients of the data (information) and describes how each would use it. The answer is clearer when the writer includes the description of how each recipient would use the data. This is entry-level data and, therefore, is essential for beginning planning.

Domain IV/Assignment B

Sample Essay

Language play assists students in developing oral language and is especially helpful in enhancing oral abilities of ethnically diverse students. The teacher could use nursery rhymes for oral language play. Steps for instruction and student activities may include:

- **Read nursery rhymes**—and play with substituting sounds.
- **Choral speaking**—students recite nursery rhymes with teacher.
- **Dramatization**—students recite and act out nursery rhymes.
- **Pair-Share**—students take turns reciting the nursery rhyme with a partner.

A variety of nonthreatening language play experiences will assist all students in positive oral language development.

Evaluating the Essay

The essay addresses the task of describing at least three instructional strategies the teacher would use to build students' oral language ability. The strategies are all oral activities as the task is to build oral language abilities. The first and last sentences in the essay describe aspects of language play. Instructional strategies are listed clearly in bullet fashion for clarity and to be frugal with word use. Four instructional strategies are listed with a short description of each strategy. This essay is a good example of giving a great deal of information while being frugal with words.

Domain II/Assignment C

Sample Essay

To identify the student's decoding need, the teacher would use a phonics survey such as the BPST. The BPST may reveal that the student has difficulties recognizing long vowel patterns such as –ake, –eed, –ike, –oat, or –une.

The instructional strategy to address this need would be direct instruction of the vowel pattern such as –ike. After blending the sound, the teacher would guide the student in practicing reading the word family for –ike.

- bike
- hike
- mike
- pike
- like

The next step would be guided practice with the word family in a meaningful manner in connected text, i.e., decodable text. The student activity would be independent practice with the word family. The first activity would be to use a word wheel to substitute initial consonants in reading the word family. The next step in the student activity would be to practice automaticity reading the word family in connected text that is a decodable text.

The above process would assist the student to attain automaticity in decoding. With practice in automaticity, the student would become able to read grade level text with fluency.

Evaluating the Essay

The essay clearly states the three steps the teacher must take in addressing the problem. These three steps or tasks guide the writing of the case study and often structure the questions in one or more essay questions. These "Big Three" guiding steps are:

1. Tell what's happening: data, findings, strengths, needs.
2. Tell what you (teacher) will do: instructional strategies, student tasks (intervention).
3. Tell why you chose to do the steps 1 and 2. Give a rationale.

To clearly describe the three tasks the author uses a bullet format. This format demonstrates the sequence of steps from assessment to instruction, practice, and finally the explanation or rationale.

Domain III/Assignment D

Sample Essay

The student, Jane, is demonstrating a need to understand the role of prefixes and suffixes in decoding multisyllabic words. The instructional strategy the teacher would use in addressing this need is direct instruction of prefixes and suffixes. In addition, she would explain the meaning of prefixes and suffixes and how they would change the meaning of words. For example; *un-* means not, *-est* means most, and *-less* means without. The teacher would model reading a word with an affix by covering the prefix or suffix and having Jane decode the root word first. Guided practice may include repeatedly blending the prefix or suffix before adding it to the root word. This will build automaticity in decoding the affix. The student activity for independent practice would include dividing the prefix or suffix from the given root word by using a slash. The student would then do a word sort by creating a paper with two columns: words with prefixes and words with suffixes. Jane would then categorize words appropriately in the two columns. This process will be effective because students must be directly taught what is necessary to become accurate, fluent readers, (Charles H. Clark 1995). Practice toward automaticity in decoding will ensure that the student will reach grade-level fluency.

Evaluating the Essay

The task addressed in the essay is "The Big Picture": tell what is happening, what the instructor will teach and have students practice, and why (rationale) will the selected tasks meet the identified need. Using The Big Three as a guide, the author begins in the first sentence addressing the identified need. Examples are given related to each of the three steps. Examples add detail and help to make each step more understandable. Note, the identified need is to understand and use prefixes and suffixes. It is a skill need; therefore, the instructional strategy to use first is direct, explicit skill instruction.

Case Study Information

Your case-study essay should have included some of the following information.

This student's 94% accuracy rate makes it an ideal text for guided reading instruction. In analyzing her running record, it shows that when confronted with an unknown word, Brianna relies primarily on meaning and structure cues. She rereads the text to check for understanding, using her knowledge of language. She uses structure and visual cues when self-correcting. She is able to self-correct one out of three errors.

In some of the student's errors, the miscue had a similar meaning to the correct word, (cold/cool, coldness/coolness, darkness/blackness). She was able to retell the story accurately to her teacher and so was able to preserve meaning. She also demonstrated an awareness of English structure or grammar several times (night's/night sc, happy/happily sc, it's/it is).

In recommending areas for additional instruction or practice, Brianna could benefit from rereading familiar text to improve her fluency rate and increase her speed. Her teacher can also encourage her to read more like she talks. Even though she was able to use expression and phrasing, her teacher noted that she read very slowly. In addition, the running record shows some confusion with some vowel digraph patterns: "oo" in cool, "ou" in could. These skills could be part of a word study program in her class. Brianna also needs to be encouraged to look at the whole word, not just at the beginning of words, (expression/excitement, cold/cool, coldness/coolness, darkness/blackness). She could also benefit from practice with suffixes like "ily" happily. Suffixes are usually a second-grade skill so she should have many opportunities to work in these areas.

Brianna's running record suggests that she is on her way to being a fluent reader. She needs to continue to be encouraged to use meaning and structure to decode words, and her skills in word knowledge and vocabulary need to be developed and strengthened. A teacher should also continue to expand her comprehension strategies and vocabulary skills as she reads more complex text. In order to improve fluency, Brianna needs to read a lot of familiar material and write about what she is reading. Her teacher might model the reading behavior that she wants to make the instruction more explicit.

Some suggested activities for Brianna might be: preparing for oral speaking parts, participating in *Readers Theater,* practice for reading aloud to another child or an adult, or practice reading before reading into a tape recorder and making a "Brianna's Very Best Reading" tape. A program of word study coupled with at least an hour of reading on her independent level will develop her fluency rate, improve her reading rate, extend her vocabulary, and advance her comprehension.

Analyzing Your Test Results

Use the following charts to carefully analyze your results and spot your strengths and weaknesses. Complete the process of analyzing each subject area and each individual question for Practice Test 1. Examine your results for trends in types of error (repeated errors) or poor results in specific subject areas. This re-examination and analysis is of tremendous importance for effective test preparation.

Practice Test 1 Analysis Sheets

Multiple-Choice Questions				
	Possible	*Completed*	*Right*	*Wrong*
Domain I	15			
Domain II	23			
Domain III	17			
Domain IV	15			
Total:	70			

Analysis/Tally Sheet for Multiple-Choice Questions

One of the most important parts of test preparation is analyzing why you missed a question so that you can reduce the number of mistakes. Now that you've taken Practice Test 1 and corrected your answers, carefully tally your multiple-choice mistakes by marking in the proper column.

Reasons for Mistakes				
	Total Mistakes	*Simple Mistake*	*Misread Question*	*Lack of Knowledge*
Domain I				
Domain II				
Domain III				
Domain IV				
Total:				

Open-Ended Questions (The Essays)

See the discussion of essay scoring beginning on page 2 to evaluate your essays. Have someone knowledgeable in reading instruction read and evaluate your responses using the checklists that follow.

Domain I/Assignment A

RICA Practice Essay Evaluation Form

Use this checklist to evaluate your essay:

1. To what extent does this response reflect an **understanding of the relevant content** and academic knowledge from the applicable RICA domain?

thorough	**adequate**	**limited or no**
understanding	understanding	understanding

2. To what extent does this response **fulfill the purpose of the assignment?**

completely	**adequately**	**partially**
fulfills	fulfills	fulfills or fails to

3. To what extent does this essay **respond to the given task(s)?**

fully	**adequately**	**limited or inadequately**
responds	responds	responds

4. How **accurate** is the response?

very	**generally**	**inaccurate**
accurate	accurate	

5. Does the response **demonstrate an effective application** of the relevant content and academic knowledge from the applicable RICA domain?

yes	**reasonably**	**no**
effective	effective	ineffective and inaccuracies

6. To what extent does the response **provide supporting examples, evidence, and rationale** based on the relevant content and academic knowledge from the applicable RICA domain?

strong	**adequate**	**limited or no**
support	support	support

Domain IV/Assignment B

RICA Practice Essay Evaluation Form

Use this checklist to evaluate your essay:

1. To what extent does this response reflect an **understanding of the relevant content** and academic knowledge from the applicable RICA domain?

thorough	**adequate**	**limited or no**
understanding	understanding	understanding

2. To what extent does this response **fulfill the purpose of the assignment?**

completely	**adequately**	**partially**
fulfills	fulfills	fulfills or fails to

3. To what extent does this essay **respond to the given task(s)?**

fully	**adequately**	**limited or inadequately**
responds	responds	responds

4. How **accurate** is the response?

very	**generally**	**inaccurate**
accurate	accurate	

5. Does the response **demonstrate an effective application** of the relevant content and academic knowledge from the applicable RICA domain?

yes	**reasonably**	**no**
effective	effective	ineffective and inaccuracies

6. To what extent does the response **provide supporting examples, evidence, and rationale** based on the relevant content and academic knowledge from the applicable RICA domain?

strong	**adequate**	**limited or no**
support	support	support

Domain II/Assignment C

RICA Practice Essay Evaluation Form

Use this checklist to evaluate your essay:

1. To what extent does this response reflect an **understanding of the relevant content** and academic knowledge from the applicable RICA domain?

thorough	**adequate**	**limited or no**
understanding	understanding	understanding

2. To what extent does this response **fulfill the purpose of the assignment?**

completely	**adequately**	**partially**
fulfills	fulfills	fulfills or fails to

3. To what extent does this essay **respond to the given task(s)?**

fully	**adequately**	**limited or inadequately**
responds	responds	responds

4. How **accurate** is the response?

very	**generally**	**inaccurate**
accurate	accurate	

5. Does the response **demonstrate an effective application** of the relevant content and academic knowledge from the applicable RICA domain?

yes	**reasonably**	**no**
effective	effective	ineffective and inaccuracies

6. To what extent does the response **provide supporting examples, evidence, and rationale** based on the relevant content and academic knowledge from the applicable RICA domain?

strong	**adequate**	**limited or no**
support	support	support

Domain III/Assignment D

RICA Practice Essay Evaluation Form

Use this checklist to evaluate your essay:

1. To what extent does this response reflects an **understanding of the relevant content** and academic knowledge from the applicable RICA domain?

thorough	**adequate**	**limited or no**
understanding	understanding	understanding

2. To what extent does this response **fulfill the purpose of the assignment?**

completely	**adequately**	**partially**
fulfills	fulfills	fulfills or fails to

3. To what extent does this essay **respond to the given task(s)?**

fully	**adequately**	**limited or inadequately**
responds	responds	responds

4. How **accurate** is the response?

very	**generally**	**inaccurate**
accurate	accurate	

5. Does the response **demonstrate an effective application** of the relevant content and academic knowledge from the applicable RICA domain?

yes	**reasonably**	**no**
effective	effective	ineffective and inaccuracies

6. To what extent does the response **provide supporting examples, evidence, and rationale** based on the relevant content and academic knowledge from the applicable RICA domain?

strong	**adequate**	**limited or no**
support	support	support

Case Study/Assignment E

RICA Practice Case Study Evaluation Form

Use this checklist to evaluate your essay:

1. To what extent does this response reflect an **understanding of the relevant content** and academic knowledge from the applicable RICA domain?

   | **thorough** | **adequate** | **limited** | **little or no** |
   | understanding | understanding | understanding | understanding |

2. To what extent does this response **fulfill the purpose of the assignment?**

   | **completely** | **adequately** | **partially** | **fails to fulfill** |
   | fulfills | fulfills | fulfills | |

3. To what extent does this essay **respond to the given task(s)?**

   | **fully** | **adequately** | **limited** | **inadequately** |
   | responds | responds | responds | responds |

4. How **accurate** is the response?

   | **very** | **generally** | **partially** | **inaccurate** |
   | accurate | accurate | accurate | |

5. Does the response **demonstrate an effective application** of the relevant content and academic knowledge from the applicable RICA domain?

   | **yes** | **reasonably** | **limited** | **no** |
   | effective | effective | generally ineffective | inaccurate and ineffective |

6. To what extent does the response **provide supporting examples, evidence, and rationale** based on the relevant content and academic knowledge from the applicable RICA domain?

   | **strong** | **adequate** | **limited** | **little or no** |
   | support | support | support | support |

Essay Review

Compare your essays to the ones given and review the Evaluation Forms, which you have had a reader complete, for each assignment. From this information, circle what you feel is the appropriate level of response for each assignment. This should help give you some general guidelines for your review.

Open-Ended Questions			
Level of Response			
Assignment A (Domain I)	good	average	poor
Assignment B (Domain IV)	good	average	poor
Assignment C (Domain II)	good	average	poor
Assignment D (Domain III)	good	average	poor
Assignment E (Case Study)	good	average	poor

Practice Test 2 Answer Document

Multiple-Choice Answer Sheets

1 Ⓐ Ⓑ Ⓒ Ⓓ	36 Ⓐ Ⓑ Ⓒ Ⓓ
2 Ⓐ Ⓑ Ⓒ Ⓓ	37 Ⓐ Ⓑ Ⓒ Ⓓ
3 Ⓐ Ⓑ Ⓒ Ⓓ	38 Ⓐ Ⓑ Ⓒ Ⓓ
4 Ⓐ Ⓑ Ⓒ Ⓓ	39 Ⓐ Ⓑ Ⓒ Ⓓ
5 Ⓐ Ⓑ Ⓒ Ⓓ	40 Ⓐ Ⓑ Ⓒ Ⓓ
6 Ⓐ Ⓑ Ⓒ Ⓓ	41 Ⓐ Ⓑ Ⓒ Ⓓ
7 Ⓐ Ⓑ Ⓒ Ⓓ	42 Ⓐ Ⓑ Ⓒ Ⓓ
8 Ⓐ Ⓑ Ⓒ Ⓓ	43 Ⓐ Ⓑ Ⓒ Ⓓ
9 Ⓐ Ⓑ Ⓒ Ⓓ	44 Ⓐ Ⓑ Ⓒ Ⓓ
10 Ⓐ Ⓑ Ⓒ Ⓓ	45 Ⓐ Ⓑ Ⓒ Ⓓ
11 Ⓐ Ⓑ Ⓒ Ⓓ	46 Ⓐ Ⓑ Ⓒ Ⓓ
12 Ⓐ Ⓑ Ⓒ Ⓓ	47 Ⓐ Ⓑ Ⓒ Ⓓ
13 Ⓐ Ⓑ Ⓒ Ⓓ	48 Ⓐ Ⓑ Ⓒ Ⓓ
14 Ⓐ Ⓑ Ⓒ Ⓓ	49 Ⓐ Ⓑ Ⓒ Ⓓ
15 Ⓐ Ⓑ Ⓒ Ⓓ	50 Ⓐ Ⓑ Ⓒ Ⓓ
16 Ⓐ Ⓑ Ⓒ Ⓓ	51 Ⓐ Ⓑ Ⓒ Ⓓ
17 Ⓐ Ⓑ Ⓒ Ⓓ	52 Ⓐ Ⓑ Ⓒ Ⓓ
18 Ⓐ Ⓑ Ⓒ Ⓓ	53 Ⓐ Ⓑ Ⓒ Ⓓ
19 Ⓐ Ⓑ Ⓒ Ⓓ	54 Ⓐ Ⓑ Ⓒ Ⓓ
20 Ⓐ Ⓑ Ⓒ Ⓓ	55 Ⓐ Ⓑ Ⓒ Ⓓ
21 Ⓐ Ⓑ Ⓒ Ⓓ	56 Ⓐ Ⓑ Ⓒ Ⓓ
22 Ⓐ Ⓑ Ⓒ Ⓓ	57 Ⓐ Ⓑ Ⓒ Ⓓ
23 Ⓐ Ⓑ Ⓒ Ⓓ	58 Ⓐ Ⓑ Ⓒ Ⓓ
24 Ⓐ Ⓑ Ⓒ Ⓓ	59 Ⓐ Ⓑ Ⓒ Ⓓ
25 Ⓐ Ⓑ Ⓒ Ⓓ	60 Ⓐ Ⓑ Ⓒ Ⓓ
26 Ⓐ Ⓑ Ⓒ Ⓓ	61 Ⓐ Ⓑ Ⓒ Ⓓ
27 Ⓐ Ⓑ Ⓒ Ⓓ	62 Ⓐ Ⓑ Ⓒ Ⓓ
28 Ⓐ Ⓑ Ⓒ Ⓓ	63 Ⓐ Ⓑ Ⓒ Ⓓ
29 Ⓐ Ⓑ Ⓒ Ⓓ	64 Ⓐ Ⓑ Ⓒ Ⓓ
30 Ⓐ Ⓑ Ⓒ Ⓓ	65 Ⓐ Ⓑ Ⓒ Ⓓ
31 Ⓐ Ⓑ Ⓒ Ⓓ	66 Ⓐ Ⓑ Ⓒ Ⓓ
32 Ⓐ Ⓑ Ⓒ Ⓓ	67 Ⓐ Ⓑ Ⓒ Ⓓ
33 Ⓐ Ⓑ Ⓒ Ⓓ	68 Ⓐ Ⓑ Ⓒ Ⓓ
34 Ⓐ Ⓑ Ⓒ Ⓓ	69 Ⓐ Ⓑ Ⓒ Ⓓ
35 Ⓐ Ⓑ Ⓒ Ⓓ	70 Ⓐ Ⓑ Ⓒ Ⓓ

CUT HERE

Note: On the actual RICA you will NOT be tearing out any pages as your answers and essay will be written in separate documents or booklets.

CUT HERE

Assignment A

CUT HERE

Assignment B

CUT HERE

Assignment C

_____

_____

_____

_____

_____

_____

_____

_____

_____

_____

_____

_____

_____

_____

_____

_____

_____

_____

_____

_____

_____

_____

_____

CUT HERE

CUT HERE

Assignment D

CUT HERE

CUT HERE

Practice Test 2 Case Study Response Booklet

Assignment E

CUT HERE

CUT HERE

CUT HERE

Practice Test 2

General Directions

The RICA test is composed of two sections: a multiple-choice question section, which contains 70 multiple-choice questions, and an open-ended assignment section. This assignment section contains five assignments, A to E, requiring written responses. The weight of each section toward the total examination score is approximately 50%. Therefore, your performance on both sections is equally important.

The directions for each section appear immediately before that section. The multiple-choice questions and the open-ended assignments may be worked on or completed in any order that you choose. On the actual RICA test you will be given a checklist to help you keep tract of the sections you have completed. Plan your time carefully to make sure that you can complete the entire test within the time allotted.

For security reasons, you may not take notes or remove any of the test materials from the room. Since no scratch paper is allowed, you may use the margins of this test booklet for your scratch work. Keep in mind that only the responses recorded in your Answer Document and your Case Study Response Booklet will be scored.

Following the last open-ended assignment (E) you will see the words "End of Test." You may go back and review your answers at any time during the testing session if time permits. When you are sure you have answered all the multiple-choice questions, completed all the assignments, and properly recorded all of your responses in your Answer Document and Case Study Response Booklet, let the proctor know by raising your hand. At that time, your test materials will be collected, and you will be allowed to leave.

If you have any questions when you are taking the actual RICA test, be sure to ask them before beginning the test.

GO ON TO THE NEXT PAGE

Directions for Section I: Multiple-Choice Questions

Questions 1 to 70

This section is composed of seventy multiple-choice questions. Each of the questions is followed by four answer choices. You should read each question carefully and choose the **one** best answer. Make sure that you record each answer on page 1 or 2 of the Answer Document in the space that corresponds to the question number. Completely fill in the circle having the same letter as the answer you have chosen. *Use only a No. 2 lead pencil.*

Sample Question:

1. Which of the following cities is farthest south?

   A. Los Angeles
   B. Sacramento
   C. San Diego
   D. San Francisco

The correct answer to this question is C. You would indicate that on the Answer Document as follows:

1 Ⓐ Ⓑ ● Ⓓ

You should try to answer all the questions. If you have some knowledge about a question, try to answer it. You will not be penalized for guessing.

DO NOT GO ON UNTIL YOU ARE TOLD TO DO SO.

1. A second-grade teacher assesses reading development by listening to her students read aloud. The teacher observes Shaniqua reading quickly, with a lot of expression. She notes Shaniqua reading *home for house, child for kid,* and *puppy for dog*. The teacher analyzes her assessment and decides that Shaniqua is:

   A. reading at her instructional level and needs direct instruction in phrasing and fluency.
   B. reading a story that is too difficult for her and should be given instruction in using her structure cues.
   C. relying on meaning and structure cues and needs practice using her visual cues rather than relying on context clues.
   D. reading a story at her instructional level and focuses on other reading errors because it is clear that Shaniqua understands the meaning of the text.

2. Mrs. Harvey is using results of an IRI (Informal Reading Inventory) to determine every child's independent, instructional, and frustration reading level. She will then group students according to their reading needs. She should remember that:

   A. *frustration level* refers to books above the child's current grade. Students are frustrated and cannot comprehend the material because it is too difficult.
   B. knowledge of independent, instructional, and frustration reading levels is important. However, she needs to select standards-based material for all learners.
   C. instructional level refers to students being able to read 90–95% of words correctly and answer most comprehension questions accurately. This material can be read with instructional help from the teacher.
   D. independent reading level refers to what children can independently read. They should be able to choose books they are interested in and retell them to their friends. Students should be able to read 90% of the words accurately.

3. When planning guided reading instruction so that student reading development is supported, a teacher should be aware of the importance of:

   A. creating well-balanced and diverse groups.
   B. providing high-interest, grade level reading material.
   C. meeting with each student an equal amount of time per week.
   D. planning flexible groups in which students read at approximately the same level.

4. Irena is an English Language Learner who arrives in Ms. Hightower's seventh-grade class mid-year. Following a round of assessments, Ms. Hightower determines that Irena decodes extremely well and reads fluently. However, her comprehension performance is inconsistent. Sometimes she seems to understand everything in a grade level text, while other times she has difficulty retelling a story with accuracy. Ms. Hightower then informally assesses Irena's vocabulary knowledge and notes some weak areas. What are some logical next steps for instruction?

   A. Provide Irena easier reading material that is at her instructional reading level.
   B. Place Irena in a group with other English Language Learners. They should focus on vocabulary and phonics instruction.
   C. Provide systematic vocabulary and phonemic awareness instruction. Irena needs more exposure to the sounds of the English Language.
   D. Use this information to further assess and plan appropriate vocabulary and comprehension strategy instruction in relation to Irena's specific reading needs.

5. Ms. Eisenman is a sixth-grade teacher. She frequently asks students to respond to literature through purposeful writing opportunities. When creating writing lessons, it is most important that Ms. Eisenman's lessons and activities:

   A. address at least two writing skills specified in the reading and writing standards.
   B. involve different learning modalities and connect reading, listening, speaking, and writing.
   C. reflect the state, district, and grade level norms.
   D. relate to the specific instructional needs of her students.

GO ON TO THE NEXT PAGE

6. Ms. Jackson regularly listens to her students read, administers running records frequently, and follows up with comprehension questions related to the passage. The best reason for this type of assessment is to:

    A. use on-going data to communicate with parents and plan at-home reading interventions.

    B. analyze data to determine student strengths and weaknesses and use data to guide instruction.

    C. rank students according to grade level and help teachers plan classes for the next school year.

    D. plan phonics interventions and design appropriate groupings for her learners.

7. A second-grade teacher conducts reading assessments of her lower performing students more frequently than her students who are achieving at grade level. Her reason for doing this could be because:

    A. frequent informative assessments help the teacher to guide instruction and make decisions for providing any intervention for lower performing students.

    B. she can more easily help them make informed decisions about choosing independent reading material.

    C. more frequent assessment of lower performing students is often required by school districts and is sent to the state department to better evaluate how schools are performing.

    D. frequent assessments are necessary for reporting to parents.

8. What are some differences between formal and informal reading assessments?

    A. Formal assessments provide more reliable student reading information than informal reading assessments.

    B. Formal assessments use standardized tests, such as published norm-referenced tests, and informal assessments use many types of nonstandardized measures such as teacher-prepared tests, informal reading inventories, and student/parent interviews.

    C. Formal assessments include tests that are given on a regular basis, and informal tests are administered less frequently.

    D. Formal tests are more useful in determining a student's reading ability, and informal assessments provide different information.

9. The State of California recommends using a balanced, comprehensive literacy program. This indicates:

    A. a systematic phonics-based program that builds from simple to complex in a logical manner. This may also include guided reading.

    B. a well-balanced literature program, which includes fiction and non-fiction texts, as well as books from all the major literature genres.

    C. systematic, comprehensive instruction based on content and performance standards in all of the subject areas.

    D. direct, explicit instruction of reading skills and strategies based on content and performance standards in all of the major language arts areas. This may also refer to content-area reading.

10. Mrs. Chu is a beginning fourth-grade teacher setting up her classroom for the first time. Her class is comprised of students from many different linguistic and ethnic backgrounds. She knows that she wants to create an environment that supports literacy. A portion of her classroom will be devoted to a classroom library. Included in her daily instructional plan will be time for sustained, silent reading time. She is eagerly acquiring books for her classroom library. She should be most concerned with finding books that are:

    A. at her students instructional level and reflect the cultures of her diverse group of students.

    B. at a fourth-grade reading level and considered to be literature.

    C. at varied reading levels and include a variety of topics, types of texts, reference books, and genre.

    D. from the school-adopted literature series and/or reflect the content areas.

11. The best purpose for continued and frequent reading assessment of students is:

    A. to inform parents.

    B. to be an informed teacher.

    C. for grading purposes.

    D. to keep the administration informed.

12. At the beginning of each school year, Ms. Ohuru, a first-grade teacher, creates a general plan for reading and writing instruction. She develops long-range goals related to first-grade academic content standards and the district-adopted reading language arts text and materials. In addition, on a weekly basis, she regularly assesses her students and adjusts her teaching according to student need. Ms. Ohuru is most likely to make a change to her weekly and daily plans based on:

   A. covering a large amount of material in a short amount of time.

   B. considering California and District Standards as well as grade-level guidelines.

   C. developing curriculum based on student interest.

   D. examining results of ongoing assessments, developmental level of students, and individual student needs.

13. Which of the following can be used by teachers to inform instruction and determine a student's reading level?

   A. informal reading inventories and cloze tests

   B. criterion-referenced and reading fluency tests

   C. high frequency word tests and phonemic awareness inventories

   D. interest inventories and phonic tests

14. It is the beginning of the school year in Mr. Jones' third-grade class. He is examining the results of a standardized reading test that includes norm-referenced, grade-equivalent scores. One student's score was 5.2. This student's score indicates that her reading performance on this test:

   A. corresponds to what an average fifth grader in the second month of school would achieve.

   B. represents a top third-grade stanine score for students in the same school.

   C. places her in the fifty-first percentile of all students who have taken this norm-referenced test.

   D. was as good as or better than 51 percent of students in the same grade nationwide.

15. A first-grade teacher notices that one of her students, Henry, is having difficulty during a variety of phonemic awareness activities. Although her assessment is made by observation and is informal, she does have an indication of his general weaknesses. Which of the following strategies is likely to be most effective in addressing his phonemic awareness weaknesses?

   A. practicing alliteration, rhymes, blends, and, segmentation

   B. brainstorming lists that start with a particular letter

   C. sorting word cards by sounds

   D. practicing letter identification, and hearing sounds in words

16. A second-grade student often writes *rane* for rain, *nite* for night, and *fead* for feed. In order to correct this, the teacher should implement:

   A. weekly spelling tests focusing on long vowel patterns.

   B. systematic phonemic awareness instruction focusing on long vowel sounds.

   C. direct instruction in long vowel patterns that includes word sorts and word study notebooks.

   D. systematic spelling instruction that emphasizes morphology, etymology, and long vowel patterns.

17. Mr. Jackson notes that Kim is in the transitional stage of spelling, that is, the stage where the student knows most sounds and patterns but has difficulty with sounds that can come from several letter combinations. In order to continue developing Kim's spelling in a systematic manner, Mr. Jackson is apt to teach:

   A. words for specific content areas, highly irregular words, as well as spelling patterns for multisyllabic words.

   B. morphology and etymology of words as well as alternative spellings for the same sound.

   C. sound-symbol correspondence, as well as rimes, prefixes, and suffixes.

   D. concepts about print, phoneme awareness, phonics, and alphabetic principle.

GO ON TO THE NEXT PAGE

18. What intervention technique would be the most effective for a teacher to use with a student who is having difficulty becoming a fluent reader?

   A. The teacher can read with the student on an individual basis.

   B. The teacher needs to ability group the student with readers on his level.

   C. The teacher needs to give the student additional practice worksheets to be completed carefully at home that are related to his reading difficulty.

   D. The teacher can give the student many opportunities to reread books while providing books on the student's independent reading level.

19. The students in Ms. Tyler's class individually read a chapter on insects from their science books. During a follow-up discussion about ants, one sixth-grader continually contributes incorrect information. Ms. Tyler is uncertain whether the misunderstanding stems from an inability to comprehend a particular grade-level text, or a different reason. She uses an assessment to help determine his ability to comprehend the grade-level science book. Ms. Tyler is most likely to:

   A. use teacher observation to build anecdotal records of his reading behaviors. She notes when he retrieves information easily and when he has difficulty decoding grade-level material.

   B. administer a cloze test from a chapter in his sixth-grade science book. She chooses an unread passage and omits every fifth word. The child is told to read the passage and try to fill in the missing words.

   C. examine his science journal. She notes how he responded to previous science textbook passages and which pages have the best examples of six-trait writing based on the sixth-grade rubric.

   D. give the sixth-grade Informal Reading Inventory. She registers how many words he is able to read correctly off the grade-level reading list. Then she gives the student a passage, asks him to read silently, and asks him to retell the passage in his own words.

20. At the beginning of the school year, Mrs. Wilkerson administers the Observational Survey by Marie Clay. It becomes clear that Tali, a kindergartener, does not understand that print conveys meaning. Tali is most likely to benefit from:

   A. practicing printing while writing about meaningful experiences such as a class trip to a museum.

   B. dictating an account of a particular experience to an adult who records it word for word. Then the child and adult can read the story aloud.

   C. retelling stories, sequencing, and other comprehension skills in order to become more aware of text meaning.

   D. using both tactile and kinesthetic methods in order to understand that print carries meaning.

21. Ms. Haupeakui knows that reading, writing, and spelling are interrelated. During a unit on geology, Ms. Haupeakui creates a geology word wall. On the wall, she alphabetically records geology words taken from the texts her students are studying. Later on in the unit, students will find additional geology words from their readings and record them on this wall. Students will refer to these words when writing geology reports. The instructional strategy that is most likely to develop spelling is the:

   A. memorization of difficult words such a *metamorphic*.

   B. practice of spelling content area words in context and accurately spelling words when writing.

   C. development of fluency by quickly reading alphabetical thematic word lists and recording words in a journal.

   D. spelling of content area words using the look-see-say method as part of a systematic program of spelling instruction.

22. At the beginning of each year, Mr. Carrington administers the Yopp-Singer phonemic awareness exam to his first grade class. He determines that many of his students are having difficulty segmenting the sounds in words. One appropriate instructional strategy would be to:

A. write words on the board. Then ask the children to segment the words into letters and letter sounds.

B. say words aloud and then break them up into sounds. For example, after hearing "*chat*," students would say "*ch/ - /a/- /t/*."

C. ask students to move magnetic letters as they say the sounds in words. For example, after hearing "*bl/ - /a/ - /ck/*," students would move the matching letters with their sounds to form *black*.

D. say words aloud and then break them up into syllables. For example, after hearing *computer*, students would say "*com - pu - ter*."

23. Mrs. Samir is planning her phonemic awareness instruction. Her lesson plans might include:

A. rhyming, blending sounds, alliteration, deleting sounds, syllable awareness, and word awareness.

B. letter identification and letter clusters, segmentation, and sound substitution.

C. blending sounds, syllabication, phoneme deletion and addition, and alphabet recognition.

D. onsets, rimes, alliteration, rhyming, word boundaries, morphemes, and graphemes,

24. Hien, a first-grade English Language Learner, can identify the letters of the alphabet. She can automatically read some words such as *cat* and *dog*. However, when asked to read similar words such as *hat* and *fog*, she freezes. One instructional strategy would be providing:

A. activities that help her to develop listening comprehension.

B. systematic, explicit instruction in word strategies.

C. direct instruction in rhyming and sound substitution.

D. audio cassettes for her to listen to in the class listening center.

25. In the following conversation, a kindergarten teacher is preparing a student for a phonemic awareness test. After reading, answer the question that follows.

Teacher: I'm going to say the sounds in a word. The sounds are /k/.../i/.../t/. When I put those sounds together, they say *kit*. Now I'm going to say some more sounds, and I want you to put them together to make a word. This time, the sounds are /f/.../i/.../t/. Can you put those sounds together to make a word?"

Student: /f/.../i/.../t/. That says fit!

Teacher: That's right, fit. Now, I'd like you to do this for some more words.

This assessment would be an appropriate way to measure which of the following phonemic awareness tasks?

A. identifying phonemes and their letters

B. blending the phonemes in a given word

C. matching phonemes in rhyming words

D. segmenting the phonemes in a given word

26. A first-grade teacher plays the song, *Willoby Walloby*. One verse says, *Willoby, Walloby Wustin, an elephant sat on Justin*. Next she uses this to introduce a game to her students. She looks at Tammy and sings, *Willoby, Walloby Wammy, an elephant sat on Tammy*. She then encourages the class to sing along as she looks at Pedro and sings, *Willoby, Walloby Wedro, an elephant sat on Pedro*. The next day, she sings *Zippedy, Doo, Dah* and then asks students to sing along when she sings *Pippedy Poo Pah, Rippedy, Roo Rah*, etc. This activity is *most* likely to promote the reading development of students primarily by helping them:

A. understand the principles of spoken words.

B. develop the /w/ sound while studying the letter W.

C. have fun while writing.

D. manipulate the initial sounds in words.

GO ON TO THE NEXT PAGE

27. A first-grade teacher is organizing her phonemic awareness instruction. She should make sure to do all of the following *except:*

    A. create flexible phonemic awareness groups.

    B. prepare systematic, structured instruction based on the needs of her students.

    C. introduce big books and songs during phonemic awareness activities in order to make connections between oral language and print.

    D. assess students and provide systematic, direct instruction in word identification strategies.

28. A first-grader seems to have visual discrimination difficulties and often confuses similar letters. The student may learn to distinguish between frequently confused letters by:

    A. writing capital and lower case letters and recording them in a learning log.

    B. drawing letters in a salt tray and using her body to make the shape of the letters while saying their letter names.

    C. saying letters aloud while the teacher reads aloud from shared reading.

    D. working with a partner to find b's, d's, p's, q's, and other tricky letters "hidden" in books.

29. Mrs. Rashid is teaching her students to read words such as *do, through,* and *goes.* The most helpful strategy for word identification of these words would be to teach students:

    A. selected words as sight vocabulary.

    B. to decode such words phonetically.

    C. selected words as part of an organized context clue program.

    D. to unlock unknown words using syntax.

30. A first-grade teacher is working with her class during morning circle time. She is teaching a mini-lesson on onsets and rimes. The teacher uses the word "hair" as an example. Which of the following best represents an understanding of onsets and rimes?

    A. hare and hair.

    B. hair and care.

    C. /h/ and /air/.

    D. hair and chair.

31. Which of the following statements about phonics instruction is *false?*

    A. Phonics instruction is important because it leads to an understanding of the alphabetic principle.

    B. Effective phonics programs provide ample opportunities for students to apply what they are learning about letters and sounds to the reading of words, sentences, and stories.

    C. Systematic phonics is the most important component of literacy and should be taught by itself during reading instruction.

    D. Explicit phonics is most effective when it begins in kindergarten or first grade.

32. Which of the following strategies would a first-grade teacher instruct her students to use when figuring out unknown words?

    A. use phonetic clues, find parts of words you can read, use picture clues

    B. skip the word you don't know, ask the teacher for help, ask a peer

    C. spell the word aloud, use the sentence context to figure out the word, use onsets and rimes

    D. use a word wall, reread the story, use phonemic awareness

33. Mr. Ovadia is evaluating several supplemental reading programs for his second-graders. He is particularly interested in providing systematic effective phonics instruction. Mr. Ovadia is most likely to select:

    A. a literature-based program that emphasizes reading and writing activities in an unstructured, yet interesting way, to students.

    B. an explicit program that helps teachers instruct students to relate letters and sounds, to break spoken words into sounds, and to blend sounds to form words.

    C. a basal reading program that focuses on whole-word or meaning-based activities.

    D. a sight-word program that begins by teaching a sight-word vocabulary of fifty to one hundred words followed by children receiving instruction in the alphabetic principle.

34. Tabitha is an eighth-grade student who reads very slowly. During a parent-teacher conference, her mother notes that she wishes Tabitha would read "more smoothly." Tabitha's teacher gives her direct instruction and guided practice in reading fluently. Tabitha is likely to make the greatest gains in overall fluency by:

A. participating in activities such as *Readers Theater,* reading into a tape recorder, partner reading, and choral reading.

B. studying organized word lists and studying flash cards in order to develop automatic word recognition.

C. having multiple opportunities for silent, independent reading at her independent level in the classroom.

D. being timed and calculating words-per-minute as she reads from grade-level reading lists.

35. In the word *blustery,* which of the following pairs of letters is a consonant blend?

A. st
B. er
C. bl
D. ry

36. A second-grade teacher is teaching her students different ways of spelling the long e sound. She gives her students flash cards with long e words printed on them and asks her students to sort them by spelling patterns. The flash cards include the following words: *key, leaf, bee, sheep, we, beast, me, believe, cheese, cede, see,* and *tea.* After the sorting activity, the teacher asks her students to complete a follow-up activity. The greatest benefit to her students would result from promoting:

A. growth across the content areas by writing and illustrating a story in their learning logs using mostly long e words.

B. application of spelling strategies and knowledge transfer by giving students a long e spelling test.

C. vocabulary development by asking students to record long e words in a word study notebook complete with illustrations.

D. spelling patterns and generalizations by asking students to read results aloud and record categorized words in a word study notebook.

37. Which of the following is *not* an effective strategy for encouraging reading at home?

A. Students complete at-home reading logs and receive rewards as incentives.

B. Students take home book bags with classroom books on their independent reading level.

C. The teacher regularly gives comprehension quizzes on reading completed at home.

D. The teacher provides lists of books that can be checked out of the public library.

38. Jemma is a sixth grader experiencing difficulty in comprehension. Her teacher has noted that her reading fluency is weak despite her proven ability to decode words accurately. The teacher might help improve Jemma's fluency by:

A. providing direct, explicit instruction in fluency. Jemma can then practice reading aloud books at her independent level to a partner or small group.

B. modeling phrasing and reading with expression. Jemma can practice orally retelling stories in order to build her text fluency and comprehension.

C. providing direct instruction in phonics in order to build decoding skills and automaticity before reading aloud. Jemma can practice reading aloud to a younger student in order to help build her confidence.

D. providing meaningful opportunities for Jemma to listen to classmates reading aloud fluently. When Jemma is ready, she will read with expression.

39. On Monday Mrs. Valdez notices that many of her sixth-grade students have difficulty comprehending nonfiction texts. The next day, Mrs. Valdez introduces an unseen expository text. The following instructional strategy would be most effective in facilitating comprehension of expository text:

A. using cooperative learning so that a greater number of students will understand the text.

B. using graphic organizers for students to complete using information from text.

C. teaching comprehension strategies such as note taking and outlining for understanding nonfiction text.

D. asking students to complete non-fiction book reports.

GO ON TO THE NEXT PAGE

40. Focusing on roots to help students understand the meaning of words is based on:

   A. being familiar with languages that are historically related to English.

   B. knowing how to use prefixes and suffixes to analyze words.

   C. comparing English words with many Asian words.

   D. understanding.

41. Ms. Hidalgo is teaching a unit on fairy tales to her diverse fourth-grade class. To begin with, students read and discuss *Cinderella*. The teacher then assigns The *Golden Slipper,* a Vietnamese version of the classic *Cinderella* story. Following the two stories, students are asked to complete a Venn Diagram and include as many aspects of the stories as possible. This instructional strategy is most likely to promote student reading proficiency by:

   A. guiding students to compare and contrast several aspects between stories.

   B. fostering an understanding of cultural relativism and diversity.

   C. supporting the needs of the Vietnamese students in the classroom.

   D. helping students diagram the relationships between characters in both stories.

42. Anwar is a fourth grader who reads at grade level. When asked to choose a book from the classroom library, he generally selects texts that are at his frustration level. It is clear that he is unable to read his chosen material. The teacher's best response to this behavior would be to:

   A. choose easier material for Anwar so that he is able to accurately decode and comprehend the text.

   B. continue allowing Anwar to select books at his frustration level for as long as he appears to be enjoying his choices.

   C. teach Anwar the five-finger rule of reading so that he will be able to monitor his own reading selections. When Anwar makes more than five errors per page, he will know that the book is too difficult for him and choose another.

   D. review Anwar's book selections during Guided Reading. Give mini-lessons on difficult reading concepts so that Anwar will be able to read on his instructional level.

43. Of the following, the most effective "before reading" practices for a primary teacher to use are:

   A. brainstorming, connecting prior knowledge, predicting what the book will be about.

   B. reviewing new vocabulary, discussing the author's background, naming other books by the same author.

   C. listing words by phonic elements, comparing similar books, sequencing pictures.

   D. dramatizing story elements, labeling favorite parts, asking questions.

44. The students in a second-grade classroom are asked to "retell" the story that they have just heard. The teacher asks them to tell the story events in sequence and tell about the story characters. The teacher is trying to gain information about:

   A. the children's understanding of the text and their developing comprehension.

   B. the children's use of story vocabulary and whether they recall phrases from the text.

   C. whether the students liked the story and whether it should be reread.

   D. finding the appropriate reading level for independent reading.

45. In choosing books for fourth graders to read on their own, the teacher finds stories with similar themes. Why would a teacher do this?

   A. The students can compare and contrast the books providing links for dialogue and topics for discussion.

   B. This technique enables the teachers to save planning time by researching only one theme.

   C. This technique opens the door to many interaction opportunities for students.

   D. The teacher can connect the independent literature to themes that the students dislike studying in their classrooms.

Use the information below to answer the two questions that follow.

Ms. Chang's fourth-grade class has been studying amphibians. Her class includes a large number of English Language Learners. Ms. Chang designs and implements the activity described below.

Before she gives directions to the students, the teacher leads a whole-class discussion on the life cycle of a frog. Next, the teacher creates mixed-ability cooperative learning groups with four students in each group.

Student Directions

1. The students in each group continue discussing the subject.

2. Students take turns writing what happens first, second, third, or fourth in the life cycle on sentence strips.

3. Each group then sequences the sentences in order to form a proper paragraph. At the same time, they correct any errors.

---

46. When planning whole-class activities, it is important to consider the needs of second-language learners. During this activity, Ms. Chang should be most concerned with:

   A. helping second language learners gain a solid understanding of the text.
   B. covering the most material in the shortest amount of time.
   C. meeting the needs of all her students.
   D. providing motivating assignments for her learners.

47. Ms. Chang's organizing and writing activity is most likely to develop student reading by helping students:

   A. build knowledge in a systematic manner.
   B. improve reading comprehension skills.
   C. increase automaticity and fluency.
   D. transfer oral language skills to written language.

GO ON TO THE NEXT PAGE

48. Several students have been reading *Nate the Great* books during guided reading. In the books, the main character and his friends use detective skills to solve mysteries. Which of the following activities would allow the teacher to informally evaluate each student's ability to make a personal connection to the text and recognize features of mystery writing?

    A. Each student cites passages from one of the stories that show suspense.

    B. Students use graphic organizers to retell one of the mysteries in their own words.

    C. Students create a class web and brainstorm traits commonly found in *Nate the Great* mystery stories.

    D. Each student pretends to be a character in a *Nate the Great* book and writes a new mystery.

49. Which of the following is *not* a true statement?

    A. Effective fluency instruction is ongoing, well-planned, targeted, and direct.

    B. Fluency instruction needs to use progressively difficult text as well as provide opportunities for rereading familiar text.

    C. The type and quantity of reading practice are equally important for fluency development.

    D. Fluency occurs automatically when students become skilled readers.

Use the information below to answer the two questions that follow.

Students in a middle-school class frequently use K-W-L charts when reading expository texts. Before beginning a unit on the Periodic Table, students are asked to form small groups and list everything known about the Periodic Table. Then the whole class meets to share their lists on a class K-W-L chart.

K	W	L

50. This strategy is likely to be particularly useful in helping the teacher evaluate her class's ability to:

    A. organize textual information by analyzing similarities and differences.

    B. activate, think about, and organize prior knowledge.

    C. clarify known and unknown vocabulary.

    D. use QARs to teach inferential and evaluative comprehension.

51. The middle school students are then told to read a passage on atoms from their science text. The teacher distributes to each student a copy of the K-W-L chart that was previously filled out by the class. She could best help students use the chart to learn and retain facts from their reading by asking them to:

    A. memorize all of the known information before starting the passage.

    B. complete the L (learned) section of the chart. Students can go on the Internet or search other reference materials to find all unanswered questions from the "want to learn" category.

    C. add continuously to the K-W-L chart as they absorb new information from the passage.

    D. work with a partner to form known fact categories.

52. Which of the following is *not* a component of Reciprocal Teaching?

   A. The teacher explains how a particular reading strategy should be used, models its use, and helps children use the strategy independently.

   B. Students participate in questioning, summarizing, clarifying, and predicting.

   C. Students self-monitor their own reading and understanding in a passage.

   D. The teacher helps students reflect on passages and develop a sense of how the written word is formed.

53. A fourth-grade class is studying California missions. Students are told to open to the chapters that discuss missions in their social studies books and locate all references to Native Americans. They are explicitly being taught:

   A. skimming.
   B. scanning.
   C. in-depth reading.
   D. structured reading.

54. What are some effective ways that teachers can promote independent reading?

   A. provide reading logs for students to list the books that they read outside of class and give extra credit for turning the log in to the teacher

   B. invite parents and special guests in to class to read books to students, ask the principal to participate in classroom read-alouds, take students to their local library

   C. offer incentives to students to participate in the local library's summer reading program, find ways to stock the classroom library with many books, read aloud to students

   D. allot classroom time for independent reading, provide a well-stocked classroom library for students, give students opportunities to see others immersed in books

55. As part of a Dr. Seuss author study, Mrs. Miyashta begins to read aloud *The Butter Battle* book. Halfway through the book, she stops reading. The teacher wants to facilitate comprehension while encouraging students to connect elements in the text to their background knowledge. They complete one of the following activities before Mrs. Miyashta finishes the end of the story. Which activity is likely to be most effective?

   A. Students are asked to confirm whether or not they correctly predicted the book's outcome.

   B. Students write what they think might happen next in the story and are encouraged to justify their predictions to the class.

   C. The students preview a set of comprehension questions that they will answer at the end of the book.

   D. The students rewrite the first part of the story and then record all their background knowledge about Dr. Seuss.

56. Chad is a behaviorally-challenged seventh grader who performs significantly below average in reading. A teacher plans to assess his comprehension of a short story through oral retelling. After Chad silently reads the short story, his teacher prompts his retelling and understanding by asking open-ended questions. Chad behaves well and thoughtfully answers the questions. The best use of this assessment is to inform:

   A. other seventh-grade teachers, resource specialists, and the principal about the need for a Student Study Team.

   B. parents about his academic performance on the school standards-based report card.

   C. his teacher about his comprehension needs so that she can provide effective individualized reading interventions.

   D. Chad about his challenging reading behavior.

GO ON TO THE NEXT PAGE

57. Before beginning a writing assignment, a fifth-grade teacher asks her students to share orally with their neighbors about the suggested topic. Students are instructed to discuss their ideas for writing with their group. Which of the following reasons is least likely to explain why she uses this strategy?

A. The discussion helps students make connections between their oral language and writing.

B. Students may become more interested in writing about the topic following discussion with partners.

C. Student writing tends to be more detailed following discussion.

D. Oral language helps second language learners develop spelling skills.

58. A second-grade teacher gives students pieces of a puzzle to put back in proper order. The "puzzle," comprised of words and phrases that form a single, complex sentence, is taken directly from their reading. The cut-up pieces have been taken from sentence strips that were printed with the sentences. Partners are told to sequence the cut-up words and phrases into a proper sentence. After correctly ordering one sentence puzzle, students mix up the parts again and trade with their classmates. They then begin sequencing a new sentence.

This instructional activity is likely to be most effective in helping students:

A. strengthen their ability to assemble sentences, sequence words, and use language conventions when reading and writing complex sentences.

B. improve general inferential comprehension skills through sequencing and analysis of semantic and orthographic patterns.

C. organize instructional materials in a systematic, direct manner in order to clarify text meaning.

D. use deliberate multi-sensory techniques that contribute to vocabulary development and reinforce reading development in context.

59. An eighth-grade teacher designs the following instructional activity. Students are given the word *sweltering*. Students brainstorm the definition, synonyms, an antonym, and create a sentence using the word *sweltering*. The teacher uses their suggestions to complete the diagram below on the board.

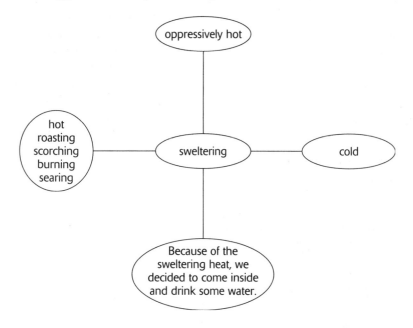

This activity is most accurately called a:

A. concept diagram.
B. syntactic structure.
C. graphic organizer.
D. semantic map.

GO ON TO THE NEXT PAGE

60. Structural analysis would be an especially appropriate strategy for determining meaning in which of the following words?

    A. pigeon

    B. misinformation

    C. lethal

    D. guava

61. Which of the following statements regarding vocabulary instruction is least likely to be true?

    A. Children learn the meanings of most words indirectly, through regular experiences with oral and written language. However, some vocabulary must be taught directly.

    B. Students learn vocabulary directly when they are explicitly taught individual words and word-learning strategies. Repeated exposure to vocabulary in many contexts aids word learning.

    C. Teachers can facilitate student comprehension of all unknown words. Children need encouragement to look up every word in the dictionary when reading an unknown word.

    D. Teachers can encourage indirect learning of new vocabulary by reading aloud to students. Reading aloud is especially helpful when teachers help students relate new words to prior knowledge and experiences.

62. Which of the following is the most effective way to teach students to learn word meanings?

    A. Introduce all new vocabulary before reading.

    B. After reading a selection, teachers and students post interesting words that are related to the passage content around the classroom.

    C. Use worksheet exercise, matching words, and word searches to teach root words.

    D. Use weekly vocabulary lists in which students memorize word meanings.

63. Mr. Bilorusky, a fourth-grade teacher, displays the following sentences on a piece of chart paper:

- Even though he had been *reminded,* D'Andre still forgot to call his mother.
- The electrician *rewired* the ceiling lights so that they would stop blinking off and on.
- Harrison *retold* the story to his teacher after recess.
- Meisi *rewrote* her essay when she had finished editing it.
- The weaver *rewove* the loose piece of yarn into the rug.

Students are told to read the sentences and reread the italicized words. Individual children are chosen to come to the wipe board and highlight the common element. Mr. Bilorusky facilitates the class working together to arrive at the meaning of the *underlined* words.

In order to provide continued vocabulary development, Mr. Bilorusky could follow up by:

- **A.** continuing to study the origin and development of common Greek words. Students are asked to print words on index cards and use guide words to find their meanings in the dictionary.
- **B.** providing direct instruction in breaking down words into word parts. Students then look for other examples of *re* words in their independent reading and record them on a class list.
- **C.** continuing teaching prefixes, root words, and antonyms. Antonyms are added to the prefixes and root words in order to form new words. Students record new words in a word study notebook.
- **D.** providing additional words that have *re* as a prefix. Students then sort the words into alphabetical order.

GO ON TO THE NEXT PAGE

Use the following passage to answer the three questions that follow.

Mrs. Feinberg, a first-grade teacher, engages with students about the stories they are reading. Printed below is an excerpt from a conversation with Rosa, an ELL student. After this conversation, Rosa will write a story about her bike.

Mrs. Feinberg:	What did you like about the bikes in this book?
Rosa:	The colors bikes are pretty.
Mrs. Feinberg:	Oh. You liked the pretty colors on the bikes. What else did you like about the bikes?
Rosa:	I like the bikes big and the bikes fast.
Mrs. Feinberg:	I also liked the big bikes and the fast bikes. Do you know anybody who has a bike?
Rosa:	I have a new bike. It is pretty.
Mrs. Feinberg:	I would love to hear more about your bike. I want you to write in your journal about your *fast, new* bike.

64. After reading this conversation, it is likely that Mrs. Feinberg knows the importance of:

   A. using metacognitive strategies to clarify meaning during reading and writing.

   B. drawing on a variety of cues to help English Language Learners identify unfamiliar English words.

   C. supporting English Language Learners in learning grammar and syntax through modeling.

   D. helping beginning readers who have difficulty with words that are not already part of their oral vocabulary.

65. The most appropriate follow-up activity for Rosa would be:

   A. a worksheet filled with nouns and adjectives.

   B. direct, explicit instruction in grammar, syntax, and prepositional order.

   C. a pile of index cards with adjectives and the words *car, skateboard,* and *bus* written on them. An English only student places them on a pocket chart and uses them to describe the vehicles in proper English grammar.

   D. direct, explicit instruction during a mini-lesson in use of adjectives and their placement in relation to nouns.

66. Which assessment is likely to be most helpful to Mrs. Feinberg in evaluating Rosa's ability to use appropriate English grammar in the classroom:

   A. qualitative assessment based on Rosa's written and oral language.

   B. six-trait writing rubric evaluating Rosa's language skills.

   C. CELDT test.

   D. analytic quantitative assessment based on Rosa's journal entry about her bike.

67. Ms. Palacios regularly has her class participate in Language Experience Approach activities. LEA instruction is *least likely* to promote student understanding of:

   A.   sentence, word, and letter representation.
   B.   directionality and tracking of print.
   C.   print conveying meaning.
   D.   sound/symbol correspondence.

68. Fifth-grade students are studying traditional literature. As part of the fable section, students will perform a reader's theater version of *Androcles and the Lion* for a second-grade class. This type of activity helps teachers informally gather data about fifth-grade student ability to:

   A.   change the way they speak to fit main character traits while reading and develop automaticity at an independent level.
   B.   develop listening skills in younger students.
   C.   learn roles and read lines with fluency and expression
   D.   work with younger students while performing literary analysis.

69. Mr. Kassisseah is helping his seventh-graders understand the similarities and differences between language structures used in spoken and written English. He can help students master academic language by providing:

   A.   direct instruction in systematic oral and written language development.
   B.   direct instruction in academic language used in literature texts.
   C.   a balanced language approach when speaking and writing across the curriculum.
   D.   modeling and guided practice to teach oral and written language structures.

70. A seventh-grade teacher decides to introduce the following words during an instructional activity: cyclone, cyclical, tricycle, and encyclopedia. She explains that *cycl* comes from the Latin meaning "circle or wheel." The teacher then asks students if they can think of other English words that include *cycl*. She lists their answers on the board. This brainstorm activity is likely to promote vocabulary development primarily by helping students:

   A.   build word banks and sort words into categories.
   B.   break down the components of a word to derive its meaning.
   C.   using morphemic analysis to determine word history and origin.
   D.   identify prefixes and suffixes for comprehension.

END OF SECTION I

Proceed to Section II of the test.

Directions for Section II: Open-Ended Assignments

Assignments A to E

This section of the test consists of four focused educational problems and instructional tasks and one case study. You are required to prepare a written response for each of these assignments and record each in the appropriate area provided in the Written Response Sheet in the Answer Document or, for the case study, in the Case Study Response Booklet.

Before you begin to write your response to an assignment, read the assignment carefully. Take some time to plan and organize your response. Blank space is provided in this test booklet following each assignment so that you can make notes, write an outline, or do any pre-writing necessary. *Your final responses, however, must be written on the appropriate page(s) of the Answer Document. The case study must be written in the Case Study Response Booklet.*

The evaluation of your written responses will be based on how well the responses demonstrate knowledge and skills important for effective delivery of a balanced, comprehensive reading program. Make sure that you address all aspects of each given assignment. The evaluation criteria will include your attention to: fulfilling the purpose; effectively applying relevant content and academic knowledge; and supporting your response with appropriate evidence, examples, and rationales.

Considering that the complete RICA is 100% and the multiple-choice section is weighted 50%, each of the individual assignments will be weighted approximately as follows:

Assignment A	5%
Assignment B	5%
Assignment C	10%
Assignment D	10%
Assignment E	20%
Total	50%

The assignments are intended to assess knowledge and skills of reading instruction and, although writing ability is not directly assessed, your responses must be written clearly enough to allow for a valid judgment of your knowledge and skills. As you plan your responses, keep in mind that the audience is composed of educators knowledgeable about reading instruction. Each written response should conform to the conventions of edited American English.

Your responses to the assignments should be your original work. They should be written in your own words and not copied or paraphrased from some other work. Citations, however, may be used when appropriate.

To maintain your anonymity during the scoring process of the written assignments, the multiple-choice section of the Answer Document containing your name will be removed from your written responses. Do not write your name on any other portion of the Answer Document, and do not separate any of the sheets from the document.

You may work on the assignments in any order you choose, but be sure to record your final responses in the appropriate locations, as listed in the directions for each individual assignment.

Assignment A

Record your written response to Assignment A on the Assignment A Response Sheet on page 3 of the Answer Document. The length of your response is limited to the lined space available on the Assignment A Response Sheet.

Use the information here to complete the exercise that follows.

A fifth-grade teacher is setting up her classroom at the beginning of the school year. She has students from diverse cultural, ethnic, and academic backgrounds. What should she do to prepare for teaching spelling to her fifth graders?

<u>Examinee Task</u>

Write a response in which you describe strategies and resources the teacher should use to prepare for teaching spelling.

Remember to record your final response on the **ASSIGNMENT A RESPONSE SHEET**
on page 3 of the Answer Document.

**(On the actual RICA test you will be warned NOT TO REMOVE THIS OR ANY OTHER PAGE,
or any portion of any page, from the test booklet.)**

You may use the space below to make notes. These notes will not be scored.

GO ON TO THE NEXT PAGE

Assignment B

Record your written response to Assignment B on the Assignment B Response Sheet on page 5 of the Answer Document. The length of your response is limited to the lined space available on the Assignment B Response Sheet.

Use the information here to complete the exercise that follows.

A seventh-grade teacher is working on a plan to support written language development in her class.

<u>Examinee Task</u>

Write a response in which you identify and describe some of the methods the teacher should include in her plan.

Remember to record your final response on the **ASSIGNMENT B RESPONSE SHEET**
on page 5 of the Answer Document.

**(On the actual RICA test you will be warned NOT TO REMOVE THIS OR ANY OTHER PAGE,
or any portion of any page, from the test booklet.)**

You may use the space below to make notes. These notes will not be scored.

Assignment C

Record your written response to Assignment C on the Assignment C Response Sheet on pages 7 and 8 of the Answer Document. The length of your response is limited to the lined space available on the Assignment C Response Sheet.

Use the information here to complete the exercise that follows.

It is important to have an implementation plan when teaching specific skills—for example, phonemic awareness. Study the Curriculum Implementation Plan that follows.

Curriculum Implementation Plan

1. ASSESS
Informal / Formal:
- Fluency
- Sight Word Check Off
- Decoding Test (BPST)
- Other Assessments

2. PLAN
Data Use:
- Standards & Framework
- Grouping
- Scheduling
- Instructional Strategies
- Student Tasks
- Technology
- Individual Needs

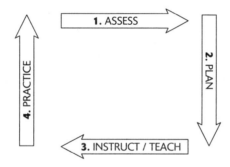

4. MEANINGFUL PRACTICE
Instructional Tasks:
- Highly Structured Practice
- Guided Practice
- Independent Practice
- Decodable Text
- Leveled Readers

3. INSTRUCT / TEACH
Direct & Explicit Instruction:
- Decoding
- Sight Word Mastery
- Comprehension Strategies
- Comprehension Skills
- Writing Skills
- Other Instructional Strategies

GO ON TO THE NEXT PAGE

Examinee Task

Based on the information given and your knowledge of reading, write a response in which you: (1) explain how phonemic awareness is related to reading achievement and (2) describe the steps or instructional process a teacher must take to teach phonemic awareness to his/her kindergarten class.

Remember to record your final response on the **ASSIGNMENT C RESPONSE SHEET**
on pages 7 and 8 of the Answer Document.

**(On the actual RICA you will be warned NOT TO REMOVE THIS OR ANY OTHER PAGE,
or any portion of any page, from the test booklet.)**

You may use the space below to make notes. These notes will not be scored.

Assignment D

Record your written response to Assignment D on the Assignment D Response Sheet on pages 9 and 10 of the Answer Document. The length of your response is limited to the lined space available on the Assignment D Response Sheet.

Use the information here to complete the exercise that follows.

There are three levels of comprehension skills—literal, inferential, and evaluative comprehension. A number of comprehension strategies are appropriate to teach each level of comprehension.

<u>**Examinee Task**</u>

Using your knowledge of reading comprehension, write a response in which you: (1) describe the three levels of comprehension skills and (2) describe two comprehension strategies that would be appropriate to teach each level.

Remember to record your final response on the **ASSIGNMENT D RESPONSE SHEET**
on pages 9 and 10 of the Answer Document.

**(On the actual RICA test you will be warned NOT TO REMOVE THIS OR ANY OTHER PAGE,
or any portion of any page, from the test booklet.)**

You may use the space below to make notes. These notes will not be scored.

GO ON TO THE NEXT PAGE

Assignment E

Case Study

Record your written response to the case study in the Case Study Response Booklet. Your response is limited to the lined space available in the Case Study Response Booklet.

This case study focuses on a student named Tara, who is 11 years old and in the sixth grade. The information and data on the following pages describe Tara's performance on assessments and observations. Using these materials, write a response in which you apply your knowledge of language arts assessment and instruction to analyze this case study. Your response should include three parts:

1. identify three of Tara's important reading strengths and/or needs at this point, citing evidence from the documents to support your observations;

2. describe two specific instructional strategies and/or activities designed to enhance; and

3. discuss Tara's literacy development by addressing the needs and/or building on the strengths you identified, and explain how each strategy/activity you describe would promote Tara's reading proficiency.

Remember to record your final response in the **CASE STUDY RESPONSE BOOKLET.**

(On the actual RICA you will be warned NOT TO REMOVE THIS OR ANY OTHER PAGE, or any portion of any page, from the test booklet.)

You may use the space below to make notes. These notes will not be scored.

Interest Survey

Tara's teacher created an interest survey for her students to complete at the beginning of the year. Printed on the following page are Tara's responses to the survey.

GO ON TO THE NEXT PAGE

Interest Survey

1. What do you like to do? _Cheerleading, play basketball and softball_

2. What is your favorite subject in school? _History and science_

3. What is your least favorite subject in school? _Math_

4. What are you good at doing? _Drawing cartoons_

5. What would you like to do better? _Write and spell_

6. Do you like to read? Why? Or Why not? _Yes. When the book is interesting._

7. Are you a good reader? _I'm ok_

8. What kinds of things do you like to read? _Mysteries and instructional books._

9. Are you a good writer? _Yes_

10. What do you like to write about? _Me and my hobbies_

11. What do you want to be when you grow up? _A designer_

12. What will you need to do to prepare yourself for your future career? _Learn a lot of math, and be a better writer and speller_

Phonics Test

Tara's teacher gave her a phonics inventory in which she tried to decode nonsense words containing the most common spelling patterns. The purpose was to determine which phonics elements she could read, and on which ones she needed to work. She was able to recognize consonant blends and digraphs; she was able to identify the short vowels and the sounds they make, but she had difficulty with the following short vowel nonsense words: fis, gud, and hin. She also read "nail" for nel, and "doke" for dook. She could read some nonsense words with prefixes and suffixes, although the words with suffixes were more difficult for her. She could read the nonsense compound words correctly, but had some problems with words with silent letters and r-controlled vowels. She could correctly divide multisyllabic words into syllables four out of seven times. On all the tasks she did not read the words with automaticity.

On another phonics assessment, Tara had difficulty with vowel diphthongs saying:

> "mail" for maul
> "coal" for cowl
> "owl" for awl
> "rock" for rook

She did not read the words on this assessment with automaticity.

GO ON TO THE NEXT PAGE

Running Record

Tara's teacher took a running record of her reading various grade-level passages. A running record is an informal assessment of reading performance to assess the rate and accuracy with which a student reads aloud. Self-corrections are also noted. For this assessment, Tara read aloud short, graded selections, and the teacher made notes about her performance. Following are the results of the fourth-grade passage she read. After reading each passage, Tara was asked to retell what the selection was about, to check for comprehension, and she was able to retell this passage with great accuracy, although she had to be prompted to supply details.

RECORD OF READING BEHAVIOUR

Name: Tara		Title: **My Favorite Lunch**	
Age: **11**	Grade: **6**	Running Words: **99**	Seen
Date: **10/01/05**		Grade Level: **4**	(Unseen)

Calculations	**Understanding from Retelling/Questioning**		
Error Rate $\frac{SC}{E}$ = 1:**42**	Characters	(Yes) .... No
Accuracy % **92**	Setting	(Yes) .... No
S/C Rate $\frac{E - SC}{SC}$ = 1:**5**	Plot	(Yes) .... No
Level: Easy (Instr) Hard	Inferences	(Yes) .... No

Competencies (circle predominant behaviours)

(1 on 1 matching)   (Directionality)   Fluent Reading
No-reads
very slowly

At an unknown word

Makes no attempt   Seeks help   Reruns   (Reads on)

Attempts using   (Letter/sound knowledge)   Meaning   Syntax

After an error

(Ignores)   Seeks help   Reruns   Attempts s/c

Self-corrects using   Letter/sound knowledge   (Meaning)   Syntax

	E	SC	E msv	SC msv
✓ ✓ ✓ ✓ ✓ ✓R ✓				
✓ ✓ ✓ ✓ ✓ ✓ ✓ ✓			M**S**V	
✓ $\frac{can}{can't}$ ✓ ✓ ✓ $\frac{wait/sc}{want}$ ✓✓✓R	1	1	M**S**V	**MSV**
✓ ✓ ✓ ✓ $\frac{everywhere}{everything}$ ✓ ✓	1		M**S**V	
✓ ✓ ✓ ✓ ✓ ✓ ✓ ✓				
✓ ✓ ✓ $\frac{hummingbird}{hamburger}$ ✓ $\frac{search}{scratch}$	2		M**S**V	
✓ ✓ $\frac{pull}{put}$ ✓ ✓ ✓ ✓	1		M**S**V	
✓✓✓ $\frac{double/sc}{doorbell}$ ✓ $\frac{granted}{greeted}$ ✓ ✓	1	1	M**S**V	**MSV**
✓ ✓ $\frac{concentrated}{concerned}$ ✓✓✓✓	1		M**S**V	
✓ ✓ ✓ ✓ ✓ ✓ ✓ ✓ ✓	1		M**S**V	
✓ ✓✓R ✓ ✓ ✓ $\frac{very}{-}$ ✓				
✓ ✓ ✓ ✓ ✓ ✓ ✓ ✓ ✓			**M**SV	

GO ON TO THE NEXT PAGE

Qualitative Spelling Inventory

Tara's teacher gave her a qualitative spelling inventory to find out where she is making spelling errors and what spelling features she already has in place. When Tara missed five out of the first seven words on the Upper Elementary Spelling Inventory, her teacher administered Bear's Elementary Qualitative Spelling Inventory to her to determine her spelling stage. Tara's spelling test and analysis of errors on the Feature Guide are on the two following pages.

Qualitative Spelling Checklist

Student **Tara**   Observer **Ms. Mellon**

Use this checklist to help you find what stages of spelling development your students are in. There are three gradations within each stage—early, middle, and late. The words in parentheses refer to spelling words on the first Qualitative Spelling Inventory.

This form can be used to follow students' progress. Check when certain features are observed in students' spelling. When a feature is always present check "Yes." The last place where you check "Often" corresponds to the student's stage of spelling development.

Emergent Stage   Dates:____ ____ ____

Early
- Does the child scribble on the page?   Yes ✓   Often___   No___
- Do the scribbles follow the conventional direction?
  (left to right in English)   Yes ✓   Often___   No___

Middle
- Are there letters and numbers used in pretend
  writing? *(4BT for ship)*   Yes ✓   Often___   No___

Late
- Are key sounds used in syllabic writing *(P for ship)*   Yes ✓   Often___   No___

Letter Name—Alphabetic

Early
- Are beginning consonants included *(B for bed, S for ship)*   Yes ✓   Often___   No___
- Is there a vowel in each word?   Yes ✓   Often___   No___

Middle
- Are some consonant blends and digraphs spelled correctly?
  (ship, when, float)   Yes ✓   Often___   No___

Late
- Are short vowels spelled correctly? *(bed, ship
  when, lump)*   Yes ✓   Often___   No___
- Is the *m* included in front of other consonants? *(lump)*   Yes ✓   Often___   No___

Within Word Pattern

Early
- Are long vowels in single-syllable words "used but
  confused"? (FLOAT for *float,* TRANE for *train*)   Yes___   Often ✓   No___

Middle
- Are most long vowels in single-syllable words
  spelled correctly but some long vowel spelling and
  other vowel patterns "used but confused"
  (COTE for caught)   Yes___   Often___   No ✓
- Are most consonant blends and digraphs spelled correctly?   Yes ✓   Often___   No___
- Are most other vowel patterns spelled correctly?
  (caught, chased, preparing)   Yes___   Often ✓   No___

Syllables and Affixes

Early
- Are inflectional endings added correctly to base vowel
  patterns with short vowel patterns? *(popping, beaches)*   Yes ✓   Often___   No___
- Are consonant doublets spelled correctly? *(cattle, cellar)*   Yes ✓   Often___   No___

Middle
- Are inflectional endings added correctly to base words?
  (inspection, cellar)   Yes___   Often ✓   No___

Late
- Are less frequent prefixes and suffixes spelled correctly?
  (confident, ripen, cellar, opposition, puncture)   Yes___   Often___   No ✓

Derivational Relations

Early
- Are most polysyllabic words spelled correctly?
  (fortunate, confident)   Yes___   Often___   No ✓

Middle
- Are unaccented vowels in derived words spelled correctly?
  (confident, civilize, opposition)   Yes___   Often ✓   No___

Late
- Are words from derived forms spelled
  correctly *(pleasure, civilize)*   Yes___   Often___   No ✓

Words Their Way Appendix © 2000 by Prentice-Hall, Inc.

GO ON TO THE NEXT PAGE

Spelling Test

Name **Tara**

1. bed
2. ship
3. drive
4. bump
5. when
6. trane ✓
7. closet
8. chase
9. flot ✓
10. beaches
11. prepairing ✓
12. popping
13. cattle
14. cote✓
15. inspecsion ✓
16. pouchser ✓
17. seller ✓
18. pleasher ✓
19. squirrel
20. forcanet ✓
21. confident
22. civilize
23. flexible
24. oposeion ✓
25. enfasize ✓

Writing Samples

Tara's teacher examined three writing samples. She was instructed to choose any topic about which she wanted to write. She wrote about her cheerleading competition, her family, and sports. Her writing did not include many details and was incomplete because she ran out of time. Her sentence structure was simple and to the point. She spelled words with common long vowel spelling patterns incorrectly.

GO ON TO THE NEXT PAGE

Elementary Inventory Error Guide

Stages	Early Letter Name	Letter Name	Within Word Pattern	Syllable Juncture	Derivational Constancy
1. bed	b bd	bad	(bed)		
2. ship	s sp shp	sep shep	sip (ship)		
3. drive	irv drv	griv driv	drieve draive (drive)		
4. bump	b bp bmp	bop bomp bup	(bump)		
5. when	w yn wn	wan whan	wen (when)		
6. train	j t trn	jran chran tan tran	teran traen (tran) train		
7. closet	k cs kt clst	clast clost clozt	clozit closet (closet)		
8. chase	j jass cs	tas cas chas chass	case chais (chase)		
9. float	f vt ft flt	for (flot) flort	flowt flount floate		
10. beaches	b bs bcs	bechs becis behis	bechise beches beeches (beaches)		
11. preparing	preparing	preparng preypering	(preparing)(prepairing) preparing		
12. popping	popping	popin poping	(popping)		
13. cattle	cattle	catl cadol	catel cattle cattel (cattle)		
14. caught	caught	cot (cote) cout cought caught			
15. inspection	inspection	inspshn, inspectin	inspecshum, (inspecsion) inspection		
16. puncture	puncture	pucshre pungchr puncker	punksher punture puncure		
17. cellar	cellar	sulr selr celr seler	(seller) cellar celler cellar		
18. pleasure	pleasure	plasr plager plejer pleser plesher (pleasher)	plesour pleasure	pleasure	
19. squirrel	squirrel	scrl skwel skwerl	scqori sqrurel squirle (squirrel)		
20. fortunate	fortunate	furhnat frehnit foohini (forcenet)	forchenut fochininte forchenut	fortunate	
21. confident				confedent confedint confedent confedent conphident (confident)	confident
22. civilize				sivils sevelies sivilicse cifillazas sivelize sivalize civalise civilize (civilize)	civilize
23. flexible				flecksibl flexobil fleckuble flecible flexeble flexable flexibal flexible	(flexible) flexible
24. opposition			(oposeion) opasion opasishan opozcison opishien opssition	opasion oppasishion oppisition	opposition opusition
25. emphasize				infaxize imfacize emphasize (emfasize) emphasise	emphasize emphasize

Words Their Way, 1996

Teacher Comments

Tara's teacher made the following notes about her:

Tara is a positive and enthusiastic learner with a great sense of humor.

Frequently aware of mistakes she is making in reading and spelling, but lacks the strategies to correct them.

A one-to-one learning situation helps her to learn.

Is open about her feelings.

Is willing to try new learning methods and strategies and tries to apply them.

Tara is able to work independently and is able to concentrate on a task for a long period of time without losing interest.

End of Test

Answers and Explanations for Practice Test 2

Answer Key and Charts for Practice Test 2

Multiple-Choice Questions

1. C (Domain 1)		**36.** D (Domain 2)	
2. C (Domain 1)		**37.** C (Domain 3)	
3. D (Domain 1)		**38.** A (Domain 3)	
4. D (Domain 1)		**39.** C (Domain 3)	
5. D (Domain 1)		**40.** A (Domain 3)	
6. B (Domain 1)		**41.** A (Domain 3)	
7. A (Domain 1)		**42.** C (Domain 3)	
8. B (Domain 1)		**43.** A (Domain 3)	
9. D (Domain 1)		**44.** A (Domain 3)	
10. C (Domain 1)		**45.** A (Domain 3)	
11. B (Domain 1)		**46.** C (Domain 4)	
12. D (Domain 1)		**47.** D (Domain 4)	
13. A (Domain 1)		**48.** D (Domain 3)	
14. A (Domain 1)		**49.** D (Domain 3)	
15. A (Domain 2)		**50.** B (Domain 3)	
16. C (Domain 2)		**51.** C (Domain 3)	
17. B (Domain 2)		**52.** D (Domain 3)	
18. D (Domain 2)		**53.** B (Domain 3)	
19. B (Domain 3)		**54.** D (Domain 3)	
20. B (Domain 2)		**55.** B (Domain 3)	
21. B (Domain 2)		**56.** C (Domain 3)	
22. B (Domain 2)		**57.** D (Domain 4)	
23. A (Domain 2)		**58.** A (Domain 4)	
24. C (Domain 2)		**59.** D (Domain 4)	
25. B (Domain 2)		**60.** B (Domain 4)	
26. D (Domain 2)		**61.** C (Domain 4)	
27. D (Domain 2)		**62.** B (Domain 4)	
28. B (Domain 2)		**63.** B (Domain 4)	
29. A (Domain 2)		**64.** C (Domain 4)	
30. C (Domain 2)		**65.** D (Domain 4)	
31. C (Domain 2)		**66.** A (Domain 4)	
32. A (Domain 2)		**67.** D (Domain 4)	
33. B (Domain 2)		**68.** C (Domain 4)	
34. A (Domain 2)		**69.** D (Domain 4)	
35. C (Domain 2)		**70.** B (Domain 4)	

Practice Test 2 Explanations

Section I: Multiple Choice

1. C. All of Shaniqua's known errors involved reading a synonym for the correct word. Therefore, she is using her meaning and structure cueing systems. She is relying on context rather than using decoding skills to "unlock" an unknown word. Choice A is incorrect because Shaniqua already is reading with expression. Choice B is not correct because the story is not too difficult for her and she doesn't need structure cue (syntax) instruction. Although her mistakes imply an understanding of the text, the goal must be to have students reading all words accurately. Additionally the responses are counted as errors in the student's accuracy score on the running record. Therefore, Choice D is also incorrect. It is impossible to make assumptions about her instructional level without more data. (Domain 1)

2. C. Awareness of independent, instructional, and frustration reading levels is crucial for creating flexible reading groups. Knowing a students' instructional level is important because it provides the teacher with information on selecting text for guided reading groups for the student. It means that the student is making decoding errors on enough words to create an opportunity for instruction and support. If too many errors are made, it becomes frustrating for the student to read and text meaning is lost. Frustration means reading 89% or less correctly; instructional refers to 90–95% accurately; and independent means reading 96–100% correctly. If the student is making four errors or less in a 100-word passage, this signifies that this text can be read independently by the student. This is a good passage to provide reading practice for the student. Generally, at least 70% of the comprehension questions must also be answered accurately. (Some experts cite a different percentage of comprehension questions, but you can assume that the vast majority must be correctly answered. (Domain 1)

3. D. In organizing reading groups, the teacher must target her plan to meet the identified instructional level of all her students. In order to accomplish this goal, she should form flexible groups according to students' instructional reading level and then provide individual and/or differentiated instruction. Reading groups should be leveled according to ability, yet remain flexible to accommodate the constantly shifting abilities of the students. Historically, some teachers have chosen to place students according to levels at the beginning of the year and seldom waiver from those leveled groups. By continually assessing student ability, the teacher can be certain that each child is placed in the group that best matches his/her instructional reading level. Choice B is not correct because during guided reading, it is important to provide materials at the instructional level, which is not necessarily grade level. Choice C is incorrect because a teacher might meet with lower performing students more often than other children. Although classrooms are comprised of diverse learners and reading levels, guided reading groups should be based on student instructional reading level. Therefore, Choice A is not appropriate. (Domain 1)

4. D. As mentioned previously, Irena is a second language learner. However, it is important to remember that what is best for *each* student is a central theme in teaching. Do *not* assume that all English Language Learners have the same needs and must be assigned to the same groups. Because she already decodes well, reads fluently, and frequently retells accurately, we can conclude that Irena would benefit from effective vocabulary instruction before reading complex passages. Phonemic awareness instruction would not effectively remediate this problem. (Domain 1)

5. D. Choices A, B, and C are all good things to keep in mind when lesson planning. However, only Choice D refers specifically to planning according to the needs of the individual and class. As specified in the Contents Standards, "the goal of reading instruction is to develop reading competence in all students." Because reading and writing are interrelated, the responding to literature does help develop reading competence. (Domain 1)

6. B. Although running records can be used to communicate with parents and rank students in a grade level as in Choices A and C, Choice B is the best answer. The main reason to do assessment is to provide specific information on what students know and don't know. The teacher can consistently use assessment data to then plan her reading program based on student strengths and identified needs. This idea should be kept in mind throughout the RICA exam. Running records can also be used to determine instructional reading level and provide information on student decoding strategies. Choice D is incorrect because it focuses only on phonics, rather than all of the skills necessary for reading. (Domain 1)

7. A. The Reading Advisory states that schools and school districts should provide all teachers with a variety of assessment tools and strategies necessary to inform daily instruction. They help teachers to assess which children are at risk and to guide instruction.

Some assessments include the following:

- screening assessments
- checklists
- running records
- writing rubric
- reading logs
- comprehensive assessments
- collection, of student work

The purpose of more frequently assessing lower performing students is to collect information on student strengths and weaknesses, to better inform instruction, to identify at-risk students, and to inform decisions for early interventions. (Domain 1)

8. B. Norm-referenced tests, one type of formal assessments, are developed for large numbers of students. The norms allow educators to compare the performance of students with that of a sample group. Additional types of informal assessments can be: published informal reading inventories, reading behavior checklists, attitude/habit measurements, and interviews with teachers or parents. (Domain 1)

9. D. Choices A and B are important components of a balanced, comprehensive literacy program, but are not complete on their own. Choice C is close but refers to all subject areas rather than a literacy focus. Choice D is also more detailed than Choice C because it includes direct, explicit instruction, a necessary part of a balanced literacy program. (Domain 1)

10. C. The teacher should know how to "select and use instructional materials and create a learning environment that promotes student reading." When creating a library, it is important to have varied, motivating texts at students' independent and instructional reading levels, regardless of grade level. Choices A, B, and D are not complete answers because they limit the types of books to be found in the classroom library. (Domain 1)

11. B. Assessment allows teachers to see the results of their teaching and allows them to make informed decisions regarding the next steps in their teaching. (Domain 1)

12. D. When planning long-term instruction, the beginning teacher should plan instruction based on California and District Standards as well as text and grade-level guidelines, Choice B. However, the question specifically asks about weekly and daily planning, which makes Choice D the correct answer. Although a teacher may consider time and student interest, identified individual student needs should take precedent in weekly/daily plans. (Domain 1)

13. A. Although the choices include assessments that can help a teacher plan her instruction, only Choice A includes tests that can determine a student's reading level. (Domain 1)

14. A. When using this type of scoring, the first number refers to the grade. The second number refers to the month of school. (Domain 1)

15. A. Students must develop an awareness that words are made of individual speech sounds. The teacher must provide direct instruction in phonemic awareness. This instruction should be both implicit and explicit. Alliteration, rhyming, blending, and segmenting are all examples of phonemic awareness activities. Although Choice D is partially correct because it mentions "hearing sounds in words," letter identification is a phonics, rather than phonemic awareness activity. Choices B and C, also phonics activities, rely on visual skills rather than a primary emphasis on hearing and/or articulating sounds. (Domain 2)

16. C. Systematic spelling instruction should be related to students' spelling development. A good assessment to determine a student's spelling development level is the "Qualitative Spelling Assessment." It is helpful for the teacher to use multi-sensory techniques to teach and reinforce spelling patterns. Word sorts and games that involve long vowel sounds would be appropriate for this student. It is also important that the student works on skills that are at his or her spelling development level. While morphology and etymology are important in a systematic spelling program, Choice D, they don't address spelling long vowel patterns. Choice B is inappropriate because phonemic awareness refers to sounds that are articulated and heard, rather than spelled. Choice A is incorrect because success on spelling tests doesn't necessarily translate to proper spelling in written work. (Domain 2)

17. B. Choice B refers to teaching in the transitional stage. Choice C would be appropriate for the phonetic stage, and Choice D would help develop skills in the pre-phonetic stage. Only part of Choice A corresponds to developing spelling for the conventional spellers. (Domain 2)

18. D. Fluency comes from lots of easy reading and the opportunity to practice reading. (Domain 2)

19. B. All of the answers describe assessment tools. You can rule out Choice A because it mentions decoding rather than overall comprehension. Although decoding may contribute to his problem, Choice B is better because it specifically relates to comprehension of his grade-level science text. Choice C is incorrect because it is based on six-trait writing, which does not assess his comprehension. Choice D is an attractive distracter because an IRI is an effective way of measuring grade-level reading. However, since the question specifically asks about student ability to comprehend the *science text,* Choice B is the better assessment tool. (Domain 3)

20. B. Print is oral language, or talking, put onto paper. Choice D is close, but is not as clear as Choice B. Choice D does not specify how tactile and kinesthetic methods will lead to improved concepts about print. Choice A is incorrect because the emphasis is on printing, rather than understanding that print carries meaning. Choice C addresses general comprehension but not her lack of understanding that print conveys meaning. (Domain 2)

21. B. The teacher should teach spelling in context and students can apply their spelling skills across the curriculum. Choice A is incorrect because we cannot know whether a child is actually learning to spell the word. Choices C and D do not specifically address the question. (Domain 2)

22. B. Phonemic awareness indicates awareness of sounds that make up spoken words. Choice A addresses phonics rather than phonemic awareness needs. Phonics is related to the written form of language while phonemic awareness deals specifically with hearing and articulating sounds. Choice C involves the phonemic awareness task of blending, rather than segmenting. Choice D focuses on syllabication, breaking words into syllables, instead of phonemes in words. (Domain 2)

23. A. Choice A is the only answer that includes only phonemic awareness. All others also deal with phonics and/or vocabulary concepts in addition to phonemic awareness tasks. (Domain 2)

24. C. Choice A refers to comprehension, which is not Hien's known area of need. Choice B sounds close, but "word strategies" is not a literacy phrase. Choice D can be an appropriate activity but would not target the specified problem. Choice C is the only one that addresses her instructional needs. (Domain 2)

25. B. Blending phonemes is the only choice that matches the phonemic awareness task listed. Phoneme blending is the act of listening to a "sequence of separately spoken phonemes and then combining the phonemes to form a word." (*Put Reading First,* developed by the Center for the Improvement of Early Reading Achievement.) (Domain 2)

26. D. Choice B is incorrect because the /w/ sound should not be taught in isolation. Choice C is irrelevant because it mentions writing, which is not a component of the activity. The focus is primarily on manipulating the initial sounds in words. This is a phonemic awareness element that helps promote reading development. (Domain 2)

27. D. Choices A, B, and C all should be included in a systematic phonemic awareness program. Word identification is not a phonemic awareness skill. (Domain 2)

28. B. The beginning teacher should use engaging, multi-sensory techniques to assist children in recognizing letter shapes and names. Choice B is most effective because it engages visual, auditory, kinesthetic, and tactile modalities at the same time. Choice D is not the best answer because it engages only the visual modality. Although group work is often appropriate, in this case the first grader may rely on her partner to do the work for her. (Domain 2)

29. A. These words are commonly found in the English language. However, they do not follow typical phonetic rules. We want students to know these words automatically. Using syntax and context clues will not necessarily lead to automaticity. (Domain 2)

30. C. An onset is the initial consonant or consonant blend in a syllable, as /*sh*/ in *shook*. A rime is a vowel and any of the following consonants of a syllable, as /*ook*/ in *shook*. (Domain 2)

31. C. Choices A, B, and D are all true statements. Although systematic phonics is extremely important, Choice C is incorrect because the answer suggests that phonics should be taught in isolation. Learning to encode (spell) and decode phonetically must be combined with other areas of reading instruction. In order to fully understand reading material, students must be taught strategies for comprehension, fluency, and vocabulary acquisition along with phonics instruction. (Domain 2)

32. A. A first-grade teacher could instruct her students to use phonetic clues, find parts of words you can read, and use picture clues to figure out unknown words. These are all often used and successful strategies. (Domain 2)

33. B. Choice B is the most effective, systematic phonics program. The other programs are not systematic. (Domain 2)

34. A. Although silent, independent reading may increase fluency, direct instruction combined with oral reading practice is most likely to develop Tabitha's reading. Choice B is incorrect because automaticity, or the ability to read a word quickly and accurately, is only one component of fluency. Likewise, timed reading from a word list, Choice D, may not help her. Phrasing, intonation, reading with speed and expression, and automaticity are *all* necessary fluency skills. (Domain 2)

35. C. A consonant blend is a combination of sounds in one syllable made by blending two or more consonants together. (Domain 2)

36. D. Choice A is incorrect because it does not focus on orthographic patterns, and limits writing by specifying long e words. Choice B is wrong because correct spelling on a test does not necessarily transfer to proper spelling in authentic writing situations. Choice C is close but focuses on developing vocabulary for fairly basic words rather than paying attention to spelling patterns, a necessary component in an organized word study program. The activities noted in Choice D could be part of an organized word study program. This helps decoding skills as well as spelling. (Domain 2)

37. C. Regular quizzes will not help promote enjoyment of independent reading. Choices A, B, and D are all ways to support at-home reading. (Domain 3)

38. A. Choice B is partially correct because it mentions modeling phrasing and reading with expression. However, retelling a story orally will not be as helpful in developing reading fluency. In addition, both Choices B and D are incorrect because Jemma is never given the opportunity to read aloud, an appropriate strategy for building fluency. The question states that Jemma decodes accurately. Although reading aloud to a younger student would be an appropriate strategy, Choice C is wrong because the focus should not be on phonics. (Domain 3)

39. C. The beginning teacher should model and teach various comprehension strategies that included, but are not limited to, self-monitoring, rereading, note taking, outlining, summarizing, mapping, and using learning logs. Note that the strategies in Choice C apply to comprehending both fiction and non-fiction. Although Choices A, B, and D all might help students understand the text, teaching actual comprehension strategies specifically for expository text is most effective. (Domain 3)

40. A. Many words and roots come from languages that are historically related to English and have similar spellings and meanings in English. (Domain 3)

41. A. Choices B and C are focused on culture, rather than what is the best instructional strategy. Choice D is close, yet only refers to comparing characters, rather than comparing and contrasting several aspects of the two stories. (Domain 3)

42. C. Choice C is the best answer because the five-finger rule is an effective tool that Anwar can use to self-monitor his reading selections. Choice A is incorrect because Anwar, rather than his teacher, should be allowed to select motivating material in the library. Providing a mini-lesson and reviewing material does not necessarily make a book an appropriate selection for guided reading. Therefore, Choice D is also wrong. The teacher might also install a system of book leveling in the classroom for students to use when making independent reading choices. (Domain 3)

43. A. Brainstorming, connecting prior knowledge, and predicting what the book will be about, are all very effective "before reading" practices. The teacher might also "do a picture walk." (Domain 3)

44. A. "Retelling" and the details that the student provides, are an effective means of assessing the student's comprehension. (Domain 3)

45. A. Selecting books with similar themes—like stories of courage, adventure, or books about stereotypes—can provide wonderful opportunities for comparing and contrasting, furthering reading comprehension. (Domain 3)

46. C. Although it is important to motivate students and help English Language Learners, Choices A and D, Choice C is the best answer. Choice B is not an appropriate rationale for any classroom activity. (Domain 4)

47. D. The teacher should plan instruction in which reading, writing, and oral language are interrelated. It is important to provide meaningful writing opportunities in all the content areas. Automaticity and fluency are not likely to be developed during this activity, Choice C. Although comprehension may increase as a result of this activity, Choice B is not as complete as Choice D. Choice A refers to scaffolding, a common English Language Learner strategy, but the knowledge acquired is not systematic. Choice A is an attractive distracter; close, but not quite right. (Domain 4)

48. D. Choices A , B, and C do not address personal connections. Choice C may at first appear correct. However, the work is done as a class rather than individually. Therefore, the teacher will not be able to accurately evaluate individual student understanding. Choice D is the only answer that provides information about the individual student and how he/she makes personal connections to the literature. (Domain 3)

49. D. Choice D is correct because it is not a true statement. Fluency development, as well as comprehension and decoding, require effective instruction within the reading classroom. Choices A, B, and C are components of effective fluency instruction. (Domain 3)

50. B. Choice C may help to clarify vocabulary. However, a K-W-L chart does more than develop vocabulary. The letters stand for K = know, W = want to know, and L = learned. Choice B focuses on prior knowledge, what students already know. (Domain 3)

51. C. The purpose of a K-W-L chart is to help students use prior knowledge, read with a purpose, and clarify what they learned. Choice A is wrong because the focus in only on rote memorization, rather than facilitating understanding. Choices B and D are close, yet neither is quite right. Because the focus is to retain facts from the chosen passage, searching other reference materials will not necessarily transfer to learning the teacher-selected material. Choice D is not the best answer because the focus in unclear. (Domain 3)

52. D. Reciprocal teaching is an instructional comprehension strategy for helping students approach reading in the same way that successful readers do. It provides practice in the use of four comprehension strategies: questioning, summarizing, clarifying, and predicting. It also uses "scaffolding" to enable the students to assume responsibility for understanding text. Choices A, B, and C are all components of Reciprocal teaching. (Domain 3)

53. B. Choice A, skimming, is usually done before or after reading a text. The reader quickly searches for key words, phrases, and/or sentences in order to get a general overview. The reader may also focus on headings or areas printed in bold. Choice B, scanning, is quickly seeking specific words or details from the passage. (Domain 3)

54. D. Students who read on their own become better readers, and teachers can encourage independent reading. Choice D contains the most effective ways for teachers to encourage reading. (Domain 3)

55. B. Choice A is wrong because you cannot completely confirm your prediction before the end of the story. Recording information about the author would not help achieve the teacher's comprehension goal. Therefore, Choice D is also incorrect. Choice C prepares students to answer specific questions rather than a wider, more evaluative understanding of the text. (Domain 3)

56. C. The beginning teacher should use both formal and informal assessment strategies to provide effective instruction in reading comprehension. Choices A and D are not correct because for the purpose of passing the RICA exam, your primary focus should be on what the teacher does to effect change, rather than communicating with parents or a team of specialists. Although this type of communication is mentioned in Domain 1, the focus tends to be on the teacher. Chad's challenging behavior is not as important as how he actually performs when reading. Although Chad should be informed of his strengths and weaknesses, Choice C is the most thorough answer. (Domain 3)

57. D. Choice D is correct and is the only false statement. Reading, writing, speaking, and listening are interrelated, and students must connect their experiences to their reading and writing. Giving students meaningful opportunities to express their ideas orally and get peer feedback helps promote writing proficiency. (Domain 4)

58. A. In order to complete this activity, students must pay attention to the phrasing, sequencing, and other English language conventions including punctuation and grammar. A basic understanding of these elements helps improve reading competence. This activity does not directly relate to orthography or inferential comprehension, Choice B. Choices C and D are both attractive distracters. Choice C sounds appropriate, but is not as thorough as Choice A. Choice D is incorrect because the focus is on vocabulary development. (Domain 4)

59. D. Choice C is close, because the teacher has drawn a type of graphic organizer. However, Choice D is the exact name of the diagram. (Domain 4).

60. B. A student can break down the components of the word to derive its meaning. (Domain 4)

61. C. Beware of any answer that says *all* or *every*. In addition to searching through the dictionary, students should be taught other strategies for gaining meaning from unknown words. Choices A, B, and D are all appropriate strategies. (Domain 4)

62. B. Choice B is the only answer that would be an effective way to teach vocabulary. Choice A is incorrect because you would not want to introduce *all* new vocabulary, but rather key vocabulary. (Domain 4)

63. B. One of the goals of knowing common prefixes and suffixes is to help students learn the meanings of many new words. It is preferable that students be taught strategies for deriving meaning from unknown words in addition to dictionary analysis. Students must not be limited to only studying Greek word origins. For both of those reasons, Choice A is wrong. Choice C is wrong because antonyms are not a part of word parts. Choice D is an attractive distracter. Although it would be appropriate to provide additional words that have *re* as a prefix, sorting the words alphabetically would not necessarily help develop vocabulary. (Domain 4)

64. C. Although all of the choices are important when working with students, Rosa's specific needs have to do with usage errors. Mrs. Feinberg is providing clear examples of English grammar through reading, writing, and oral language. (Domain 4)

65. D. Choice A, simply using a worksheet, is not the appropriate follow-up activity for Rosa. Choices B and D are similar. Choice B is wrong because it mentions prepositional order. Choice C would be an appropriate activity if Rosa completed the task, either alone or with a partner. However, the answer specifies that another student is responsible for executing the activity. (Domain 4)

66. A. Six-trait rubrics only partially focus on grammar. Choice C is a second language assessment, but only is based on student performance in a one-on-one, non-classroom setting. Choice D focuses on many parts of writing, rather than grammar only. (Domain 4)

67. D. Language Experience Approach will teach most of the concepts about print. Although LEA can promote student understanding of sound/symbol correspondence, phonics, Choice D, is best learned when explicitly taught. This question is tricky because it asks for the *least likely* answer. (Domain 4)

68. C. This strategy encourages rereading of familiar text and enhances students' phrasing and oral expression. Choices A and D are partially correct. Although the teacher could assess how a student changes his speech to reflect the main character, Choice A is wrong because it mentions independent reading levels. Choice B is incorrect because second grade listening skills are not the focus of the question. Choice D is incorrect because students are not completing literary analysis. (Domain 4)

69. D. Choice A is incorrect since oral and written language development would not necessarily address language similarities and differences. Choice B is incorrect because it refers only to academic language used in literature rather than in all the content areas. Although "a balanced language approach" sounds right, it is not a recognized teaching term for specifically addressing academic language. (Domain 4)

70. B. Choice A is an excellent vocabulary activity. However, it does not correspond to the method introduced by the teacher. Determining word history and origin, Choice C, should not be the main focus. Choice D is too vague to be correct. (Domain 4)

Section II: Open-Ended Questions

Sample Essays and Evaluations

Domain I/Assignment A

Sample Essay

A spelling inventory such as the Qualitative Spelling Inventory (Bear, 1998) is a tool to determine each student's developmental spelling level. This information, linked with evaluating student writing samples, will give the teacher insight into instructional spelling needs for individual students. Using data from these two sources, the teacher will plan direct instruction lessons to target identified needs.

Evaluating the Essay

The essay fulfills the task by describing strategies and resources. Because students in fifth grade may have a variety of spelling levels and spelling needs, the teacher must determine what each student knows as well as what each one needs to know. The essay clearly points out that using the two assessment tools mentioned will give data on developmental spelling levels as well as phonic pattern needs. The teacher will then target the gaps with direct instruction in identified needs.

Domain IV/Assignment B

Sample Essay

In writing her plan, the teacher should make sure that she includes giving direct instruction in the writing process. She should carefully explain and let the students practice the steps of prewriting, writing, and proofreading. The teacher should also use a variety of activities such as experience stories and charts to demonstrate or model that oral language can be recorded in written language. It is important that the teacher's direct instruction is followed by guided practice where students can get immediate feedback and positive reinforcement.

Evaluating the Essay

The essay fulfills the task by clearly identifying some methods that the teacher should include in her plan. The author starts by recommending giving direct instruction in the writing process, and then briefly mentions the specifics that should be explained and practiced. The author then suggests the use of a variety of activities and gives two examples—experience stories and charts—to demonstrate that oral language can be recorded as written language. Finally, the author points out that guided practice should be followed by immediate feedback and positive reinforcement, a very important point. The methods mentioned and described should definitely be part of the teacher's plan.

Domain II/Assignment C

Sample Essay

Phonemic awareness, as noted in Marilyn Adam's research, is one of the three predictors of success in early reading. Adams notes that if a student does not attain mastery of phonemic awareness he/she will probably never be able to read on grade level. Keith Stanovich's research has shown that phonemic awareness is a core causal factor separating normal from disabled readers.

To teach phonemic awareness the teacher must first assess, using a phonemic awareness survey such as the Yopp-Singer Survey, to determine student skill needs in phonemic awareness. The teacher would use the results (data) from the assessment to plan and target instruction in such sub-skill areas as identifying phonemes, blending phonemes, or deleting/adding phonemes. Planning for instruction would address teaching one or two sub-skills at a time and would include a variety of variables such as grouping (small groups are best for PA Instruction), individual student needs, and resources. Students should have many opportunities to practice phonemic awareness skills, first with the teacher and then independently. The teacher monitors practice and provides intervention as needed. Skill mastery is noted in retesting with the original assessment tool, e.g., Yopp-Singer. Large group and individual practice in phonemic awareness is ongoing throughout the year in songs, games, and other activities.

Evaluating the Essay

The essay must address the two tasks stated in the question. In the first paragraph the writer tells how phonemic awareness is related to reading achievement. The work of two researchers is noted in support of the explanation given in the first paragraph.

The second paragraph addresses the second question. The author describes each step in the instructional process. Following the description of each step in the instructional process (diagnostic instruction) is a sentence or two that give examples to support the description. The last sentence in the essay is a summary statement concerning phonemic awareness teaching.

Domain III/Assignment D

Sample Essay

Literal comprehension is "reading the lines." It is identifying factual ideas that are explicitly stated. This could include the comprehension strategies such as identifying main idea, details, or cause and effect. Literal comprehension involves answering who, where, what, and when questions. Memory questions and recall are often used to determine literal comprehension.

Inferential comprehension is about inferring, figuring out ideas that are implied in a text. Inferential questions, "reading between the lines," require students to think beyond the facts of the text. In inferential comprehension questions the student is often asked to answer how and why questions. Comprehension strategies appropriate for this "what is implied" level of comprehension include drawing conclusions and making predictions. Inferential comprehension is about implied meanings. Interpretive questions (a higher level than memory/recall) as well as applying facts to new contexts aid students in practicing inferential comprehension.

Evaluative comprehension requires the reader to make a judgment about the text and to base these judgments on what he or she knows/understands both literally and inferentially. Making distinctions e.g., fact/opinion, identifying propaganda, identifying bias, helps students in evaluative comprehension. Comprehension strategies such as distinguishing between facts and opinions, reacting to a text's content, characters, and use of language are all appropriate strategies for evaluative comprehension. In evaluative comprehension students ask higher order questions, analyze new situations with new knowledge, synthesize information among texts, and evaluate texts.

Evaluating the Essay

The essay clearly fulfills the two tasks. The first task is to describe the three levels and the second task is to describe two comprehension strategies appropriate to teach each level. The author chose to write three paragraphs. Each paragraph addresses a level of comprehension. First, there is a description of what the level is—a definition. Following the description of the level is the description of two comprehension strategies appropriate for that level. The last sentence in each paragraph gives a snapshot view of the level of comprehension.

Case Study Information

Your case-study essay should have included some of the following information.

Since you are asked to identify three strengths and weaknesses and describe two teaching strategies, you will not be able to respond to every issue presented in this case study. You must select the weaknesses that are the most prominent, the most severe, and the most basic. To find strengths, look at the student's interest survey to find out what she likes to do, and what she says she is good at doing. Then, look at the teacher's comments for strengths.

In determining the most salient weaknesses, look for concerns that show up in more than one piece of data. In this case study, fluency was slow both on Tara's phonics tests and on her running record. Tara had difficulty with decoding basic words on both her phonics test and running record. You would recommend that Tara work on reading fluency, and suggest one or more strategies for working on fluency. She could also be working on decoding basic words at the same time, by practicing reading easy material and decodable books.

Tara had difficulty with spelling on her spelling assessment and in her writing samples. Furthermore, on her interest survey, she wrote that she wants to be a better speller. Specifically, she has difficulty spelling words with long vowels, as evidenced in her spelling test and writing samples. You would identify her spelling stage in the Beginning Within Word stage and you could recommend that she work on long vowel spelling patterns through word study, activities, spelling games, and study of common spelling patterns. You might also suggest activities in which Tara contrasts words with long vowels and words with short vowels.

Examine Tara's running record to see what information you can get from it. It was a fourth-grade selection, and she read it at the instructional level, so her instructional level is fourth grade. Since she is in sixth grade, she is two years behind in reading, so she needs help. Her comprehension was good, so that is a strength, as she is able to comprehend at a higher level. On the running record, Tara had trouble decoding multisyllabic words, as well as on her phonics tests. She does not possess strategies for decoding multisyllabic words and would benefit from practice in decoding them. On her running record, you can also see that her decoding errors are mostly substitutions and that she uses the beginning of the word to decode without attending to the rest of the word. She is using visual cues without attending to meaning. She needs to be taught to look at the whole word and read for meaning as well. The assessments definitely suggest that Tara would benefit from improving her word recognition skills.

To improve Tara's decoding and fluency, you could suggest that she practice reading daily from books that are at her independent level. Additionally, reading a lot will help her improve her spelling and writing because she will be getting much needed exposure to the correct spellings of words, and to good written structures. To capitalize on her strengths, she could read books on topics about which she is interested. You can get her interests from the interest survey. For Tara it would be cheerleading, sports, mysteries, and instructional books. On her writing samples, Tara wrote about those topics, and she should continue to do so, and she should be encouraged to write mysteries and instructions. Tara's self-correction rate on her running record was low, so she needs to be encouraged to self-monitor her reading and read for meaning.

Next, look at the other assessment data. From the phonics assessments, you learned that Tara had difficulty reading nonsense words with short vowel sounds, multisyllabic words, and words with diphthongs. You would want to leave the diphthongs alone for now, because you need to work on the multisyllabic words and long vowel words identified in the other assessments first. Tara's difficulty with short-vowel nonsense words indicates that she reads words better in context than out of context.

From the writing samples you learned that Tara's sentences are simple, and she doesn't include many details. Once again, reading a lot will help her to see good writing patterns and formats. You could suggest writing lessons in which Tara would add details to sentences or fill in sentence frames with various formats. You also could suggest that Tara use graphic organizers or story planning charts to plan her writing, and as part of her prewriting.

Analyzing Your Test Results

Use the following charts to carefully analyze your results and spot your strengths and weaknesses. Complete the process of analyzing each subject area and each individual question for Practice Test 2. Examine your results for trends in types of error (repeated errors) or poor results in specific subject areas. This re-examination and analysis is of tremendous importance for effective test preparation.

Practice Test 2 Analysis Sheets

Multiple-Choice Questions				
	Possible	*Completed*	*Right*	*Wrong*
Domain I	14			
Domain II	20			
Domain III	20			
Domain IV	16			
Total	70			

Analysis/Tally Sheet for Multiple-Choice Questions

One of the most important parts of test preparation is analyzing why you missed a question so that you can reduce the number of mistakes. Now that you've taken Practice Test 2 and corrected your answers, carefully tally your multiple-choice mistakes by marking in the proper column.

Reasons for Mistakes				
	Total Mistakes	*Simple Mistake*	*Misread Question*	*Lack of Knowledge*
Domain I				
Domain II				
Domain III				
Domain IV				
Total:				

Open-Ended Questions (The Essays)

See the discussion of essay scoring beginning on page 2 to evaluate your essays. Have someone knowledgeable in reading instruction read and evaluate your responses using the checklists that follow.

Domain I/Assignment A

RICA Practice Essay Evaluation Form

Use this checklist to evaluate your essay:

1. To what extent does this response reflect an **understanding of the relevant content** and academic knowledge from the applicable RICA domain?

thorough	**adequate**	**limited or no**
understanding	understanding	understanding

2. To what extent does this response fulfill the purpose of the assignment?

completely	**adequately**	**partially**
fulfills	fulfills	fulfills or fails to

3. To what extent does this essay **respond to the given task(s)?**

fully	**adequately**	**limited or inadequately**
responds	responds	responds

4. How **accurate** is the response?

very	**generally**	**inaccurate**
accurate	accurate	

5. Does the response **demonstrate an effective application** of the relevant content and academic knowledge from the applicable RICA domain?

yes	**reasonably**	**no**
effective	effective	ineffective and inaccuracies

6. To what extent does the response **provide supporting examples, evidence, and rationale** based on the relevant content and academic knowledge from the applicable RICA domain?

strong	**adequate**	**limited or no**
support	support	support

Domain IV/Assignment B

RICA Practice Essay Evaluation Form

Use this checklist to evaluate your essay:

1. To what extent does this response reflect an **understanding of the relevant content** and academic knowledge from the applicable RICA domain?

thorough	**adequate**	**limited or no**
understanding	understanding	understanding

2. To what extent does this response fulfill the purpose of the assignment?

completely	**adequately**	**partially**
fulfills	fulfills	fulfills or fails to

3. To what extent does this essay **respond to the given task(s)?**

fully	**adequately**	**limited or inadequately**
responds	responds	responds

4. How **accurate** is the response?

very	**generally**	**inaccurate**
accurate	accurate	

5. Does the response **demonstrate an effective application** of the relevant content and academic knowledge from the applicable RICA domain?

yes	**reasonably**	**no**
effective	effective	ineffective and inaccuracies

6. To what extent does the response **provide supporting examples, evidence, and rationale** based on the relevant content and academic knowledge from the applicable RICA domain?

strong	**adequate**	**limited or no**
support	support	support

Domain II/Assignment C

RICA Practice Essay Evaluation Form

Use this checklist to evaluate your essay:

1. To what extent does this response reflect an **understanding of the relevant content** and academic knowledge from the applicable RICA domain?

thorough	**adequate**	**limited or no**
understanding	understanding	understanding

2. To what extent does this response fulfill the purpose of the assignment?

completely	**adequately**	**partially**
fulfills	fulfills	fulfills or fails to

3. To what extent does this essay **respond to the given task(s)?**

fully	**adequately**	**limited or inadequately**
responds	responds	responds

4. How **accurate** is the response?

very	**generally**	**inaccurate**
accurate	accurate	

5. Does the response **demonstrate an effective application** of the relevant content and academic knowledge from the applicable RICA domain?

yes	**reasonably**	**no**
effective	effective	ineffective and inaccuracies

6. To what extent does the response **provide supporting examples, evidence, and rationale** based on the relevant content and academic knowledge from the applicable RICA domain?

strong	**adequate**	**limited or no**
support	support	support

Domain III/Assignment D

RICA Practice Essay Evaluation Form

Use this checklist to evaluate your essay:

1. To what extent does this response reflect an **understanding of the relevant content** and academic knowledge from the applicable RICA domain?

thorough	**adequate**	**limited or no**
understanding	understanding	understanding

2. To what extent does this response fulfill the purpose of the assignment?

completely	**adequately**	**partially**
fulfills	fulfills	fulfills or fails to

3. To what extent does this essay **respond to the given task(s)?**

fully	**adequately**	**limited or inadequately**
responds	responds	responds

4. How **accurate** is the response?

very	**generally**	**inaccurate**
accurate	accurate	

5. Does the response **demonstrate an effective application** of the relevant content and academic knowledge from the applicable RICA domain?

yes	**reasonably**	**no**
effective	effective	ineffective and inaccuracies

6. To what extent does the response **provide supporting examples, evidence, and rationale** based on the relevant content and academic knowledge from the applicable RICA domain?

strong	**adequate**	**limited or no**
support	support	support

Case Study/Assignment E

RICA Practice Case Study Evaluation Form

Use this checklist to evaluate your essay:

1. To what extent does this response reflect an **understanding of the relevant content** and academic knowledge from the applicable RICA domain?

thorough	**adequate**	**limited**	**little or no**
understanding	understanding	understanding	understanding

2. To what extent does this response fulfill the purpose of the assignment?

completely	**adequately**	**partially**	**fails to fulfill**
fulfills	fulfills	fulfills	

3. To what extent does this essay **respond to the given task(s)?**

fully	**adequately**	**limited**	**inadequately**
responds	responds	responds	responds

4. How **accurate** is the response?

very	**generally**	**partially**	**inaccurate**
accurate	accurate	accurate	

5. Does the response **demonstrate an effective application** of the relevant content and academic knowledge from the applicable RICA domain?

yes	**reasonably**	**limited**	**no**
effective	effective	generally ineffective	inaccurate and ineffective

6. To what extent does the response **provide supporting examples, evidence, and rationale** based on the relevant content and academic knowledge from the applicable RICA domain?

strong	**adequate**	**limited**	**little or no**
support	support	support	support

Essay Review

Compare your essays to the ones given and review the Evaluation Forms, which you have had a reader complete, for each assignment. From this information, circle what you feel is the appropriate level of response for each assignment. This should help give you some general guidelines for your review.

Open-Ended Questions			
Assignment A (Domain I)	good	average	poor
Assignment B (Domain IV)	good	average	poor
Assignment C (Domain II)	good	average	poor
Assignment D (Domain III)	good	average	poor
Assignment E (Case Study)	good	average	poor

PART IV

FINAL PREPARATION AND SOURCES

This short section is designed to help you put everything together to do you best on the RICA test. The Final Touches emphasizes what you should do as you get close to the test day.

This section also acknowledges the sources of the assessments, tests, surveys, inventories, lists, glossaries, and charts used in this book.

The Final Touches

1. Make sure that you are familiar with the testing center location and nearby parking facilities.

2. Spend the last week of preparation on a general review of key concepts and test-taking strategies and techniques.

3. Don't cram the night before the exam. It is a waste of time!

4. Arrive at the testing center in plenty of time. At least 30 minutes early.

5. Remember to bring the proper materials: identification, admission ticket, four or five sharpened Number 2 pencils, an eraser, and a watch.

6. Start off crisply, working the questions you know first, and then go back and try to answer the others.

7. On the multiple-choice questions, try to eliminate one or more choices before you guess, but make sure that you fill in all the answers. There is no penalty for guessing!

8. Underline key words in the questions. Write out important information and make notations on diagrams. Take advantage of being permitted to write in the test booklet.

9. On multiple-choice questions, cross out incorrect choices immediately: This can keep you from reconsidering a choice that you have already eliminated.

10. Make sure that you answer what is being asked.

11. On the open-ended assignments (essays), take a few minutes to jot down notes to organize your thoughts. Remember, you are writing a response to the task(s) and to show the readers how much you know about the given assignment.

12. On the essay assignments, even if you don't know the answer, at least try to give a partial response. Always write something; you could get partial credit.

13. Don't get stuck on any one question. Never spend more than $1\frac{1}{2}$ minutes on a multiple-choice question. Spend about 15 minutes each on Assignments A and B, and about 25 minutes each on Assignments C and D. Be sure to leave about an hour for Assignment E, the case study.

14. The key to getting a good score on the RICA Written Examination is reviewing properly, practicing, and getting the questions right that you can and should get right. A careful review of Parts I and II of this book will help you focus during the final week before the exam.

Sources

Sincere appreciation is given to the following authors and companies for allowing the use of their assessments, tests, surveys, inventories, lists, glossaries, and charts from their outstanding works.

Page 70, Word Recognition Assessment: San Diego Quick Assessment—Lapray, Margaret Helen, & Ross, Ramon Royal (January 1969). The graded word list: Quick gauge of reading ability. *Journal of Reading,* 12, 305–307. Reprinted with permission of the International Reading Association. All rights reserved.

Page 72, Informal Reading Assessment: Fry Oral Reading Test—Record Form from "Building Reading Success 4–8" by Edward Fry, Ph.D. Copyright 1995 by Edward Fry. Copyright 1999 by Core.

Page 74, Fluency Assessment: Grade 5 Probe 3 from "Collections for Young Scholars" Volume 5, Book I copyright 1995.

Page 76–77, Phonics Test: Cunningham Names Test by Patricia Cunningham form California Reading Professional Development Institute copyright 1999.

Page 80, Qualitative Spelling Inventory: Upper Elementary Spelling Inventory by Bear, Donald R.; Invernizzi, Marcia; Templeton, Shane R.; Johnston, Francine; Words Their Way: Word Study for Phonics, Vocabulary, and Spelling Instruction, 1st Edition copyright 1996. Reprinted by permission of Pearson Education, Inc., Upper Saddle River, NJ.

Page 92, Home Survey: My Child as a Reader and Writer—copyright 1996 Wright Group Publishing, Inc.

Page 94, Student Survey: Myself as a Reader—copyright 1996 Wright Group Publishing, Inc.

Page 96–97, Running Record: Book Evaluation—The Busy Mosquito from Early Detection of Reading Difficulties (Heinemann).

Page 99, High Frequency Words: Fry's Sight (Instant) Word Recording Sheet by Edward Fry, Ph.D. Copyright 1995 by Edward Fry.

Page 137–141, Glossary of Terms and Concepts Source: California Department of Education, 1430 N Street, Sacramento, CA 95814. The Guide to the California Reading Initiative of 1996 is out of print and no longer represents California Department of Education Policy.

Page 187, Reading Attitude Survey: Assessment Handbook.

Page 189, Family Survey: Assessment Handbook.

Page 191–192, Running Record: Moon Mouse from Early Detection of Reading Difficulties (Heinemann).

Page 259–260, Running Record: from Early Detection of Reading Difficulties (Heinemann).

Page 264, Writing Samples: Elementary Inventory Error Guide.